Women Composers
of Classical Music

Women Composers of Classical Music

*369 Biographies from 1550
into the 20th Century*

MARY F. MCVICKER

McFarland & Company, Inc., Publishers
Jefferson, North Carolina, and London

LIBRARY OF CONGRESS CATALOGUING-IN-PUBLICATION DATA

McVicker, Mary Frech
    Women composers of classical music : 369 biographies
from 1550 into the 20th century / Mary F. McVicker.
      p.   cm.
    Includes bibliographical references and index.

    ISBN 978-0-7864-4397-0
    softcover : 50# alkaline paper ∞

    1. Women composers.   I. Title.
ML390.M4647   2011
780.92'2 — dc22   2011000213

BRITISH LIBRARY CATALOGUING DATA ARE AVAILABLE

Cover images ©2010 Shutterstock

Manufactured in the United States of America

McFarland & Company, Inc., Publishers
   Box 611, Jefferson, North Carolina 28640
   www.mcfarlandpub.com

Table of Contents

Introduction

A select group of male composers and their repertoires define music periods and styles. This can be misleading since only a few forged new styles. More typically, classical music has been an evolutionary process, often closely linked with the developing technology of more complex musical instruments. Most in that select group slightly redirected the path and put it on a different, angled direction. Often overlooked are the many composers who provided the fabric of much of the evolution of classical music.

This book is about the women in that fabric. Of course, gender issues underlie the book, but it's not the theme of the book. The theme is women composing music. And there were many.

A consideration of women composers invariably generates some frustration and resentment on their behalf. They worked within the confines of limited or no access to education, performance, and the music community, particularly of composers, as well as limited or no opportunities for rehearsal and performance. These limitations meant that many of them worked without the means to fully develop their skills and hone their skills and, in some cases, their brilliance.

Artists have always faced barriers in terms of economics and public interest. The history of the arts mirrors economic history. When times are good there are patrons and audiences, and the arts are more likely to flourish.

Women have had the additional barrier of gender and lack of opportunity for education and for audience. The significance of these barriers cannot be underestimated. How many women chose not to follow a life in classical music because of them? But at various times in various countries between 1550 and 1900 good economic times and somewhat better acceptance for their music have coincided, and there have been brief windows of opportunity and sunshine for women composers.

Many, perhaps most, women wrote small pieces for small ensembles, which has often been a subject of criticism or has been cited as "proof" that they couldn't write larger forms of music. But those small, limited venues were all they had available. Their lack of access to working with an orchestra and hearing their orchestral music played confined many women to producing works for solo instruments or small ensembles. And, except for a few rare windows of openness, opera was a field denied to them. It's little wonder, then, that few women composed symphonic or operatic works. Both the symphonic tradition and the tradition of grand opera were closed to them because of societal and (more importantly) professional barriers. Professional composing on a large scale was a closed club. Yet, in spite of everything, women composers persevered.

Women composers also had to face the problem of the unwarranted conviction that they write "feminine" music. This is reinforced by the fact that the three composers most frequently heard — Clara Schumann, Fanny Mendelssohn, and Amy Beach — wrote music in the style of Romanticism. But they weren't writing "feminine" music; they were writing the music of their era, as did the men composers of that era.

In any "blind" testing where listeners would be asked to determine the gender of the composer of unknown music, the correct answer is a matter of probability, not derived from characteristics deemed inherent in the music. Not all women wrote good music, any more than all men composers wrote good music.

These women, their music, and their composing are part of the vast mosaic of classical music. We should pay attention to more of their music — and more of the music of some lesser-known male composers as well. If we don't, we are depriving ourselves of much of the richness of classical music.

Women and men composers from all eras suffer from the demands of an audience wanting masterpieces and composers with name recognition. This has long been an issue. Deems Taylor in his book *The Well Tempered Listener*, taken from his radio broadcasts, quotes from a letter from a listener, Fraser Macdonald of Lacombe, Alberta: "Don't you think there is too much attention paid to the composer and not enough to the composition?"* Taylor agrees.

But in the overwhelming majority of situations, composers without masterpiece name recognition aren't likely to be heard ... period. The compositions of these forgotten, unknown women contain gems of music — and we are poorer for not hearing them.

This book celebrates women composers and their achievements, perseverance, and pushing the limits — and those moments of sunshine.

This quotation is taken from page 102 of Deems Taylors' The Well Tempered Listener. Taylor quotes a substantial portion of Macdonald's letter in the "Guest Speaker" section of his book.

The Format of the Book

Women Composers of Classical Music is a chronological survey of women composers of classical music. It looks at the lives and careers of the women composers in the contexts of setting and time. In cases where it is unclear how a composer's name should be listed in an alphabetical reference, the beginning letter of the appropriate name is underlined.

Through the centuries a startling number of operas by women composers were performed. An opera timeline illuminates the vast array of these works — which represent perhaps half of the operas actually written by these women (that we know about).

In the earliest period, the Renaissance, the sole focus is on Italy, the center of development in music. As the decades progress, women composers from other countries and areas join the chronology. The designation "country" is used loosely; for centuries the present-day country name denoted the area rather than a political entity.

The introduction to each period has a brief look at the musical culture of each country or area represented by a composer in that section. The geographic diversity increases through time. By the last chapter, "Into the 20th Century," many countries are represented. Undoubtedly there were composers from other areas and countries throughout this history; inclusion is a matter of information available.

The choice of what section a woman should be included within is based on the time period of their first major composition, if known, since the book focuses on their music. Some women came to composing later in their lives; some started composing at a young age and were particularly long-lived. Consequently, a given time period could include a range of life spans, and many women composed over several time periods.

For many women there is scant or no biographical information; they are known to us only through their work. For many of these women, you wish to know more of their stories. And for so many, you want to play or hear their music. Much music is inaccessible. And, sadly, much is lost.

More must surely be out there.

Source Abbreviations

ANB   Garraty, John A., and Mark C. Carnes, editors. *American National Biography*. New York: Oxford University Press, 1999.

CCH   Glickman, Sylvia, and Martha Furman Schleifer, editors. *From Convent to Concert Hall: A Guide to Women Composers*. Westport, CT: Greenwood Press, 2003.

Cohen   Cohen, Aaron I., editor. *International Encyclopedia of Women Composers*, 2nd ed. New York: Books & Music, 1987.

Elson   Elson, Arthur. *Woman's Work in Music; Being an Account of Her Influence on the Art, in Ancient as Well as Modern Times; A Summary of Her Musical Compositions, in the Different Countries of the Civilized World; An Estimate of Their Rank in Comparison with Those of Men*. Boston: L.C. Page, 1903.

Grove's   Blom, Eric, editor. *Grove's Dictionary of Music and Musicians*, 5th ed. London: Macmillan, 1954.

New Grove   Sadie, Stanley, and John Tyrrell, editors. *The New Grove Dictionary of Music and Musicians*, 2nd ed. London: Macmillan, 2001.

Norton Grove   Sadie, Julie Anne, and Rhian Samuel. *The Norton/Grove Dictionary of Women Composers*. New York: W.W. Norton, 1994.

Oxford   Matthew, H.C.G., and Brian Harrison, editors. *Oxford Dictionary of National Biography*. Oxford: Oxford University Press, 2004.

WON   Laurence, Anya. *Women of Notes: 1000 Women Composers Born before 1900*. New York: Richards Rosen Press, 1978.

WWO   Letzer, Jacqueline, and Robert Adelson. *Women Writing Opera: Creativity and Controversy in the Age of the French Revolution*. Berkeley: University of California Press, 2001.

Chapter One

The Renaissance Transition, 1550–1600

Women were part of the flourishing of music in Renaissance Italy. Too often their roles are unknown, overlooked or understated, but from the Renaissance to the present day women have been part of the development of music.

Music suffers from being ephemeral instead of visual. Manuscripts — the most visual aspect of music — don't convey much of the development of music to most of us. In contrast, books and works of art are readily visible in our museums and libraries, and we can see the historical line of development of techniques, styles, and palates.

Fortunately for us, people of the Renaissance tended to document and record, and because of this we know more about the education and activities of a number of women composers. They were well educated, and they wrote, composed and published. They were an important part of music making in the church and the court, and they were recognized for this.

As with all the arts and trades, music tended to have a family business aspect to it, and composers and musicians often came from musical families. The church was particularly important as a center of education in music, both for people entering the religious life and those choosing to be secular. The family also was a significant source for education. The family aspect is particularly prominent in this section.

Music in Italy in the late 1500s was dominated by the Roman Catholic Church, which trained and housed musicians and composers and was the setting for performances. There was secular music as well, including traditional folk music and dances, and pageants with music that often were performed by touring companies. The church tended to be dubious about secular music and was wary about the possibility of secular music entering the church. Later, as musical genres developed, there would be an uneasy fine line between oratorio and opera.

Hildegard of Bingen

Hildegard of Bingen is one woman who has some name recognition as a composer. The resurgence of research and interest in her life and works has established her as the forerunner of woman composers. Although her life span is earlier than our time frame, we begin with her.

Ironically, we know more about the life and music of **Hildegard of Bingen** (1098, Bemersheim–September 17, 1179, Rupertsberg, near Bingen) than we know about many later composers. Because of her writings, her poetry, her mystical experiences, her public renown and her education, much of her life and work was documented. She was the tenth child of a noble couple who promised her to the service of the Church, and when she was eight she went to live with the recluse Jutta of Spanheim at the Benedictine monastery of Disibodenberg. She took her vows when she was fifteen.

Her education included music and singing and a good reading knowledge of Latin. A number of the nuns in the monastery had gradually formed into a group, and when Jutta, who was the Sister Superior, died, Hildegard, who was in her thirties, became Sister Superior of the nuns.

She had begun seeing visions when she was young; these continued more intensely as she got older. Eventually she felt strongly drawn to recording her visions, which she did often using song texts. She began her first book after having a vision from God ordering her to write it. The book was never finished, but it became known. As her fame spread, women sought to join her order. Finally, in 1148 she asked permission to move her order but was refused.

Eventually the group seceded from the monastery; Hildegard founded the monastery near Bingen between 1147 and 1150, when she was in her late forties, and lived there the rest of her life.

As she got older she became even more widely known for her prophecies and her mysticism. She was sought for her wisdom by popes, rulers, clergy and lay people not only for her mystical abilities and wisdom, but also for her diplomacy and political wisdom. Her correspondence was widespread, reaching many in government and religious life, and people sought out her writings. She also was learned in natural history and medicine and wrote on both subjects.

We know she composed lyrical poetry when she was in her forties, and she may have composed earlier. She wrote music of her time, but much of her music is more individual and less predictable than that written by her contemporaries. She did not draw from plainchant as most composers did. Some of her compositions are more complex in format and with some antiphony, giving it a different harmony.

Principal sources: CCH; Norton Grove.

Italy

Maddalena Casulana (c. 1544 near Siena, fl. Vicenza 1566–1583) is one of the best-known female secular composers of the late 1500s. Most of what we know of her life stems from the dates of publications and performances. Sources vary on some of these dates.

Her earliest education and performance were in Florence. In 1566 she published a book of four madrigals, which apparently was the first work by a woman of European music to be printed. At that time she was already well known as a composer of madrigals and music for voices.

Her second book of madrigals in 1688 contained a dedication to Isabella de Medici Orsini, who was an amateur musician and a strong patron of music:

> ... not only to give witness to my devotion to Your Excellency, but also to show to the world (to the degree that it is granted to me in this profession of music) the foolish error of men, who so greatly believe themselves to be the masters of high intellectual gifts that [these gifts] cannot, it seems to them, be equally common among women [from Norton Grove, p. 110].

Maddalena often utilized her own poetry as well as classical poems for her texts. Her last known book was published in 1583; however, she may have written more poetry. She was also a talented singer and played the lute.

Principal source: CCH

The difficulty of sorting out scanty data is personified by the sisters **Vittoria Aleotti** (c. 1575, Ferrara–?) and **Raphaela Aleotta** (c.1570?–1646?). Apparently there has been some confusion about their being two separate people or just one person with a confusion of names.

Raphaela Aleotta (c.1570?–1646?) was the eldest of five daughters, all musically talented. She published a volume of sacred motets in 1593, the earliest-known publication of sacred music by a woman composer. Raphaela, who resided at the convent of San Vito, trained the nuns in music, directed their singing, and directed their instrumental playing. As was often the case, the nuns gave public performances.

Principal sources: CCH; Grove's

Vittoria Aleotti (c. 1575, Ferrara–?) was one of five daughters who all were musically talented. At the age of four she showed great interest in music, being always present at the music lessons being given to an older sister, probably Raphaela. She showed such interest and talent that when she was six or seven she went to the convent of San Vito to continue her musical studies. In 1591, one of her madrigals was published in an anthology of works by composers of Ferrara. Her own collection of madrigals was published in 1593.

When she was fourteen she decided to enter the convent permanently. No more compositions or musical activity are known.

Principal sources: CCH; Grove's

Accounts **Taruinia Molza** and **Clementine de Bourges** are unfortunately rather typical: we know of them through their music, and biographical information is sparse at best.

Taruinia Molza (16th century, Modena) was a very talented musician and singer, and a poet as well. She was at the Este court at Ferrara where she served as singer and violinist. She also composed for the lute, viol and harp. Under Duchess Margarita she led a woman's orchestra. However, she fell out of favor with the Duchess because of a love affair and was dismissed.

Principal source: WON

Clementine de Bourges (date not known, Lyon?–1561, Lyon) was said to have been master of many instruments and of great intellectual prowess. Little is known about her life. Her many compositions include choral works and organ music.

Principal source: CCHs

Chapter Two

The Age of Harmony, 1600–1685

While the impact of the Renaissance spread throughout Europe, Italy continued to be the focal point of the arts, including music. Italy was the equivalent of a tourist destination, for pilgrims visiting the holy sites and the churches, merchants taking advantage of the international trade with the East, and people who wanted to participate in or simply enhance their appreciation of the arts. All this, of course, contributed to Italy's prosperity and fueled more economic development as well as support of the arts. Everyone wanted to keep up with changes and styles in Italian music and art, and one of the most significant developments was the evolution of Italian opera.

Opera was a logical outgrowth of such entertainments as religious pageants. Its development was driven by the prevailing creative energy in the arts and the thirst for entertainment among the nobility. Opera caught on quickly. The first public opera house opened in Venice in 1637. From the first, opera appealed to the demand of a moneyed nobility and upper class for entertainment, spectacle, and social gathering — a demand that seemed insatiable. The popularity of opera quickly spread, and Italian opera would dominate for many decades.

The church continued to be a primary source for music education in Italy. Four *ospedali* were established in Venice. These *ospedali*, sometimes called *Mendacanti*, held a significant position in the musical life of Venice. Often referred to as conservatories, they were religious-based charitable institutions that served a variety of people in need: the sick, homeless, and those unable to care for themselves. They also were major venues for musical training and performance and were well known for the quality of their music and education.

Students received thorough instruction in music — training in the fundamentals of music, sight-singing, ear-training, performance practice, and instruction on at least two instruments. Some of the teaching was by secular male teachers from outside the institution, who were chosen to ensure that the music and training were current with musical trends in Europe.

A student who completed the training became a teacher and was required to remain in the *ospedale* to perform and to instruct younger students. The woman could, with permission of the governor, leave and marry or stay as a permanent resident, possibly teaching outside pupils for pay, and she could retire at the *ospedale*.

Originally the *ospedali* were designated as orphanages. However, they soon became known as the source for a good education, and an exceedingly good musical education, and there was demand for them to open their admission to girls from other backgrounds and families. As a result the schools would admit, upon audition, young women from families to study music. Girls were not required to join the religious order. After a ten-year course of study, a girl could become an instructor at the *ospedale*. The *ospedali* would also provide a dowry for a girl who wanted to marry.

Francesca Caccini is one of the very few women composers who may show up in an index of a book on music history, particularly the history of opera. She usually is mentioned in connection with her father, who was one of the originators of early Italian opera. Missing, of course, is reference to the fact that she was the first woman known to compose opera and was the composer of the first opera to be given outside Italy.

Changes in music spread quickly, particularly to France, Germany and England. While Italian music held the premier place, different areas in Europe began to formulate their own style of music. Generally, music and music education were concentrated in noble courts, in the church, or in the family. Music was part of a noblewoman's accomplishments, and many composed songs. In much of Europe royal courts were the center for music performance — and for employment in music. Music also opened up career opportunities for women. Some became professional singers, often having a position with a royal court, then later with an opera house.

The setting in France at that time was the reign of Louis XIV. He adored entertainments of all kinds, and during his long reign, from 1643 to 1715, music and theater flourished. His policy was to keep the nobility occupied and amused so they didn't have the time, energy or inclination to stir up trouble — and he knew how to divert them. The entertainments were non-stop, and everything — government, society, the arts — was centered at Versailles.

At the same time, though, Paris wasn't entirely a wasteland. While the nobility needed to be resident at Versailles, many people involved in the arts moved between Versailles and Paris. Versailles might be the center of the French world, but the life of the arts remained robust in Paris.

Jean-Baptiste Lully managed everything musical at Versailles. He was the court composer, musician, "manager" of musical events at court and director of opera. The impact of Italian music remained strong, and much French music from this period reflects Italian influence. But Italian music never completely took over, and French music always retained its individuality, particularly in opera.

Music publishing had been established in France in the early 1500s, and for decades, if not centuries, France and particularly Paris would be the center for music publishing. Similarly there had been instrument makers and organ builders in Paris for many decades.

Together, Versailles and Paris drew talented musicians and composers (as well as writers, playwrights, and artists) from all over France, leaving a virtual cultural vacuum in the rest of the country, the provinces.

In the midst of the very patriarchal society, government and legal system, many women in the arts, women of letters, women of the salons, women who were brilliant at conversation and wit were held in great esteem.

Elisabeth Claude Jacquet de la Guerre had a remarkable career as a composer in France, successfully negotiating the politics of the Court of Louis XIV as well. Her work was well known and recognized during her lifetime. Other French women were recognized for their musical/composing achievements. Marie-Anne-Catherine Quinault was the first woman whose composing earned her the decoration of the Order of St. Michel.

Music, which had had a particularly important place in the court of Queen Elizabeth, continued to thrive in England in the first part of the 1700s. However, after the English Civil War and during the time of Cromwell, the music world essentially shut down. The return of Charles II in 1660 reversed that. While living at the French court he had developed a strong taste for all things French, including French music and French musicians, and he returned music to English life. With French music being heavily influenced by Italian music, so, too, was English music.

England was prosperous, and music performances, first primarily focused on the court, became more widespread with performances in public concerts, in private musicales, on stage and in specially built concert rooms, such as the still-surviving Holywell Music Room in Oxford, and in music houses, which were similar to coffee houses.

German music also experienced a strong Italian influence, and music was no longer the province of native composers writing in a "German style" of music. Composers and musicians were coming to Germany from the Low Countries (roughly present-day Netherlands and Belgium), from England, and of course from Italy. They were drawn, in part, by the numerous courts that provided ample opportunities for patronage and employment. The rivalry between these courts gave rise to a particularly diverse musical culture. Similarly, the split between the Protestant church and the Catholic Church, which had a strong impact on church music, also contributed to this diversity.

Music in Switzerland reflected its regional differences, giving rise to a strongly diverse musical tradition and life. The Reformation had a major impact on music. Much church music was forbidden or restricted, and organs were no longer allowed in churches.

Italy

One of the best-known musical families in Florence was the Caccini family. **Francesca Caccini** (September 18, 1587, Florence–after June, 1638) and her sister Settimia (see entry) were immersed in the musical culture of Florence and had important roles in it as well.

They both lived when music, particularly opera, was at a turning point, with rapid change and development. Music, along with the other arts, was central to the culture of Florence. The court was the focus and patronage was essential to the arts; looking at that period from today, it is hard to grasp just how closely woven the arts were in the fabric of the society and culture of the time. People seem to have lived and breathed the arts, and the changes and development of music, literature, and art were heady matters.

Francesca is considered to be the first woman to compose opera. She was also the composer of the first Italian opera to be given outside Italy. She was the leading music personage (and highest paid composer) at the court of Tuscany under three Grand Dukes: Ferdinand I, Cosimo II, and Ferdinand II.

Her father, Giulio Romano Caccini, and her step-mother were both singers. Giulio had an important role in the development of early opera.

Francesca was educated both in music and literature; she was a poet (writing in Latin and Tuscan) and singer, and she played the harp, guitar and keyboard. From all accounts, she must have had an outstandingly beautiful singing voice. The entire family, talented singers all, often were featured in public performances, both religious and secular. Francesca began composing major "entertainments" for the court.

In 1604 the family went to France to perform for King Henry the IV and his Queen, Marie de Medici. Francesca was then offered a position as a salaried court singer, but as she already had a position with the court of Grand Duke Ferdinand I, she had to refuse Marie de Medici's offer.

When the family returned to Italy her father worked on negotiating a position for Francesca in Rome, one that would include a salary and a dowry. This didn't come to fruition, however, and Francesca took a position at the

Florentine court. By then she was promised in marriage to Giovanni Battista Signorini, a court singer. They were married in 1607 and had one child.

That same year Francesca composed her first music for the stage. Over the next ten years Francesca continued composing chamber music, primarily for herself and her pupils, but she also composed some incidental music for entertainments.

Francesca began publishing her compositions in 1618. By the 1620s she was the highest paid musician at court. At that time she was setting theater pieces to music, alone and in collaboration. Her one surviving opera, *La liberazione di Ruggiero dall'isola d'Alcina,* was performed in February 1625 at Carnival.

Her husband died in 1626. Six months later Francesca went off the Medici payroll, and five months after that she married Tomaso Rafielli. They had one son and were married for three years. Rafielli's death left Francesca a wealthy landowner. She returned to the Medici payroll in 1633 and continued to compose and perform.

Of the operas she wrote, only one has survived. She also wrote many sacred and secular songs, often set to her own poetry.

Operas and stage works:

La stiava, Pisa, music lost, 1607.
La mascherata, delle ninfe di Senna, balletto, Palazzo Pitti, Florence, 1611.
La tancia, incidental music, Palazzo Pitti, Florence, 1611.
Il passatempo, incidental music to balletto, Pallazo Pitti, Florence, 1614.
Il ballo delle Zingane, balletto, Palazzo Pitti, Florence, music lost, 1615.
La fiera, incidental music, Palazzo Pitti, Florence, 1619.
Il martirio de S. Agata, Florence, 1622.
La liberazione di Ruggiero dall'isola d'Alcina, musical comedy, Villa Poggio Imperiale, Florence, 1625.
Rinaldo inamorato, commissioned by Prince Wladislaw of Poland, 1626.

Principal sources: CCH; Grove's

Settimia Caccini (October 6, 1591, Florence–after 1661) was a singer and composer, as was her sister Francesca, and she also participated in the family music "business," singing in several of her father's operas and for the Medici courts in France and Florence. She was sought after as a court singer, and she held several prestigious and highly paid positions.

Her first public performance may have been in 1600 or 1602, singing in one of her father's operas, and for at least ten years she continued as part of the family singing ensemble. At times she wrote a portion of her own part. At least twice she was offered a position as a court singer; one of the terms in the contract involved a dowry and finding her a suitable husband. Her father declined the offers for her, possibly because her singing may have been part of the contractual agreement her father had with the Medici.

Her husband, Alessandro Ghivizzani, was a singer and composer, and the two were salaried musicians at court in 1609. Two years later they left without giving notice; they were subsequently hired by Duke Ferdinando Gonzaga to sing at the court in Mantua. They remained there for six years before returning to Lucca and then settling in Parma. When Ghivizzani died in 1632, Settimia returned to Florence and remained on the payroll until 1661.

Her compositions are vocal works. Few survive. Some music has been given questionable attribution.

Principal source: Norton Grove

Chiara Margarita Cozzolani (November 27, 1602, Milan–between May 4, 1676 and April 20, 1678, Milan) was from a wealthy merchant family. When she was seventeen she entered a monastery, as did many high-born women of her time, and she took her final vows a year later. (A monastery might house both male and female religious students.) The religious house she belonged to was renowned for its music.

Chiara clearly was one of the leading composers during her lifetime. Some of her publications, including her secular cantatas and her first publication (1640), are lost. Her first surviving publication, the *Concerti sacri* in 1642, was dedicated to Mathias de Medici. Her music shows innovation and movement away from the earlier traditional style. She was twice abbess of her house, and prioress for a period of time, which may account for there being few compositions after 1650.

Her works are for voice, and include some more complex part songs. Perhaps her best-known work is her *Messa Paschale*.

Principal source: CCH

One of the better-known women composers of the time was **Barbara Strozzi** (1619, Venice–after 1664, Venice?). She was the adopted daughter of Giulio Strozzi, who may have been her father. Her mother was his longtime servant. When Strozzi died, Barbara was his sole heir.

Like many composers of that time, Barbara was also a singer, and she frequently sang in private homes. She studied with Francesco Cavalli, as did Antonia Bembo. When her father founded the Accademia degli Unisoni in 1637, she participated both by singing at programs and meetings held by the academy and by suggesting subjects for their debates.

Her first publication of music was in 1644 when she published a volume of madrigals using texts by Giulio Strozzi. She had eight publications in all; most appeared after Giulio's death in 1652. They carry dedications to important patrons, which suggests she depended on her composing after Giulio's death. Nothing more is known of Barbara after the eighth publication.

Barbara never married. She had four children.

The Genoese painter Bernardo Strozzi painted her portrait and a copy, *Female Musician with Viola da Gamba* in the Gemäldegalerie Dresden, is thought to be the original portrait.

In addition to her books of madrigals her compositions include other works for singers, cantatas and pieces for strings, often using texts by Strozzi. Most are missing.

Principal source: CCH

Isabella Leonarda (1620–1704) was a prolific composer with twenty published volumes. When she was sixteen she joined the Ursuline Order of the Collegio di Santa Orsola, as did at least one of her sisters. Her music was first published by her teacher when Leonarda was twenty. There is a significant gap of about thirty years before the next surviving publication, op. 3, which suggests that there were likely two other volumes published earlier.

Her compositions include many individual sacred compositions, sonatas for two violins and continuo, and four Masses for four voices, two violins, and organ continuo.

Principal source: CCH

Antonia Bembo (Venice, c. 1643–Paris before 1715) was rediscovered in 1937 when a French musicologist found six bound manuscript volumes of her music in the French National Library. Although well known in her time, she had disappeared from view.

She lived in Venice during her early years. Her father was a doctor, and like Barbara Strozzi, she studied music for several years with Francesco Cavalli. In 1659 she married Lorenzo Bembo, a nobleman.

She left him and Venice, however, with an unknown person, having placed her daughter at a convent and leaving her two sons with their father. By 1676 she and the unidentified person were in Paris. She sang for Louis XIV, who was so impressed that he awarded her a pension, which allowed her to enter the religious community of the Petite Union Chrétienne des Dames de Saint Chaumont in Paris.

We know she composed from 1697 to after 1707; whether she had been composing earlier is not clear. Many of her compositions were dedicated to Louis XIV and other members of the royal family. Her compositions reflect both her musical training in Italy and the influence of French music.

Although her contemporary, Elisabeth-Claude Jacquet de la Guerre, was in Paris and well known while Antonia lived there, we have no indication that they were acquainted or knew each other's works.

Her works, which are six volumes of manuscript, include her opera *Ercole*

Amante (there may have been others), music for solo and several voices, and music for voices with orchestra and instrumental accompaniment.

Opera:

Ercole amante, 1707.

Principal sources: Norton Grove/CCH

Many women who composed were also proficient artists. **Angiola Teresa Moratori Scanabecchi** (1662, Bologna–April 19, 1708, Bologna) was one such woman (she is listed under Moratori). She was trained both in music and in painting. Apart from limited knowledge about her professional life and the fact of her marriage to Scanabecchi Monetta, we know little about her life.

She composed at least four oratorios that were performed. Unfortunately only the librettos (by Bergamori) survive, but these librettos indicate that the oratorios included recitatives, duets and arias.

She was also well known for her paintings; several may be seen in churches in Bologna and Ferrara.

Principal source: Norton Grove

Lucrezia Orsina Vizzana (July 3, 1590, Bologna–1662) entered the convent of Santa Cristina della Fondazza of the Camaldolese Order, known for its singers and musicians, when she was eight and she took her vows several years later. Two of her sisters and three aunts were also at the convent. Many daughters of wealthy families who were interested in music and art studied at or entered the convent. Although outside contact was limited (and frowned upon by church authorities), musicians resident in the convent were conversant with current trends in sacred music.

In 1623 a collection of twenty of her motets, an ornate edition dedicated to the nuns of her convent, was published in Venice. No further publications or compositions by her are known.

Principal source: CCH

Caterina Assandra (early 1590s, Pavia–1620), a nun at the Monastery of Saint Agatha of Lomella, published a collection of music that was followed by a second volume of eighteen compositions. Further publications include an eight-voice *Salve Regina*, 1611, and *Audite verbum Domini*, 1618.

Principal source: CCH

Claudia Sessa (no dates) was at the Convent of Santa Maria Annunciata in Milan. Two songs are known, published in a Venetian collection in 1613.

Principal source: CCH

Sulpitia Lodovica Cesis (1577, Modena–after 1619), a nun at the convent of San Geminiano in Modena, published a volume of music in 1619.

Principal source: CCH

England

Elisabetta de Gambarini (September 7, 1731?, London–February 9, 1765, London) was well known for singing Handel's oratorios, but she also became a presence in the world of keyboard music in England at that time. She began her singing career early. At times she included her own music in her concerts, and she may have conducted performances of her own music. She also reputedly played the organ.

Her three published volumes of harpsichord pieces and songs — which were in Italian and English — were likely the first publications of music by a woman in England. Her 1748 publication has a frontispiece portrait by Nathaniel Hone.

She's next heard of in 1761 when she had a benefit concert that included music she composed for an ode. There may have been a later concert under the name Mrs. Chazal. She is also spoken of as a painter.

She wrote at least one organ concerto and music for harpsichord and voice.

Principal sources: Norton Grove; CCH

France

One of the most remarkable composers — and not just for that particular time — was **Elisabeth Claude Jacquet de la Guerre** (baptized March 17, 1665– June 27, 1729, Paris). She was remarkable in several aspects in addition to her precocity, particularly as a harpsichord virtuoso. Her publications include works in almost every form that was popular. Elisabeth was interested in new musical trends and incorporated them into her own music. She was significant in introducing the new Italian style to France, and she was an early composer of the French cantata. What is perhaps most interesting is that she was fully recognized for her composing and musical talent.

The Jacquet family had been noted harpsichord builders for several generations. Her father was the French organist Claude Jacquet. Her mother, Anne de la Touché, also came from a musical family. Her two brothers were organists, and her sister Anne was a protégé of Marie of Lorraine, Princess of Guise, who was known for her musical ensemble that was headed by Marc-Antoine Charpentier.

Elisabeth was a precocious musician, and her early performances were written up in the press. She was considered "the marvel of our century" (*Mer-*

cure galant), as she composed, played, and accompanied at a very young age. At age eight she made her debut at Versailles, singing and playing the harpsichord, and she caught the attention of Louis XIV and Madame de Montespan, the king's mistress. Her musical ability so impressed them that she was offered the opportunity to live at Versailles and be educated there. Some of her compositions were dedicated to King Louis.

Her violin solo and trio sonatas, composed about 1695, were written within five years of the introduction of music of that form in France.

In 1684 she married Marin de la Guerre, an organist and harpsichord teacher. She then moved to Paris but still maintained her contacts with the court — to some extent giving her the best of both worlds. The next year her ballet, *Les jeux à l'honneur de la victoire*, was performed at Versailles. As early as 1687 she published a set of harpsichord pieces. She wrote an opera, *Céphale et Procris.*

During much of the reign of Louis XIV, Jean-Baptiste Lully was the court composer, musician, "manager" of musical events at court and dictator of opera. He was not always friendly to what he deemed competition. *Céphale et Procris*, which was the first opera by a woman to be performed at the Paris Opéra, was performed in 1694, seven years after Lully's death in 1687.

Her volume of cantatas, based on traditional mythological texts, was dedicated to the Elector of Bavaria and published after 1715, the year of King Louis's death.

Marin died in 1704, and their young son, who was a musical prodigy, died at about the same time. After Marin's death Elizabeth continued her musical life and composing but retired from public performance.

She published several books of harpsichord pieces, violin solo, trio sonatas, and cantatas. Her last known work was a choral Te Deum celebrating the recovery of Louis XV from smallpox in 1721.

Opera:

Cephale et Procri.

Principal sources: CCH; Grove's

Marie-Anne-Catherine Quinault (August 26, 1695, Strasbourg–1791, Paris) came from a theatrical family, but at least one other family member was also a composer. A singer, she made her debut at the Paris Opéra when she was fourteen and sang there until 1713. She also sang and acted at the Comédie Française.

Reportedly she composed motets for the royal chapel at Versailles. For one of her motets she was awarded the decoration of the Order of St. Michel, which had never before been given to a woman.

Principal source: Norton Grove

Germany

The court of Mecklenburg-Güstrow, where **Sophie Elisabeth, Duchess of Brunswick-Lüneburg** (August 20, 1613, Gustrow, Germany–July 12, 1676, Luchow) was raised, was noted for the excellence of its music. Sophie received very good musical training. However, when she was fifteen she had to flee from her home because of the threat of the Thirty Years' War. She was fortunate enough to settle at the Kassel court, which also had excellent music. Although she spent much time in exile, she received an excellent education and musical training.

She married Duke August the Younger of Brunswick-Lüneburg, who was known for his learning. They settled at Brunswick where they established a court orchestra. Six years later they moved to the castle at Wolfenbüttel; they moved again in 1665. Both moves required a reorganization of the orchestra, which she undertook.

Sophie Elisabeth began composing when she was a child and composed throughout her life. She wrote sacred songs and music for secular celebrations, as well as music for theatrical performances and ballets. Some music has survived anonymously.

Principal sources: Norton Grove; CCH

Switzerland

There are several instances of blind composers. One of the earliest we know about is **Esther Elizabeth Velkiers** (c 1640, Geneva–after 1685). Blind from infancy, she was taught to read by means of a wooden alphabet. She learned Latin, French and German, and mathematics, philosophy and theology and became known for her scholarship. Proceedings of the Royal Musical Association, 9th Session, 1882–1883, notes on page 188, "Esther Elizabeth Velkiers ... had a reputation as a musician, but a greater for languages, science, philosophy and theology."

She also played the harpsichord and composed for the harpsichord. None of her music is known to have survived.

Principal source: Norton Grove

Chapter Three

The Baroque Era, 1685–1750

One of the few firm dates in the evolution of classical music is 1685, the year Bach was born. Music had been evolving all along, of course, and changes didn't come abruptly. But Bach's brilliance had a tremendous impact on music, which clearly moved into a new era of style, notation, and composition.

Music had been undergoing change everywhere, including in Italy. For years vocal music of all kinds had dominated in Italy, and it was still a major focus, particularly operas and cantatas, but instrumental music was increasing in popularity. With the increase in the number of public theaters that were operated for profit, court theaters were losing their domination of theater life. The number of opera houses continued to increase. Private homes were the primary venue for instrumental music. Churches were still centers for education and performance.

Music, with the exception of music that was used in church services and religious observations, was entertainment. Audiences often regarded music and operas as pastimes and a setting for social activities.

Many, perhaps most musicians, came from families where music was the family business, a setting for at least initial teaching and training, and with connections that provided performance opportunities for younger family members.

Ironically, we seem to know less about the Italian women composers of this time than we did about earlier women composers in Italy.

In Austria, Italian influence dominated the musical scene earlier in the 1600s and was still strongly influential. Italian musicians were highly sought after in the royal courts, particularly since several of the Habsburg emperors were themselves noted composers. Opera began to be produced at court about 1630 and quickly became firmly established. But there was change in Austria as well as other places, as Austria developed more of an independent musical life, with influence from Germany.

Louis XIV reigned in France until 1715, with Versailles still "the city" and Paris the ostensible capital. His was a prosperous reign for the arts — if you were on the right side of the political fence. Lully's death in 1687 ended his monopoly of music, particularly in opera, and opened up opportunities for other composers, but to a great extent music was still the monopoly of Versailles.

After 1714, much changed under Louis XV, who wasn't particularly interested in music or culture. Versailles had lost its crucial importance and Paris welcomed back many of the nobles, artists, and ambitious souls from Versailles.

Opera was the rage. The Opéra Comique was founded in 1714, the year before Louis XIV's death.

The career of Elisabeth Jacquet de la Guerre lasted past the death of Louis XIV and into the Baroque. Another French woman, Mlle. Duval, wrote operas, one of which was the second opera by a woman that was composed at the Paris Opéra.

Frederick the Great assumed the throne of Prussia in 1740, after a wretched childhood under his tyrannical father. One of his many terrible transgressions in the eyes of his father was his great love of music, his playing and his composing.

Austria

We know about **Maria Anna de Raschenau** (fl. 1690s–1703, Vienna) from her oratorio, *Se sacre visioni di Santa Teresa*, which was performed in 1703, and a stage work, *Il consigilio di Pallade*. A nun, she was the choir director and perhaps a canoness at a convent in Vienna. Only the libretto of her oratorio and stage work survives, although the oratorio score was known to have existed into the twentieth century.

Stage work:

Il consigilio di Pallade.

Principal sources: CCH; Norton Grove

France

What little is known about **Mlle. Duval** (1718?–after 1775, Paris) is from her work and accounts of performances as a composer, dancer, singer, and harpsichordist. Her opera, *Les Genies, or Les caractères de l'Amour,* was the second opera by a woman to be performed at the Paris Opéra, in 1736 (Elisabeth Jacquet de la Guerre's opera *Céphale et Procris* being the first in 1694).

According to a review in the *Mercure*, Mlle. Duval accompanied her entire opera on harpsichord, seated in the orchestra (Norton Grove, p. 153). She was then eighteen. Her career and musical activities spanned many decades.

Duval is a common French name, and several Mlle. Duvals appear in lists of women composers. The composer of *Les Genies* may — or may not — be the same person as **Mlle. Louise Duval.**

Opera:

Les Genies, or Les caractères de l'Amour.

Principal sources: Grove's; Norton Grove

Germany

Anna Amalia, Princess of Prussia (November 9, 1723, Berlin–March 30, 1787, Berlin) was the youngest sister of Frederick the Great, who was himself a serious musician and composer. The children, especially Frederick, had a miserable childhood. Their father was brutal, and much of his brutality focused on Frederick. Their mother gave them what little they had that was good in their childhood, fostering Frederick's love of music by secretly providing for him to study music. He in turn passed along much of what he learned to his sisters. When Frederick became ruler he made his court a center of philosophy and the arts, particularly music.

Thus, Frederick was Anna Amalia's first music teacher; later she studied under the cathedral organist. Anna was an accomplished keyboard player and proficient as a violinist and flute player, as was Frederick. She was a popular hostess, and her soirées attracted many artists, literary figures and other notable personages.

She was in her mid-thirties when she began seriously to study composition, and she became extremely skilled in counterpoint. Her compositions include sonatas, marches, chorales, arias and songs, as well as a setting of Ramler's *Der Tod Jesu*. Her music library, now at the Royal Library in Berlin, is her most significant contribution to music.

Principal source: Norton Grove

Wilhelmina, Princess of Prussia, Margräfin of Bayreuth (July 3, 1709, Berlin–October 14, 1758, Bayreuth), sister of Anna Amalia (see previous entry) shared the miserable childhood of Frederick the Great, as did all the siblings. She was perhaps his favorite sister and was his close confidante for much of her life. She was intended to marry the Prince of Wales in a complicated arrangement that also involved the Crown Prince of Prussia and the oldest daughter of George II; this never came to fruition, in part because of British distrust of the Prussians. Her mother was most disappointed at this and felt that her marrying a mere margrave was a considerable comedown.

In 1731 she married Frederick, Margrave of Brandenburg-Bayreuth, who was an accomplished musician and flautist. They determined to make Bayreuth a great center of culture and rebuilt the Ermitage, the Baroque opera house for which Bayreuth is still famous, the Bayreuth palace, and a new opera house. They also founded the University of Erlangen. The court attracted many scholars and artists. She is known for her correspondence with Voltaire and her brother, Frederick the Great. Among the topics in the correspondence with her brother are his plans for operatic reform.

Her works include the opera *Argenore* in 1740, arias, a keyboard concerto and church music.

Her memoirs, *Memoires de ma vie*, are in the Royal Library of Berlin. An English translation was published in Berlin.

Opera:

Argenore, 1740.

Principal sources: Norton Grove; Derek McCulloch, "Royal Composers: The Composing Monarchs That Britain Nearly Had" in *The Musical Times*, vol. 22, no. 1662 (August 1981), pp. 527–528.

Italy

We know about the life of **Rosanna Scalfi Marcello** (fl. 1723–1742) primarily through a romantic legend and a legal tangle. She was a singer of Venetian *arie di battello*, which were simple songs sung in gondolas. When a nobleman and singing teacher, Benedetto Marcello, heard her sing outside his window that overlooked the Grand Canal, he was so enchanted by her voice that he took her on as one of his singing pupils. Marcello was a notable figure in music and an eminent composer, particularly of operas, church music, oratorios, hundreds of solo cantatas, duets, sonatas, concertos and sinfonias.

They wed, secretly, in a religious ceremony that was performed by the patriarch of Venice, but they were never married in a civil ceremony and thus the marriage wasn't recognized by the state. Consequently when Rosanna was widowed in 1739, although she was the primary beneficiary of Marcello's estate, she could not gain legal right to it. Three years later she filed suit against Benedetto's brother for financial support, but the suit went against her and she was left destitute.

She composed at least twelve cantatas; she was the author of the texts for several of them.

Joachim Raff (1822–1882) a celebrated German composer during his lifetime but largely forgotten today, wrote an opera titled *Benedetto Marcello* in which Rosanna has a significant role.

Principal source: Norton Grove

Maria Grimani and **Camilla de Rossi** are considered Italian composers, although much of their professional lives were spent in Vienna, Austria.

Maria Grimani (fl. early 18th century, apparently in Vienna) is known through her compositions. As a woman composer at the Viennese court, she may have been one of several canonesses who were at the court at that time. Three of her works, two oratorios and a dramatic work, were performed at the Vienna court theater between 1713 and 1718. Her name is spelled variously on her scores.

Principal sources: CCH; Norton Grove

Similarly, **Camilla de Rossi** (Rome?–fl. 1707–1710, Vienna) is known to us through her compositions. "Romana" on the title pages of her manuscripts suggests she was from Rome. Much of her music was performed at the Viennese court between 1707 and 1710, earlier than performances of Grimani's music.

We know of six oratorios she wrote: four have survived. For at least one oratorio, *Il figlinol prodigo*, she wrote the text as well as the music. She also wrote a cantata, which survives.

Principal source: CCH

The rather cryptic information we have about the home life of **Maria Teresa d'Agnesi** (October 17, 1720, dates vary, Milan–January 19, 1795) is intriguing. As was the case with many composers, she began performing at home and often played some of her own compositions. Those "entertainments" were eclectic and might have included her older sister, Maria Gaetana d'Agnesi, lecturing and debating in Latin. (Maria Gaetana, 1718–1799, was the author of a textbook on calculus, published in 1748. She is considered to be the first woman to establish herself as a mathematician.)

Maria's first theatrical work was a cantata pastorale, *Il restauro d'Arcadia*, which was successfully performed in Milan about 1747. Maria was well known outside of Milan; some of the collections of her arias and instrumental pieces were dedicated to rulers of Saxony and Austria. She married in June 1752 but had no children.

She was the librettist for her next opera, *Ciro in Armenia*, which was performed in Milan in 1753. She wrote several more dramatic works; perhaps her best known was *La Sofonisba*. Metastasio was the librettist for *Il re pastore*.

In addition to her dramatic works, her compositions include concerti, sonatas and dance music.

Her portrait is in the theater museum at La Scala.

Operas and stage works:

Ciro in Armenia, Regio Ducal Teatro, Milan, 1753.
Il re pastore, 1756.
La Sofonisba, Naples, 1765.
L'insubria consolata, Regio Ducal Teatro, Milan, possibly lost, 1766.
Nitocri, Venice, 1771.

Principal source: Grove's

Chapter Four

Early Classical, 1750–1800

The death of Johann Sebastian Bach in 1750 is a convenient date for marking the beginning of early classical music. At that time music was undergoing significant changes as musicians experimented with new instruments and utilizing different combinations of instruments in orchestras and musical groups. Compositions were taking on new forms. Audiences followed the changes in instruments and composing and performing in much the same way they kept up with changes in dress fashions.

The influence of Italian opera continued to be strong, but composers were beginning to question why opera had to be in Italian. Couldn't a German, who composed for German audiences, compose a different opera — a German opera, for instance? Furthermore, that opera shouldn't be a German imitation of an Italian opera, but an authentically different opera.

Music continued to be a "family business," and many women composers came from musical families and often married musicians. Most professional musicians and performers, both men and women, were part of the middle class.

Women who were connected with a court could utilize the advantage of living at a place where music was valued and they could get good musical instruction. While some women gave up their careers when they married, many did not.

Because the performance of opera, like other large music genres, generally requires a lot of resources — orchestras, singers, musicians, and sometimes stage settings — opportunities for women to have their operas performed were limited. However, chamber operas (to use the term broadly) were often performed in private settings. Also, other stage works didn't require the elaborate resources of a major opera.

Demand was high for stage works and operas of all types, which provided opportunities for women opera composers. Notwithstanding all of the limitations and prejudices, operas by women *were* performed, and some enjoyed great success.

Vienna was the center of the Austrian Empire. The Habsburgs ruled the Empire, and the Emperor's court, which was the Imperial Court, was the center of everything. Royal courts, where fashion was set, where decisions were made, and where there were jobs, almost always attracted many people. The Imperial Court was not only the center of power and society, but it was the center of music as well.

Many musicians and composers also were attracted to Vienna where there were positions outside the court as well. If they were lucky, they would acquire a patron who would take a strong interest in their work and their music and pay them.

The "right" patron could make a difference in whether or not a composer was successful. Having a good patron meant the composer had a support system that took care of financial needs and ensured that the composer's music would be performed.

Having a patron could be a mixed blessing, though. Many patrons dictated what kinds of music they wanted "their" composer to write, although some were willing to give the composer more of a free hand in what he or she wrote. A musician or composer who was in service to a noble person or a member of royalty was bound to that position; leaving that position could be very difficult. Consequently, musicians and composers had very little independence unless they were wealthy themselves.

Emperor Joseph II, who was concerned about seemingly secular influences on church music and the increasing presence of women singers in church, discouraged the use of instruments in church, women's performing in church or church music, and elaborate musical settings of the liturgy. His decree closed off an important venue for women, but the increasing number of secular venues and the amount of secular music helped compensate for these limitations, particularly in Vienna.

Vienna must have seemed like a magic place for music in the late 1700s. You could attend a concert or an opera every day. In fact, there were so many musical events that you couldn't possibly go to all of them.

Princes and nobles prided themselves on their private orchestras. In the summer when they lived on their estates, music was part of the daily life. When they moved to their palaces in Vienna for the winter, their musicians came with them.

Musical performances took place in salons and musical gatherings at a private home. This was the place to try out music, to build an audience before putting on an expensive recital or concert, and to perform solo music and music for smaller groups of instruments that were better suited to a small performance space. Having music at home was more elaborate than it might sound. The performances may have been considered "small" at the time, but the houses of the nobility and important people might have space for a concert for several hundred guests.

With all the music activity and composing in Vienna, music publishers did a good business. Many people worked at copying music by hand as they had before music printing became widely used. Vienna was also the place to buy good musical instruments and to try out new instruments, like the glass harmonica or the basset horn.

In contrast to the pleasantness of musical life in Austria and Vienna, by the end of the century musical life in France involved negotiating the politics of the French Revolution — and a great deal of luck.

The evolution of music during this period was inevitably caught up in the politics of the time. The bourgeoisie increasingly were having an impact on music, literature and art. As a result cultural life no longer was exclusively subject to the dictates of the court and nobility. Newspapers had appeared, and in addition to their obvious impact on the growing political turmoil, they had an increasing influence on the arts and on music.

In the late 1700s and early 1800s music schools were founded, not only the Institut National de Musique in 1793, later the Paris Conservatoire, but also in other cities where civic music schools were founded. Paris was still a center for music publishing and for instrument making, although the pro-duction of instruments now was a flourishing industry in several places other than Paris.

Yet, to a great extent music and composing were still the province of the nobility and well connected, and the Revolution was most disruptive to their careers — and their lives.

It may seem curious given the context, but in France between 1780 and 1820, women composers in general flourished — particularly those who were composers of opera. Early in the Revolution women were active and visible in public life, but this was soon squashed by more radical male revolutionaries. One change that opened a window for women was the abolition of the power and privileges of the royal theaters — the declaration of the freedom of the theaters in 1791, which meant that anyone could open a theater — and they did. This opened up great opportunities for playwrights and composers to have their work performed. That particular window was closed in 1806 and 1807 by Napoleon's reforms, which reduced the number of theaters to eight. In 1820 these restrictions were relaxed, and theater again became a more open venue for writers and composers.

The disruptions of the Revolution forced many well-born women to earn money to support their families. For some women there was a liberating element to this. And, although opera had been the purview of the aristocracy, it became a medium of political propaganda. All of these changes and attitudes were exceedingly difficult to navigate: some women did it better than others — or were luckier. The subject matter of operas was becoming broader and less confined to classical stories and themes. Audiences were seeing current subject matter with singers in current dress.

Although England enjoyed an active musical life at this time, there were no major female composers. However, many women were active in music, often as professional singers, and they also composed as well. Although they were minor composers, they represent a significant aspect of British musical life.

London certainly was the center of culture in England at that time. London also was an important location for harpsichord, and later piano, manufacturing; in 1800 pianos were being mass marketed by John Broadwood. London also had a publishing trade second only to Paris. Smaller cities had their own cultural life as well, and for women — and many men — who didn't have the mobility to move to London, their option was to utilize the opportunities at hand.

German musical culture continued its vigor and diversity, centered largely on several courts, particularly that of Frederick the Great, who had come to the throne in 1740. But music life was thriving in the cities as well, particularly among the wealthy upper and middle class. Music education and performance, both secular and sacred, made music life much more accessible in the cities. The court still leaned toward Italian music, particularly Italian opera. Civic music tended to be more diverse.

Leipzig was quickly becoming the most important city for music in Germany. Its international aspect — Leipzig had long been famous for its trade fairs — was particularly noticeable in opera. Leipzig would become the most important city in Europe for music publishing, in large part due to J. G. I. Breitkopf and his new system of printing notation. Opera continued to reign, although the style had changed from having the text predominant, often to the detriment of the music, to a style where the music had the greater emphasis.

Venice was a primary center for opera; demand continued to be almost insatiable. The city also had a geographical advantage with its proximity to northern Europe.

Italy's supremacy in music was eroding. Many other areas of Europe, particularly through royal courts, had good music education and opportunities for performance. While there still was a cachet to being an Italian musician or composer, or having been trained and educated in Italy, the predominance of Italian music and music in the Italian style was continuing to raise questions — more emphatically — about operas and instrument music, especially for the keyboard, or cantatas that reflected the culture or the area — and was written by someone native to the area.

Bohemia, like many areas of Europe, was experiencing an increasingly strong sense of nationalism and national identity. Although this was most evident in the literary and linguistic life of Bohemia, it soon had an impact on the music as well.

The geographic position of Denmark had long made it a crossroads for cultural influences. In the 1600s many foreign composers had been attracted to the court at Copenhagen. Church music and music based on sacred subjects came to dominate. For a time, the prohibition of opera had given emphasis to religious-based drama, pageants, cantatas, and oratorios. But by 1703 there was an opera house in Copenhagen, and by the middle of the century opera had taken firm hold.

In the Netherlands the traditions of prosperity and artistic support continued to draw musicians (as well as artists). Royal courts were often the center of cultural life, and centers of education and training. Various music institutions came into existence, in large part encouraged by the wealthy bourgeoisie. Public concerts were numerous and very popular.

There was certainly music in the English colonies, but a classical musical tradition didn't take hold until much later. The music was primarily what was brought from Europe, and many early American folk music was adaptations or versions of European traditional songs. Elizabeth Joanetta Catherine von Hagen was the first known woman in the early colonies of America to publish an instrumental work.

Austria

The most prominent woman composer of the time was **Marianne Martinez**, sometimes given as Martines (May 4, 1744, Vienna–December 13, 1812, Vienna). Well born, well connected socially and musically, she was a prolific composer and had an active performance life. She was one of six children in a family of Spanish minor nobility.

The family lived in a "house" that was typical of Vienna of that time, roughly an apartment house with roomy, luxurious flats on the lower floors. As you went up the stairs, the size and accommodations declined, as did the social level of the inhabitants. The attics were rented to poorer tenants: tradespeople and sometimes students.

The Martinez family lived in a spacious apartment they shared with Pietro Metastasio, who was court poet, an opera librettist and a family friend from the time Marianne's father had lived in Naples. A bachelor, he took great interest in the six Martinez children. He directed Marianne's education and, to a great extent, her career. For a time the young Joseph Haydn rented an attic room and gave Marianne harpsichord lessons in exchange for meals.

Marianne began composing at an early age. When she was fifteen her singing and keyboard playing attracted attention at court; by then she was composing large church works. In 1761 a mass she composed was performed at the court chapel, which was a great honor for her. In 1773 she became an honorary member of the Accademia Filarmonica of Bologna; she was one of only three female members. She composed three more masses.

In 1780 Emperor Joseph II, a ruler with definite ideas about music and church, ascended to the throne. He wanted to simplify church music, so he forbade the use of orchestras and elaborate instrumental pieces in church. He returned to the old rule that forbade women to "speak"—sing—in church. Marianne was commissioned by a Neopolitan poet to set several psalms to music. She also wrote *Dixit Dominus*, which was a large work for orchestra, for the Accademia Filarmonica in Bologna.

Metastasio died in 1782, bequeathing his house and estate to the Martinez family. The home continued to be a center for musical gatherings and soirées and attracted distinguished musicians. Haydn, no longer the poor student in the garret, often was a guest at these weekly gatherings, as was Mozart.

Marianne was also in demand as a performer. Mozart and Marianne played piano duets, and he wrote piano sonatas for them to play together. Marianne performed as a pianist and singer throughout her life. In the 1790s she opened a singing school in her house. Several of her students became well known and went on to have successful careers.

She composed more than two hundred works in all. She was partial to complex music and composed four masses, at least one oratorio, music for orchestra, music for voices and accompaniment, sonatas and much music for harpsichord and piano. The only form of music she didn't compose was opera.

Principal sources: Grove's; CCH

Marianne wasn't the only woman composer in Vienna at that time. One remarkable woman, who was about fifteen years younger than Marianne, was a pianist, a teacher, and a composer. Marianne and **Maria Theresa von Paradis** (May 15, 1759, Vienna–February 1, 1824, Vienna) both became known for their hospitality and the salons they hosted for people in the arts. They moved in the same circles and knew each other, but we have virtually no information about their meetings and any interactions.

Family connections played a large role in the musical life of Maria Theresa von Paradis. Her father was the royal court secretary of the Empress Maria Theresa, and Maria was named after the Empress.

When Maria Theresa was three years old she lost her sight. Her blindness occurred very suddenly, and no one knew what caused it or how to treat it. Many treatments were tried, but to no avail.

From the time she was very young it was obvious that Maria was remarkably talented in music. When she was eleven she performed in public, singing in Pergolesi's Stabat Mater and playing her own accompaniment on the organ. The Empress recognized her ability and potential and provided for a good education for Maria, with particular emphasis on musical training. She also granted Maria a stipend. (Joseph II discontinued the stipend; his successor Leopold II reinstated it.)

By the time she was sixteen Maria Theresa was a brilliant pianist. She had an amazing musical ear and memory and could memorize great amounts of music for her performances. Accounts say that she could play at least sixty sonatas and concertos from memory. Mozart, Salieri and Haydn wrote music for her.

When she was twenty she set out on a long concert tour through Europe with her mother and Johann Riedinger, a librettist who was a family friend. The tour, which lasted nearly three years, extended throughout Europe — to Brussels, Amsterdam and Prague and cities in Germany, France, England, and Switzerland. They would stay in a city for a period of time, and Maria Theresa would give performances. She gave at least fourteen concerts in Paris. Mozart sent her a piano concerto he'd written for her to perform at one of her Paris concerts, but unfortunately the concerto didn't get to her in time for her to perform it.

During the long tour she began composing piano and harpsichord music and also music for singers. Riedinger developed a peg-board system that she could use for putting down her compositions. The pegboard had different shaped pegs for different note values. A copyist would then transcribe the compositions into standard musical notation.

In Paris she met Valentin Haüy, who had devoted his life to working with the blind. (Several years later, in 1785, he opened the first school for the blind. Maria Theresa helped him develop the program of study, based on methods that had been used in her own education.)

The three years of traveling and performing must have been exhausting as well as exciting. Maria Theresa never made such an extended tour again, although she later planned tours in Russia and in Italy that did not materialize. She did return to Prague when one of her operas was produced there.

After she returned from her tour she began composing more and performing less; later she taught as well. Unfortunately, much of her music has gotten lost over the years. The records of what she wrote are incomplete, and scholars have found it difficult to determine which compositions are hers and which were written by someone else. But they have firmly identified about thirty works that she wrote, including several cantatas, five operas, choral pieces, piano concertos, seven symphonies, and music for piano and for stringed instruments.

Maria Theresa was always concerned with education, particularly for the blind. In 1808 she began a music school for girls. She taught piano, singing and theory. Many outstanding women pianists taught at the school, which accepted both blind and sighted students. The school was known for its Sunday house concerts, which attracted members of Viennese society. She continued to compose until at least 1813, but teaching had become her primary musical interest.

Operas and stage works:

Ariadne und Bacchus, described as a melodrama (Grove). Vienna? lost, 1791.
Der Schulkandidat, Vienna, an operetta or mourning cantata; a portion is lost, 1792.
Rinaldo und Alcina, Prague, based on a libretto by the blind author Ludwig von Baczko. This was not successful, and after this failure she focused more on teaching. Only the text survives; the music is lost, 1797.
Grosse militarische, lost, 1805?
Zwei landliche Opern, lost, 1792.

Principal sources: Norton Grove; CCH

Another member of musical circles in Vienna at that time was **Josepha Barbara von Auernhammer** (September 25, 1756 (baptized), Vienna–January 30, 1820, Vienna), who was a close contemporary of Maria von Paradis. She was not as significant a composer as either Marianne Martinez or Maria von Paradis.

Josepha, along with Therese von Trattner, was one of Mozart's favorite pupils. (Josepha reputedly fell in love with Mozart.) He dedicated music to her and composed a sonata for two pianos for the two of them to play; they performed together several times from 1781 to 1785. She was one of Mozart's first editors.

After her father died in 1782 Josepha went to live with Baroness Waldstätten. She married in 1786 and had one daughter, who sang and appeared with Josepha in concerts.

Josepha composed primarily piano music. She specialized in variations that show her wide-ranging knowledge of technique and use of the piano, and sonatas.

Principal sources: CCH; Norton Grove

Marianna von Auenbrugger (fl. Vienna–1786) also came from a musical family that was active in the musical life of Vienna. Her father wrote the German libretto for one of Salieri's operas, and Marianna studied with Salieri. Marianna and her sister Katharina were well-known keyboard players; Haydn dedicated six of his piano sonatas to them. The sisters were friends of the Mozart family as well.

Marianna's only known work is a sonata that was published in Vienna about 1781.

Principal sources: CCH; Norton Grove

The life of **Maria Anna "Nannerl" Mozart** (July 30–31, 1751, Salzburg–October 29, 1829) raises questions about what she might have been able to do in different circumstances and in a different family. There are many such instances with respect to historic women in a variety of circumstances, but hers is particularly visible and on the poignant side.

She was, of course, the very talented sister of Wolfgang Amadeus Mozart. Under the direction of Leopold Mozart, their father, she and Wolfgang toured and performed extensively when they were very young. They attracted attention everywhere, but particularly in royal and noble circles. Maria Anna was considered exceptionally brilliant, a precise keyboard player and very able improviser, but Wolfgang was particularly exceptional in improvising and composition.

Maria's performing value to her family was as a child prodigy. When she grew older she was no longer a *wunderkind*, and in 1769 when Wolfgang and Leopold went to Italy to tour she had to stay home and settle into the life of a proper young lady. Except for a few visits to Leipzig, she stayed in Salzburg most of her life.

She was attractive and had a congenial personality, but Leopold didn't care for her suitors and turned away one after another. Eventually he decided she could marry Johann Baptist von Berchtold zu Sonnenburg (1736–1801), a magistrate who was ill-tempered and had five children. The couple had three children, but only the eldest survived. During much of her married life Maria Anna taught music and gave lessons.

There is no doubt that she could have been a very able composer, but her potential received little attention. She never received instruction in composition.

There is a note that Wolfgang wrote to her in 1770, after she had sent him a song she had written. He comments that he had forgotten how well she could compose. He thought highly of her ability.

After her husband's death Maria Anna gave lessons to help support herself.

No compositions survive, nor do we know what she wrote aside from the song Wolfgang commented on.

Principal sources: Norton Grove; the Mozart Project web site

Nanette von Schaden (Ebelsberg–fl. 1780s and 1790s) was an excellent pianist, a singer and an artist in addition to being a composer. She grew up in the musical life of Vienna. Her husband, Joseph, was a critic and gave financial support to Beethoven. For at least part of their marriage they lived in the court of von Oettingen-Wallerstein, which had been a musical center for many years.

Of her compositions only two concertos are known.

Principal source: Grove's

Bohemia

Katerina Veronika Anna Dusikova (March 8, 1769, Caslav, Bohemia–1833, London) was part of the Dussek family, which had a long history of musicians. The family included at least three women composers. Katerina was the daughter of the organist and composer Jan Dussek and sister of Jan Ladislav Dussek. (His wife was Sophia Giustina Dussek, née Corri, also a composer, pianist, harpist and singer. See entry.)

She received much of her musical training from her father. When Katerina was about twenty-five she went to London to perform at the urging of her brother, Jan. Katerina stayed in London and became a successful pianist and teacher. She married Francesco Cianchettini, who was a music dealer and publisher. At least one of their children, their son Pio Cianchettini, was a pianist and composer.

Katerina's compositions include two piano concertos, solo piano works including three sonatas, sets of variations and short pieces.

Principal source: Norton Grove

Denmark

Countess Maria Theresia Ahlefeldt (February 28, 1755, Regensburg–December 10, 1810) is considered a Danish composer although she was born in Germany. Her father was the Prince of Thrun and Taxis, and her early years were spent at her father's court, which was known for its rich cultural life.

She was engaged to Prince Joseph of Fürstenberg for several years, but the engagement was terminated when she had an affair with Prince Philip of Hohenlohe. Four years later she married the Danish count Ferdinand Ahlefeldt. Her family strongly objected to the marriage, and she had to leave Germany to avoid arrest.

She and her husband lived for several years at the court of Anspach (Ansbach) and were undoubtedly there at the same time as Elizabeth Craven Anspach (see entry). Countess Ahlefeldt had a considerable reputation as a pianist and took part in many of the performances at the court. It was about this time she began composing.

In 1792 when the court of Anspach dissolved, she and her husband moved to Copenhagen where her husband was director of the Kongelige Theater. There she composed *Telemak på Calypsos Øe* or *Telemachus and Calypso*, an opera-ballet that was very successful. She seems to have been particularly skilled in orchestration. She wrote the libretto and possibly the music for *La folie, ou Quel conte!* While in Copenhagen she also wrote the cantata *To Harmony*.

In 1798 they moved to Dresden then, a few years later, to Prague. Nothing is known of the remainder of her life.

Opera and stage works:

La folie, ou Quel conte! Anspach, music is lost, 1789.

Telemak på Calypsos Øe or *Telemachus and Calypso*, Copenhagen Royal Theatre, opera ballet, 1792.

S. Sonnischen, c. 1795.

Principal sources: Norton Grove; Grove's

England

Maria "Polly" Barthélemon (c. 1749, London–September 20, 1799, London) was born into a family of noted singers. Both of her older sisters were successful singers. Her aunt Cecilia, an outstanding soprano, was married to Thomas Arne. Thomas and Cecilia were close to Maria's family, and at the age of six Maria traveled with them to Dublin, where she sang — perfectly — in Arne's *Eliza*. For several years Maria stayed with Cecilia in Ireland, studying music and performing in Dublin. She soon became known for her ability to play the harpsichord

She continued her singing career when she returned to London in 1762. In 1766 she married François Hippolyte Barthélemon, a violinist and composer, and they often performed together and toured.

Maria composed sonatas for piano or harpsichord with violin, hymns, anthems, and English and Italian songs.

Her daughter was Cecilia Maria Barthélemon (see entry).

Principal source: Norton Grove

The daughter of Maria Barthélemon and the grandniece of Thomas Arne, **Cecilia Maria Barthélemon** (1769/70, England–after 1840) continued the musical tradition of the family, accompanying her parents on their continental tour in 1776–1777 when she sang for Marie Antoinette. Cecilia played harpsichord, piano, organ and harp.

Her works, which were published, include sonatas for keyboard with accompanying violin, a keyboard work with soprano and chorus, and keyboard sonatas, one of which was dedicated to Haydn who was a family friend. Her performing and composing seem to have ceased after her marriage to Captain E. P. Henslowe.

Principal source: Norton Grove

Another member of the Dussek family, **Sophia Corri Dussek** (May 1, 1775, Edinburgh, Scotland–1847, London) was the daughter of Domenico Corri, who was a composer, music publisher and teacher. She was the sister-in-law of Katerina Veronika Anna Dusikova (see entry).

Her father had been born in Italy but moved to Scotland to start an opera company and be an opera conductor. This didn't work out, and when Sophia was about fifteen the family moved to London, where her father founded a publishing business.

Sophia performed in public from the time she was young, and after the move to London she studied singing with some of the best teachers. She made her singing debut in 1791. The next year she married Jan Ladislav Dussek but continued to perform as a singer, pianist and harpist, usually with her husband. Dussek joined the publishing business, now Dussek and Corri, in addition to continuing his musical career.

Accounts of the couple's life together vary, but it seems it was an unsettled marriage and possibly with liaisons on both sides. When the business went bankrupt, Sophia's husband, Jan Dussek, went to the continent, leaving behind his family, and perhaps leaving his father-in-law in debtors' prison. The business was later taken over by Sophia's brother.

Sophia and her husband had one child, their daughter, Olivia, who was also a pianist, harpist and composer (see entry).

After her husband's death, Sophia married John Alois Moral, a viola player. She continued her composing; she also established a music school.

She was a prolific composer. Her compositions include sonatas, rondos, music for piano or harp, songs and arrangements of songs.

Principal sources: Norton Grove; Ann Griffiths, "Dussek and the Harp," *The Musical Times*, vol. 109, no. 1503, p. 419.

The scanty information we have about **Jane Freer** (fl. London, 1770s) comes from the title page of her sonatas. She was raised in the Foundling Hospital in London and was completely blind. She was instructed in music, which enabled her to make her living.

Principal source: Barbara Harbach on *Jane Freer: Six Sonatas for Harpsichord or Piano* [recording], Vivace Press.

Like so many other women composers, **Elizabeth Billington** (December 27, 1765/1768, London–August 25, 1818, near Venice) was born into a musical family. Her father was an oboist and clarinetist, and her mother, a well-known singer, was a pupil of J. C. Bach. Elizabeth also studied singing with Bach. From an early age she appeared as a pianist, often with her brother Charles, a violinist. Haydn thought her a genius.

Her first husband was James Billington, who was a double bass player (and her singing teacher). After her marriage in 1783 she continued to study and maintained a successful career as an opera singer, first in London then principally in Italy.

An author, James Ridgeway, who had an ax to grind and took the moral high road, published a highly disreputable (often referred to as "scurrilous") *Memoirs of Mrs. Billington* in 1792. The book caused considerable gossip and comment. Early in 1794, perhaps because of the book and its aftermath, she left England with her brother and her husband. Eventually they settled in Italy; the story is that the King of Naples heard her sing at a private party and urged her to sing at the Teatro San Carlo. Her debut there was very successful. Shortly after, her husband died. Elizabeth remained in Naples, singing in operas, some of which were composed for her. She was in Naples during the eruption of Vesuvius. She also was there when Emma Hamilton, Lady Hamilton of Lord Nelson fame, was living there, and the two formed a friendship that lasted for many years.

She and her brother left Naples in 1796 while she toured, singing at opera houses throughout Italy. She met Josephine Bonaparte in Milan. There she met and married her second husband, Monsieur Felican or Felissent. They soon separated, and he was reportedly abusive. She returned to England in 1801, where she continued her very successful singing career. When she retired in 1811 she still had a very beautiful singing voice.

Unfortunately, Felissent came back into her life. In 1817 she left England with him. The next year she died at her estate near Venice. Some sources say that her death may have been as a result of injuries at Felissent's hand.

Her first published composition is noted as by "a Child eight Years of Age," and her second publication, six sonatas for piano or harpsichord, was published when she was eleven. The only other known compositions of hers are a series of six "lessons" for harpsichord or piano forte.

There is a dramatic painting of her as St. Cecilia by Joshua Reynolds. Principal source: Grove's

Jane Mary Guest (c. 1765, Bath–March 20, 1846, Blackheath) was performing before she was six. She lived in London, perhaps for much of her life, where she reputedly was one of J. C. Bach's last pupils. She performed publicly in 1783 and 1784. At that time she was also composing, and she published six sonatas for keyboard with flute or violin accompaniment, which were dedicated to Queen Charlotte. The fact that the subscription list for her publication (headed by Queen Charlotte) includes many names of people who were important in London society as well as names of prominent foreign musicians then in London suggests that her musicianship was well respected.

After she married she often used the name "Mrs. Miles" for her performances. During the 1790s she frequently was in Bath — a very fashionable spot at the time. In the early 1800s she was music instructor to the Princess Charlotte for several years.

She performed and composed throughout her life, and her career spanned about sixty years. Her works include keyboard and many vocal pieces, sonatas for keyboard with violin or flute accompaniment, music for organ, and piano concertos composed for her own performances.

Principal source: Norton Grove

We know little about **Jane Savage** (fl. c. 1780–1790, London) whose father, possibly her teacher, was William Savage, a Gentleman-in-Ordinary in the Chapel Royal, a well-known musician and composer of anthems. Jane, who was a very good keyboard player herself, wrote keyboard music, songs, and a cantata, possibly *Stephan & Flavia*, using poems written by her mother. She may have been married to a Mr. Rolleston.

Her music was popular in her time.

Primary sources: Grove's; R. J. S. Stevens and H. G. Farmer, "A Forgotten Composer of Anthems," in *Music and Letters*, Oxford University Press, vol. 17, no. 3, pp. 188–189.

Mme. Delaval (fl. London, 1791–1802) may have been French or English. A pianist and a harpist, she studied harp with J. B. Krumpholtz, presumably in Paris. She was active in London musical life during the 1790s; her name is on many concert programs of that time.

She wrote a cantata depicting the farewell of Louis XVI, which was produced in London in 1794, sonatas for harp, and works for mixed instruments that often featured the harp.

Principal source: Norton Grove

Maria Hester Park (September 29, 1760–June 7, 1813, Hampstead) is often confused with the singer and composer Maria F. Parke (see entry).

Nothing is known of her early life. She was active in musical life in Oxford in the 1770s; by 1885 she was living in London. Prior to her marriage Maria performed in public concerts, playing the harpsichord and piano. She also taught music. About 1790 she married the poet Thomas Park (1759–1834), who was an antiquarian and man of letters.

Her compositions include a number of sonatas for piano forte or harpsichord, songs, and a concerto for keyboard and strings.

It's not surprising that there is often confusion about the attribution of compositions to the two Maria Park(e)s.

Principal source: CCH

We know more about **Maria F. Parke** (1772/73, London–July 31, 1822, London) who is often confused with Maria Hester Park. This Maria caught the attention of Haydn. Her father was the oboist John Parke. She began her performing career, appearing both as a singer and pianist at his benefit concert when she was nine. She often appeared as a soprano soloist in concerts and oratorios.

In May 1794 she sang and played at a concert for her benefit. (Such benefits weren't uncommon.) Haydn directed the concert from the piano. After, he wrote to her father that he was taking the liberty of sending to Miss Park a "little Sonata."

In 1815 she married John Beardmore. Nothing is known of any musical activity after her marriage.

Her compositions include songs and sonatas for piano forte.

Principal source: Norton Grove

Ann Valentine (January 11, 1762, Leicester, England–October 13, 1842, Leicester) came from a musical family; her father, John Valentine, was a composer and a performer. He often worked with his cousin Henry, also a musician, and each of them had a music shop. Other family members were musicians in Leicester. Ann was appointed organist at St. Margaret's Church in Leicester and held the post for nearly fifty years. Subscription lists indicate that her compositions were quite popular.

She wrote sonatas and other music for keyboard, some pieces with instrumental accompaniment, transcriptions, and chamber works.

Principal source: Norton Grove

Many composers were noted for their "other careers," frequently as singers or actresses. Some are noted for their writing or painting. **Elizabeth Craven** née **Berkeley, Margravine of Craven**, sometimes listed as Elizabeth Anspach, or Ansbach (December 17, 1750, London–January 13, 1828, Naples) became known for her travels and writing in addition to the rich cultural life at her court at Anspach and her music.

Elizabeth, the daughter of the fourth Earl of Berkeley, was well educated. She loved amateur theatricals and music. By all accounts she was a lively person and beautiful; she was sometimes referred to as "indiscreet." She wrote several plays that were performed in London, but none were particularly well received.

She married Lord Craven when she was sixteen, and the couple had seven children. When Lord Craven fell in love with someone else, she confronted him on the matter. He went to the continent, apparently to consider the situation, then returned having reached a decision to leave her after thirteen years of marriage.

Elizabeth was determined to meet the situation head-on, and she decided she would travel, first to France, then to Italy. She spent some time in Italy then traveled to Vienna, Cracow, and Warsaw, where she was presented to the King of Poland. It was on that trip she met the Margrave and Margravine at Anspach. She was warmly welcomed to their household and treated like a sister.

The timing could come from a novel: the Margravine died, then shortly after Lord Craven died. (Elizabeth was not in the vicinity, should this sound suspicious.)

The Margrave and Elizabeth married. In 1792 when Anspach was incorporated into Prussia the court dissolved and they went to live in England where she became very active in singing, acting, writing and composing. She was always fond of amateur theatricals and gave private theatricals at their London home.

She often composed music for her plays, and she composed an opera (or part of the music for an opera) that was performed at Covent Garden. Very little of her music survives.

Opera and stage work:

The Silver Tankard, an "afterpiece," at Haymarket Theatre, 1780 or 1781.
The Princess of Georgia, in 1799 the opera was performed at Covent Garden and she composed six of the songs, 1794.

Memoirs:

Memoirs of the Margravine of Anspach. Written by Herself (London: H. Colburn, 1826).

Principal sources: *Oxford Dictionary of National Biography*; Norton Grove.

France

Many women composers of this time had a career onstage as an actress or singer. **Henriette Adelaide Villard de Beaumesnil** (August 30, 1748,

Paris–1813, Paris) began her music career at the age of seven, singing in comedies, and continued her acting and singing career onstage until she retired in 1781. She made her debut at the Paris Opéra at the age of eighteen and went on to be one of the foremost singers there. When her voice began to fail she turned to composing and focusing on opera. Her operas were performed at the Grand Opéra, Paris.

Her first composition, *Anacréon*, a one-act opera, first received a private performance in December 1781. It was submitted to the Opéra but never performed. However her next work, *Tibulle et Délie, ou Les Saturnales*, was performed publicly and had considerable success. Subsequently her two-act opéra comique *Plaire, c'est commander* was given in Paris in 1792 and ran for twenty-one performances. Her oratorio *Les Israélites pursuivis par Pharaon*, was performed in 1784.

Little is known of her life during the Revolution or subsequently. After her retirement from the Opéra she married Philippe Cauvy, an actor.

Operas:

> *Anacreon*, a one-act opera and her first composition, privately performed in 1781.
> *Tibulle et Délie, ou Les Saturnales*, performed at the Opéra in 1784 after being performed at Versailles, 1784.
> *Plaire, c'est commander* ou *le législatrices*, two-act opéra comique, Paris, 1792.
> *Le fêtes greques et romaines*, Paris Opéra, 1784.

Principal sources: WWO; Grove's

The varied life of **Amélie Julie Candeille-Simons** (July 31, 1767, Paris–February 4, 1834, Paris) included many roles: singer, actress, composer, harpist, librettist, author and instrumentalist, and her personal life was as wide-ranging as her professional life.

Her father, the composer Pierre Joseph Candeille, prepared her for a career as an opera singer, which was a prestigious and lucrative career for many women. She made her debut when she was fifteen. Unfortunately she had a small voice and a shy personality, and although her technique was considered excellent she was not successful as an opera singer. She took up acting and appeared at the Comédie Française. Her talents were best suited for comedy, and she soon become one of the stars of the comedy stage. She also performed as a pianist.

When she joined the Théâtre Français in 1792 she turned her focus to composing and to writing, particularly librettos for her operas. Her three-act opera (for which she also wrote the libretto) *Catherine, ou La belle fermière* had great success and ran for 154 performances. It was revived frequently over the next 35 years in various European cities. She then wrote a series of comedies interspersed with songs: *Bathilde, ou Le duc*, followed by *La bayadère, ou Le Français à surate*. Neither of those was well received. Discouraged, she left acting and didn't write for the theater again until 1807.

In 1794 she married a military doctor, Louis-Nicolas Delaroche; they divorced within three years. Amélie stayed active in the arts during that time, but she walked a tight political line and was often considered to be on the wrong side. At times her theatrical past was used against her. Many — perhaps most — of the problems she had getting her operas recognized and performed arose from political motives, not because of problems with the music itself. She eventually went into semi-retirement, which lasted for over a decade.

In 1798 she married Jean Simons, a rich Belgian. They separated in 1802 and she returned to Paris. In addition to giving piano lessons and publishing music, she published memoirs, historical novels and essays.

Her opera *Ida, ou L'orphelie de Berlin* in 1807 reputedly was badly received with considerable hissing and was only performed a few times. Yet it is considered by some to be her most important work. She next attempted a prose comedy, *Louis, ou la reconciliation*, in 1808; that, too, was a failure not related to the opera itself.

After the fall of Napoleon she returned to Paris where she published music, gave lessons and wrote essays, memoirs (unfinished and presumed lost, although portions are extant), and historical novels to help support her husband, who had lost his fortune under Napoleon's reforms, and her father who had lost his pension. During Napoleon's "Hundred Days" she fled to England and performed there, then returned to Paris, where she received a pension honoring her many contributions to the arts.

In 1822 she married the painter Hilaire-Henri Périé de Senovert. After the death of her husband in 1833, she returned to Paris.

She was a prolific composer, and in addition to her operas wrote orchestral works, chamber music and trios, sonatas and other music for piano. She is variously listed as Mme. Delaroche, Mme. Simons, and Mme. Perle.

Operas and stage works:

Catherine, ou La belle fermière, November 1792.
Bathilde, ou Le duc, September 1793.
Le commissionaire, 1794.
La jeune hôtesse, 1794.
La bayadère, ou Le Français à surate, February 1795.
Louis, ou La réconciliation, December 1808.
Ida, ou L'orphelie de Berlin, May 1807.

Principal source: WWO

Marie Emmanuelle Bayon, whose name is listed variously under Louis, or Bayon-Louis (August 30 or 31, 1748–March 19, 1813, Paris) was known for her salons and her connections with literary and musical figures. Prior to her marriage she composed at least one opera that was privately performed.

In 1770 she married Victor Louis, a prominent architect. The following year, she composed *La fête de Saint Pierre*, a divertissement, that was performed in Paris. Soon after they moved to Bordeaux where Victor Louis would design and construct the Grand-Theatre. Victor Louis's career and the connections he made were significant for Marie. The Louis household became known for musical and literary salons; at the same time his position with the Grand-Theatre provided opportunities for having her operas performed. Marie composed an opéra comique, *Fleur d'épine*, which had twelve performances and attracted the attention of several publishers.

In 1780 they moved back to Paris, where they again became noted for their connections with literary and musical personages. During this time she may have written another opera that was performed privately. She wrote sonatas for harpsichord or pianoforte, which was coming into vogue at this time, and she is credited with the popularity of the fortepiano in France.

Operas:

Title unknown, 1767.
Fleur d'epine, 1781.
Principal sources: CCH; Norton Grove

Anne Louise Boyvin d'Hardancourt <u>Brillon de Jouy</u>, usually listed under Brillon de Jouy (December 13, 1744, Paris–December 5, 1824, Villeers-sur-Mer, Calvados), took a very active part in the salon life of Paris and Passy from the 1760s to the early 1780s. Her salons, which often featured her music, were popular and attracted many visitors, including Benjamin Franklin, who was her neighbor in Passy, and Charles Burney. Franklin and Brillon spent much time together; chess was a favorite pastime of both of them. They were close friends for the eight years he lived there, and — as people tended to do in those days — wrote many notes and letters to each other. Her side of the correspondence still exists and gives a rich picture of life and society of the time.

She attracted much attention for her keyboard playing. This was a critical time of transition from harpsichord to piano, and her compositions are primarily for harpsichord or piano. Two of her compositions stipulate the use of both instruments. One of her compositions, *Marche des insurgents*, commemorated the victory of the Americans at Saratoga. Her collection of music by other composers is a valuable documentation of the transition from harpsichord to piano.

Principal sources: CCH; Norton Grove; Lionel de la Lawrence and Theodore Baker, "Benjamin Franklin and the Claveciniste Brillon de Jouy," *Musical Quarterly*, vol. 9, no. 2, pp. 245–259.

Sophie Gail, née Garre, sometimes listed as Edmée-Sophie Gail (August 28, 1775, Paris–July 24, 1819), began her career as a songwriter with her work appearing in song magazines. At eighteen she married the philologist Jean Baptiste Gail. They soon separated, and she never remarried.

During the Revolution she was independent but poor, and she worked as a professional musician. She was well known both as a singer and an accompanist, and she made a very successful tour as a singer in England, southern France and Spain. Having decided to compose opera, she began intensive study in composition and theory.

She composed five one-act operas that were all performed. Her first, *Les deux jaloux* was a great success. That same year, 1813, her *Mademoiselle de Launay à la Bastille* did less well, one critic attributing the lukewarm reception in part to the fact the opera was set in a prison. The next year two of her operas, *Angéla, ou L'atelier de Jean Cousin,* and *La méprise,* failed badly, but the problem was considered to be the libretti and not the music. Consequently, Sophie was careful in selecting the librettist for her next opera.

She chose Sophie Gay, a well-known intellectual who was associated with many of the great artists, musicians and intellectuals of the time. Gay helped manage a private theater, wrote popular novels, and was a pianist, harpist and composer of romances. The collaboration with Sophie Gail was Sophie Gay's first theatrical attempt. She later went on to write other libretti and dramatic works. (Sophie Gay was the mother of Delphine Gay, later Madame Émile de Giradin, who became a poet, novelist and the most-performed woman playwright in the history of the Comédie-Française.)

The result of this collaboration between the similarly named women was the very successful *La sérénade.* That, coupled with the continuing success of her first opera, won Gail considerable renown.

Meanwhile she had continued her touring, singing in London in 1816 and touring Germany and Austria two years later. She died in 1819 from a chest ailment.

In addition to her operas and stage works, she wrote nocturnes, music for piano and harp, and songs with accompaniment by mixed instruments.

Operas:

Les deux jaloux, one act, 1813.
Mademoiselle de Launay à la Bastille, one act, 1813.
Angéla, ou L'atelier de Jean Cousin, one act, 1814.
La méprise, one act, 1814.
La sérénade, one act, 1818.
Medée.

Principal sources: WWO; Norton Grove

Marie Elizabeth Clery (1761, Paris?–after 1795) had to negotiate carefully during the French Revolution. Biographical information about her is intriguingly sparse.

During the Revolution, her husband was the valet de chamber assigned to Louis XVI while he was imprisoned. He held this post until early 1793. In September of that year he was arrested but was freed in July 1794. In 1795 her husband — and we hope she — escaped to Austria where he served Louis XVI's daughter Marie-Therese-Charlotte.

A harpist, singer and composer, Marie often performed her own compositions. Her works include songs, sonatas for harp, piano, and violin, and various works for the harp. Five of her compositions are dedicated to the "illustrious prisoners in the Temple."

Principal source: Norton Grove

The Revolution also had an impact on **Helene de Nervode de Montgeroult, Countess of Charnay** (March 2, 1764, Lyons–May 20, 1836, Florence). Mme. Montgeroult was well educated; her teachers included Clementi, J. L. Dussek and Reicha. She was a virtuoso pianist and a composer. She taught at the National Institute of Music, which preceded the Paris Conservatoire, and wrote one of the earliest instruction books for piano.

Her first husband was the Marquis to Montgeroult. His death in 1793 after having served in Italy and been taken prisoner by the Austrians, left Helene a wealthy aristocratic widow and highly vulnerable to the Reign of Terror. She may have entered into a marriage of convenience to avoid persecution.

She was condemned to the guillotine. At the tribunal, Bernard Sarette insisted that her teaching and performing skills were essential to the National Institute of Music. A harpsichord was brought into the proceedings and Montgeroult played the *Marseillaise* with such spirit that "all present impulsively joined in singing, led by the President of the tribunal" (Calvert Johnson, ed., *Helene Montgeroult, Sonatas for Piano* [Pullman, Wash.: Vivace Press, 1994], score preface). After her release she fled to Germany, returning two years later to be one of the highest ranking professors at the Conservatoire. Her name disappeared from the list of professors after 1795, and her publications cease after 1795–96. She may have withdrawn from public view, perhaps through a marriage of convenience.

Her compositions include piano sonatas and nocturnes, and a comprehensive piano method.

Principal sources: Norton Grove

Caroline Wuiet (1766–1835) did not escape the wrath of the Revolution either. Her father was an organist. Caroline, trained as a pianist, was a child prodigy. Her piano playing brought her to the attention of Marie Antoinette, who became a patron, giving her a stipend to continue her studies. She studied literature under Beaumarchais, composition under Grétry and art under Greuz.

She began as a librettist while still in her teens, but the opera was rejected and not performed. She then decided to change her strategy and, building on the theater's favoring sequels of successful works; she wrote a sequel to Grétry's *L'épreuve villageoise,* which was *L'heureuse erreur,* with her music and libretto. In 1786 the opera was accepted and rehearsed at the Comédie-Italienne. Unfortunately, due to the extremely competitive politics of opera at that time it was then withdrawn. Caroline was devastated and bitter.

She was selected to write the music for *L'heureux strategème, ou le vol suppose,* for the Théâtre des Beaujolais, but because the des Beaujolais was not one of the privileged theaters, it could not perform an opéra-comique. The Théâtre got around this problem by using marionettes or child actors who mimed while singers offstage performed the arias, a half-hearted effort at best.

Caroline was also a gifted writer and pianist. Her first play was performed in 1782. In 1787 *Sophie,* a one-act comedy in prose, was published. When she found she couldn't have her operas performed, she went on a concert tour as a pianist.

She was arrested during the Revolution but fled to Holland and then England. She returned to Paris and remained in hiding for two years. To support herself she published romances and sonatas. Eventually, when the times were safer, some of these became very successful (and lucrative) and gave her access to well-connected people. She began a fashionable daily newspaper for women, editing it herself and writing much of the copy. The newspaper venture went through several identities but lasted only a short time. At the same time she was developing a reputation as a novelist and received several academic honors.

In 1807 she married Colonel Joseph Auffdiener, and they moved to Lisbon where her husband was posted. To avoid the political problems in Portugal she returned to France, but her husband stayed in Portugal to take care of his business. He was imprisoned and died.

Caroline taught and continued to write fiction to support herself. Eventually she was unable to deal with the changes under the Restoration and became known for eccentric behavior. She died insane and destitute.

She wrote sonatas, romances, songs, and opera.

Operas:

L'heureuse erreur, Paris, her libretto, rehearsed with orchestra at the Comédie-Italienne but not voted for public performance, 1786.
Music for Saulnier's *L'heureux stratagème.*

Principal sources: WWO; Norton Grove

Isabella Agneta Elisabeth de Charrière (October 20, 1740, Zuylen, near Utrecht–December 27, 1805, Neuchâtel) was one of several very cultured aristocrats, literary women who were talented musicians and composers. She was of Dutch origin but is often listed as Swiss. She is sometimes mistakenly referred to as Sophie de Charrière. Her work is often listed as Belle van Zuylen, the name by which she was known in the Netherlands.

In 1750, at age ten, she was sent to Geneva, and for a year she traveled through Switzerland and France. During that time she spoke only French, and consequently had to relearn Dutch when she returned home. French remained her preferred and principal language throughout her life. She was apparently a gifted student, and thanks to the liberal views of her parents, she had an unusually good education.

Her first novel was published in 1762, the first of various publications. Her writings include poetry, novels, and plays, but she particularly wanted to write librettos for opera. In terms of her writing she's best known for her correspondence, particularly with Benjamin Constant, James Boswell, and Madame de Staël.

In 1771, she married Charles-Emmanuel de Charrière de Penthaz, her brothers' former tutor. They settled at Le Pontet in Colombier (near Neuchâtel) in Switzerland, where they became known for their hospitality. They were generous hosts — in part to relieve the monotony. She often invited musicians to help her with her composing. Most of her compositions, which include keyboard works and an opera buffo, were published anonymously.

Her works were never performed, and perhaps never finished. Only fragments remain.

Operas:

Le Cyclope, never performed, 1786.
Les Phéniciennes, never performed, 1788.
Junon, never performed, 1790.
Les Femmes, libretto and music, never performed, 1790.
L'Olimpiade, libretto and music, never performed, 1790.
Polyphème ou le Cyclope, never performed, 1790.
Zadig, libretto and music, never performed, 1791.
Title unknown, libretto and music, never performed, 1792.

Principal source: WWO

Sophie (de) Charrière, as the authors of *Women Writing Opera* note, was often assumed to be the same person as Isabelle de Charrière. They are not and they are apparently not even related. Almost nothing is known of Sophie. She was the composer of *Julien et Juliette*, which is often attributed to Isabelle Charrière.

Opera:

Julien et Juliette, c. 1771.

Principal source: WWO

Stephanie-Félicité de Genlis (January 25, 1746, Champcéry–December 31, Paris) was one of those women who was larger than life, packing an enormous amount of achievement and living into her life. She was a very minor composer, but she merits recognition for her patronage and involvement with the successes of other women composers.

She was well educated musically; she sang, danced, and played several instruments very well. She was particularly proficient playing the harp, and her playing attracted notice when she was young. But it was her charm and wit that made her stand out in Paris salons, as well as in her performances. She was a presence in the musical life of Paris, and many compositions received an early performance at Mme. de Genlis' residence.

At age sixteen she married the Count of Genlis. They had three children. Later she was the mistress of the Duke of Orléans, "Philippe-Egalité" of the revolutionary period, and she raised his (legitimate) children as her own.

She took the post of governess with the family of the Duke of Chartres and was apparently a skilled teacher. She wrote comedies for her students, taught them botany, and used lantern slides in her teaching.

As was the situation with so many composers, she was caught by the Revolution, and in 1791 she left France for Switzerland and Germany, earning her living by giving harp lessons, writing and painting. In 1802 she returned to France and was welcomed by Napoleon. She brought with her Casimir Baeker, age eight, said to be a descendant of a noble family, whom she trained as a virtuoso harpist.

She's best known for her writings — plays, romances, novels, poetry and her memoirs. Her manual of harp instruction and works on pedagogy were advanced for her time.

Her compositions include songs with harp accompaniment and a ballet.
Principal source: WWO

Anne-Marie Krumpholtz (c. 1755, Metz–November 15, 1813, London) was a harpist and possibly the daughter of a harp maker. She studied and performed in Paris from 1779 to 1784.

In 1783 she married Johann Baptiste Krumpholtz, her harp teacher. No performances or compositions are known between 1784 and 1788, when she allegedly eloped to London with her lover, a younger man. In any event by 1788 she was performing in London, and for the next fifteen years she had an active career in London as a harpist.

She performed extensively, often taking part in her own benefit concerts where she performed with well-known artists and composers including Haydn, Jan Ladislaw Dussek and Sophia Corri, who became Dussek's wife. Many of her compositions were harp arrangements and variations of well-known tunes, which were very popular and successful. She was one of the first composers to compose music that was specifically for the harp and distinct from keyboard music. Many of her compositions are sonatas.

Her daughter was the composer Fanny Pittar (see entry). V. Krumpholtz, who also composed for the harp, may have been a younger daughter.

Principal sources: CCH; Norton Grove

Jeanne-Hippolyte Devismes (1765, Lyon–1834? Paris) was one of the earliest women to have an opera performed at the Paris Opéra.

She was married to Anne-Pierre-Jacques Devismes du Vulgay, who was director of the Opéra from 1778 to 1780, and again in 1800. His influence probably was a factor in the production of *Praxitèle, ou La ceinture*, in 1800. While the libretto, which wasn't hers, was soundly criticized, her music was highly praised. In spite of the success of the opera, as far as is known she didn't write another opera.

La double recompense, 1805, is often attributed to her but was composed by her husband.

The only other music known to be hers is one song.

Opera:
Praixtèle, ou La ceinture, opera, Paris Opéra, Paris, 1800.

Principal source: WWO

There are quibbles about the amount of composing **Angélique-Dorothée-Louise Grétry**, called **Lucile** (July 15, 1772, Paris–March 1790, Paris), actually did on her own. The second daughter of the composer Grétry, she was named after the heroine of Grétry's second Parisian opera.

Her father, André Grétry, was well known for his composing, and particularly his operas. He was unusual in that he believed strongly in the potential of women. His students included Caroline Wuiet, Sophie Bawr, and Lucile. He was the court composer, and Lucile was introduced at court when she was young. Marie Antoinette took a great interest in her musical abilities.

Her first opera, *La mariage d'Antonio* (inspired by the libretto of her father's opera *Richard Couer-de-lion*, 1784), premiered in July 1786. She composed the vocal parts, the bass and a harp accompaniment, and her father did the orchestral scoring. Because of this collaboration her identity as an opera composer is sometimes diminished. The opera was successful and had forty-seven performances in five years.

Her second opera, *Toinette et Louis*, was criticized for its libretto and had only one performance. Her family blamed its failure on Lucile's unhappy marriage. Two years later, she died of tuberculosis at age eighteen.

Operas:
Le mariage d'Antonio, 1786.
Toinette et Louis, one performance, 1787.
Principal source: WWO

Florine Dézedé (1766–1792 or earlier) is known primarily through the accounts of her father, Nicolas Dézedé, a well-known composer, particularly of opera. She composed *Lucette et Lucas*, a comédie mêlee, performed in 1786.
Opera:
Lucette et Lucas, comédie mêlee, Paris, 1786.
Principal source: WWO

Very little is known about **Helene Guerin** (c. 1739 Amiens–fl. 1755). Like several other composers she composed a successful opera when she was young, then little else. She was only sixteen when she wrote *Daphnis et Amanthée*, which was produced at Amiens in 1755 and received a favorable notice.
Opera:
Daphnis et Amanthée, 1755.
Principal source: Norton Grove

Similarly, we know of **Josephine-Rosalie-Pauline Walckiers** (1765–1837) only through her operas.
Opera and stage work:
Title unknown, divertissement, Théâtre de Schaerbeek, 1788.
La repetition villageoise, opera, Théâtre de Schaerbeek, 1792.
Principal source: WWO

Germany

The two **Anna Amalias** are easy to confuse. The Anna Amalia who was the Princess of Prussia was the youngest sister of Frederick the Great. The Anna Amalia who was the Duchess of Saxe-Weimar was a niece of Frederick the Great and a niece of the "other" Anna Amalia.

The musical contribution of **Anna Amalia, Duchess of Saxe-Weimar** (October 24, 1739, Wolfenbütel–April 10, 1807, Weimar), is not so much in her compositions but in her influence on intellectual life, particularly with respect to its flowering in Weimar at that time. She was the niece of Frederick the Great.

Anna was a well-educated, cultured person. Upon her marriage to Duke Ernst August Konstantin of Saxe-Weimar in 1756 she went to live at the court of Saxe-Weimar where she studied piano and composition under the court concertmaster and conductor. When her husband died two years later she was regent until her son (who was subsequently Goethe's patron) ascended the throne. Her court was famous as a center for scholars, poets and musicians. In 1788 she traveled to Italy, where she was much impressed by the Italian vocal style. She continued her involvement in music throughout her life.

She wrote piano music, vocal works, a concerto for twelve instruments, music for piano and strings, and a sinfonia, and perhaps an opera and stage works.

Her library/collection of volumes, primarily from Italy, is in the Zentralbibliothek der Deutschen Klassik in Weimar.

Opera and stage work:

Adolar und Hilaria; this may be of doubtful attribution.
Erwin und Elmire (Goethe); she may have written the vocal score only, 1776.

Principal sources: Norton Grove; Grove's

Maria Antonia Walpurgis, Electress of Saxony (July 18, 1724, Munich–April 25, 1780, Dresden; often listed under Maria Antonia and not under Walpurgis) was another woman from the German courts who composed and who fostered, or created, vital and sometimes powerful settings for the intelligentsia.

In addition to being a composer and accomplished musician, Maria Antonia was a painter and a poet in both French and Italian. (Her native language was German.) She was also a member of the Arcadian Academy in Rome. In 1747 she married Friedrich Christian, who was later the Elector of Saxony and located to Dresden where she continued her musical studies. She was well known as a patron, but she also wrote opera, often using her own texts. She often took leading roles in court performances, and she participated in court musical events as a singer or keyboard player.

The death of her husband in 1763 and the Seven Years' War both contributed to the decline of cultural life at Dresden, and in her correspondence with Frederick the Great she often refers to her growing isolation, both personally and artistically. She was also a correspondent of Pietro Metastasio. Some of the isolation she felt may have been due to the changes in music that were taking place with respect to the forms, instrumentation and style. She didn't care for the new music, particularly the new operatic style.

She wrote music for orchestra, voice, and keyboard.

There is a manuscript thematic catalog of her library in the Bayerische Stattsbibliothek in Munich.

Operas and stage works:

Il trionfo della fedelta, 1754.
Frederick II, 1754.
Talestri, regina delle amazoni, 1760.

Principal source: Norton Grove

Not all the prominent women composers had a courtly upbringing. **Margarethe (Maria) Danzi** (1768, Munich–June 11, 1800, Munich) grew up in a theatrical setting instead. Her father's troupe performed regularly in German cities, and from when she was young Maria acted, sang and played the piano.

From 1781 to about 1785 she and her brother Heinrich Marchand, who also became a composer, were pupils of Leopold Mozart and lived in his household. He taught her singing and piano, and obviously some composing as well, as he encouraged her composing and attempted to get her sonatas published.

Her operatic debut was in 1787 at Munich. She continued her singing throughout her life and was known for her roles in Mozart operas.

In 1790 she married the composer Franz Danzi, of the famous Danzi family of musicians. Subsequently they traveled with an opera troupe through Europe. Franziska Dorothea Danzi Lebrun was her sister-in-law (see entry).

As is the case with many composers, we only know of her work that was published: three sonatas and a piano work.

Principal source: Grove's

Franziska Dorothea Danzi Lebrun (March 24, 1756, Mannheim–May 14, 1791, Berlin) was born into one musical family, the Danzi family, and married into another. Her mother was a dancer and her father was the composer and cellist Innocenz Danzi; both held prestigious positions at the court in Mannheim. Her younger brother was the composer Franz Danzi; she was the sister-in-law of Margarethe Danzi (see entry).

Franziska (Francesca) reportedly had a remarkable voice and range. She made her singing debut when she was sixteen and immediately was engaged for leading roles. She went on to have an illustrious singing career.

In 1778 she married Ludwig August Lebrun, who was already well known as an outstanding oboist and as a composer. The two of them toured frequently and often performed together; several composers wrote music specifically for them. Francesca made guest appearances in concerts and operas throughout Europe. Her career never faltered.

From 1779 to 1781 she and her husband lived in London, and Francesca appeared regularly in concerts and operas. During that time, Gainsborough painted her portrait. Also that year, two sets of her sonatas for keyboard and violin were published and appeared in several editions. Her daughter Sophie was born in 1781; Rosine was born two years later. Francesca and Ludwig continued to travel and perform through much of the 1780s.

Her husband's sudden death in 1790 affected her own health, and she died four months later. Rosine became known as an actress and a singer. Sophie Lebrun also was a composer (see entry).

Principal source: Grove's

Like so many musicians, **Juliane Benda Reichardt** (May 14, 1752, Berlin–May 9, 1783) was born into a musical family; the Benda family had an illustrious musical tradition. Juliane was one of four musical children; her sister, Maria Carolina Benda Wolf, held a position at court and was noted for her songs. Her father was a violinist and concertmaster for Frederick the Great.

Juliane became an accomplished singer as well as a pianist. The story is that the young composer Johann Friedrich Reichardt came to Berlin as court Kapellmeister and fell in love with Juliane when he heard her sing and play the piano. (His first love had been the composer Corona Schröter, but she had refused him, see entry for Corona Schröter.) Juliane and Johann married less than a year after they met. Juliane's songs and piano music were already being published, and she continued to compose after her marriage, primarily lieder and works for piano. She died shortly after the birth of her third child. Her daughter was Louise Reichardt (see entry).

Perhaps her best-known composition is her Sonata in G Major.

Principal source: Norton Grove

Corona Schröter (January 14, 1751, Guben–August 23, 1802, Ilmenau) grew up in a musical family as well. Her father, an oboist, gave Corona her earliest musical training. She played a variety of instruments, including keyboard and guitar, but she became most noted for her singing.

When the family moved to Leipzig around 1763 she became the pupil of Johann Adam Hiller, who felt strongly that women should not be excluded from choral singing, especially in the church. He argued, reasonably, that if God gave man a melodic singing voice for praising him it was "highly unfair" to exclude women to whom God had also given a melodic singing voice from worshiping through music as well. Hiller also made a point that singers should receive good musical training, through regular rehearsals — with women included. His training was extensive, and Corona was one of his most successful pupils. She appeared in Hiller's Grand Concerts and was very popular with the audiences.

In 1767 J. R. Reichardt met — and became smitten with — Corona. However, the attraction was not mutual, and Reichardt later married Juliane Benda (see entry).

Corona's father took his family on concert tours in Germany, the Netherlands, and England. When they returned home she continued her concerts; she also became well known for her acting in amateur theatricals.

Goethe, who had admired her talent, was responsible for her being appointed as chamber musician to the Duchess Anna Amalia at Weimar. This move gave her significant prominence, as she also created many leading roles for Goethe's early dramas. At times she played opposite Goethe in the amateur court theatricals. However, in 1783 a professional company replaced the court theater, which reduced Corona's acting appearances.

She focused then on teaching singing and acting, and she confined her singing to more informal salons. She also became increasingly involved with her poetry, drawing and painting, at which she also excelled. And throughout she composed, primarily lieder and other vocal works. Two collections of her compositions were published. In her later years she was friends with Friedrich von Schiller and set some of his poems to music.

Principal sources: Marcia J. Citron, "Corona Schröter: Singer, Composer, Actress," *Music and Letters*, vol. 61, no. 1, pp. 15–27; Grove's

Italy

Although it's speculated that **Anna Lucia Boni** [also **Bon**] (1738/9? Russia?–after 1767) was born in Russia, she was an Italian composer. Her father was an artist, composer, stage designer and librettist, possibly from Venice, and her mother was an opera singer. Their home was in Venice, but both parents were with the court at St. Petersburg and Anna may have been born there.

She entered the music school of the Ospedale della Pieta in Venice at the age of four, probably as a tuition-paying pupil. In 1746 her parents were in Dresden and remained there for two years. Subsequently they were at the court of Frederick the Great in Potsdam and toured other cities as well. Anna may have joined them at some time.

She and her family were at the court of Margrave Friedrich of Brandenburg Culmbach at Bayreuth by 1755. The Margravine, Wilhelmine, a sister of Frederick the Great (see entry) was a composer of operas and instrumental music as well.

Anna's music was first published in 1756; at that time she may have held the new position of "Chamber music virtuosa" at the court of Frederick the Great of Prussia. Three collections of Anna's music were published in those years, the first, *Six Sonatas for Flute and Basso Continuo*, when she was sixteen. When the Margravine died in 1758 musical life at Bayreuth declined and the family left.

Anna's father then formed a touring opera company, with Anna and her mother as featured singers. Their performances at the court of Prince Esterházy in Eisenstadt were so successful that they were engaged to remain at the court full-time; they stayed three years. Haydn was at the court at that time, and the Italian operas he heard there encouraged him to compose his first Italian opera, *La marchesa Napola*, which was performed at the court.

Anna married a singer and was with him in 1767, but nothing is known of the marriage or of the remainder of her life. It is said she composed a mass and an opera but this is not verified. She did, however, compose pieces for flute and for harpsichord. Her six sonatas for flute are dedicated to Frederick the Great of Prussia.

Principal source: CCH

Slightly younger than Anna Lucia Boni, **Maddalena Laura Lombardini Sirmen** (sometimes listed under Sirmen; December 9, 1745, Venice–May 18, 1818, Venice) was also a product of the *ospedale* or Mendicanti. She was admitted to the *ospedale* at the age of seven through an open audition, where she was one of four chosen to be an apprentice. This was a highly prestigious placement. By the age of fourteen she had the rank of violin teacher. She was selected to travel to Padua for further study in 1760, 1761 and 1764.

She married the violinist Lodovico Maria Gaspar Sirmen when she was twenty-two. At that point she was independently wealthy, due, in part, to the traditional dowry from the Mendicanti. In 1768 her husband received permission from the Mendicanti to take her on a two-year tour that brought Maddalena much acclaim for her violin playing. In 1770 the couple made a second tour, this time to London where Maddalena performed her own concertos. The demand for repeat performances was so great that she performed the concertos 22 times during a five-month period. In all she gave over 200 performances in London as a singer and a violinist.

Lodovico returned to Italy in 1772 with their daughter to pursue his own career, but Maddalena remained in London, which, not surprisingly, gave rise to some criticism. However, this was tempered in part because a priest from the Mendicanti had been with her since her departure from the *ospedale* and in fact was her companion throughout her life.

Maddalena continued to tour and perform in Europe. In 1779 she was employed in Dresden as a highly paid singer. Four years later she was principal singer at the Imperial Theater in St. Petersburg, the first woman singer there. Lodovico joined her for a time as concertmaster. Maddalena again performed as a violinist and as a singer.

She returned to Paris in 1785 only to find that the musical fashions in Paris had changed substantially in the sixteen years since her last visit, and her playing was not well received. Subsequently she held a post in Naples; in 1789 the Venetian governors recalled her from Naples. Little is known of the remainder of her life; she lived until 1818.

Not only was Maddalena an international performer, but her compositions were published throughout Europe and in St. Petersburg. Leopold Mozart praised one of her concertos. Her work was primarily for string instruments and includes six violin concertos, a sonata for violin and cello obbligato, string trios, string quartets and violin duos.

Principal sources: CCH; Grove's

Maria Rosa Coccia (1759, Rome–November 1833) was precocious. At age fourteen she wrote a canonic exercise in the presence of four examiners, who commended her composing ability. The canon, with her portrait, was included in a publication the following year. Also around that time she received the title of Maestra di Cappella (one of three female members) from the Accademia Filarmonia of Bologna. Her compositions made a strong impression on Pietro Metastasio.

She is best known for her *Magnificat* for four voices and organ dated 1774, and a *Dixit dominus* for two four-part choirs and organ dated a year later. All of her composing seems to have been done early in her life, with the possible exception of a cantata for four voices dated in 1783. Although she was very well known in her day, little of her music remains.

Opera:

L'Isola Disabitata, libretto by Metastasio, c. 1772 (composed at age 13).

Principal sources: CCH; Grove's

Netherlands

Baroness **Josina van den Boetzelaer** (January 3, 1733, The Hague–September 3, 1797, Ijsselstein) was one of eight children born to Lord Cornelis van Aerssen and his wife, Baroness Albertina van Berjeren van Schagen.

She served as a lady of the court of the House of Orange; during that time she would have had many occasions to meet and hear the prominent musicians and composers of the day. She studied with F. P. Ricci, a violinist at court. She left her service at the court when she married Carl van den Boetzelaer. Little is known of her life.

Her compositions that have survived include arias with orchestral accompaniment, ariettas for voice and continuo and dances.

Principal sources: Norton Grove; Helen Metzelaar; "An Unknown 18th Century Dutch Woman Composer: Josina Boetzelaer (1793–1797)," *Tijdschrift van der Vereniging voor Nederlanse Muziekgeschiedenis,* D. 4ste, 2de (1990), pp. 3–56.

United States

Elizabeth Joanetta Catherine von Hagen (1750, Amsterdam?–1809 or 1810, Massachusetts) was the first known woman in the early colonies of America to publish an instrumental work.

Her husband was Peter Albrecht van Hagen. After their marriage in 1774, she and her husband came to the colonies, first settling in Charleston, then in 1789 moving to New York. There they worked as performers, teachers, and managers of a concert series. Elizabeth often performed as a pianist. Their success was uneven, and they never became fully established.

In 1796 they moved to Boston (at which point the "van" became "von") where they worked as music dealers and publishers, much as they had in New York, and with much the same unevenness.

Their son, also named Peter Albecht von Hagen, was a musician and joined in on the various family enterprises. When Elizabeth's husband, Peter, died, she and the family were left in difficulties. Elizabeth taught piano in Salem and Boston to help support the family.

Elizabeth was the first woman in America to publish an instrumental work. Her compositions are thought to include piano concertos, a piano sonata, and variations.

Primary sources: H. Earle Johnson, "The Musical von Hagens," *The New England Quarterly*, vol. 16, no. 1, pp. 110–117; Norton Grove

Chapter Five

The Beethoven Watershed, 1800–1840

The musical heritage of Mozart and Haydn was succeeded by the music of Beethoven, who settled in Vienna. He was unusual for being an independent composer, which in part was brought about by his deafness, which made a permanent court post impossible. Beethoven expanded the potential of music enormously: by harmonies, forms, even the instruments. His composing was a singular turning point in music. No composer was unaffected. The older, Baroque styles were passé.

The presence of Beethoven in Vienna attracted musicians from all over Europe; it's no coincidence that many composers spent time in Vienna, studying with Beethoven or with one of his pupils. At the same time, Salzburg lost much of its musical vibrancy as political instability led to frequent changes of rulers until it fell to the Habsburgs in 1816.

In Germany two significant political events in early 1800 had an impact on the musical culture: the Edict of the Deputation of the German Estates of 1803 and the end of the Holy Roman Empire in 1806. As many of the small courts dissolved and many monasteries closed, Germany's musical diversity began to erode. Music increasingly became centered in cities, and the affluent middle class was significantly involved and influential in music.

The groundwork for Romanticism, particularly German Romanticism, was being felt throughout Europe. Early Romanticism was marked by a growing interest in traditional music, which previously had been an oral tradition. Composers and musicians were beginning to collect and write down the traditional music, and catalogues were compiled. Traditional themes and melodies made their way into art music.

The two best-known women composers were born in Germany during this period: Fanny Mendelssohn in 1805 and Clara Schumann in 1819. Although they were relatively close in age, in many respects they were a generation apart. Fanny died young, in 1847, at the point when her composing was taking on a new sophistication and level of skill, and a real career as a composer seemed possible. By contrast, Clara lived until almost the end of the century, dying in 1897 and was a commanding personage in classical music, particularly performance. The women's lives are fascinating in their similarities and contrasts, one regrettable similarity being that the unmistakable potential of each of them for composing in more complex forms never was realized.

In the Netherlands, Gertrude van den Bergh was one of the first woman choral conductors in the Netherlands. She was also the first Dutch woman to publish a manual on the fundamentals of music theory. In 1830 she became the first woman to be made an honorary member of the Maaschappij tot Bevordering der Toonkunst (Association for the Promotion of Music). No other woman was awarded the honor until Clara Schumann's election twenty-four years later.

Czech music began to reflect its own musical tradition more strongly. By the end of the 1700s there was a strong renewal of interest in the Czech language and literature. As the 1800s advanced, composers were incorporating traditional melodies and themes more prominently in their music. Also at that time, many Czech composers were working with salon pieces, which would become very popular a little later in the century.

The impact of German Romantic music on English musical life and English music operated somewhat to the detriment of English music, which tended to be overshadowed by German music. Britain still had a vibrant musical life, however, and was a destination for concert tours from the continent. Several musical institutions of long standing came into being in the early to mid–1800s, including the long-lived periodical *The Musical Times* and the Philharmonic Society, which was founded in 1813.

In France the famous Prix de Rome was instituted in 1803. At the onset it was very insular. It was founded by six members, most of whom then won the Prix de Rome, as did their composition professors at the Conservatoire. The Prix would remain highly political for decades but it did provide enormous prestige and opportunity for its winners. By the end of the nineteenth century the prize involved several years' residency at the Villa Medici in Italy for the sole purpose of composing.

Ironically, in contradiction to some of the goals of the French Revolution, music became a very elitist matter in France. Opera retained its foothold, particularly after 1806 when large cities were permitted to have two theaters with the main theater designated for grand opera. But Paris remained the home of culture and was a draw for people all over Europe. Women were a strong element of Parisian cultural life, as participants as well as patrons. In 1842 Louise Farrenc was appointed professor of piano at the Paris Conservatoire.

She was the only woman musician in the 19th century to hold a permanent chair of such a rank at the Conservatoire.

As France, Germany and Austria had become increasingly prominent and influential in music and musical culture, the significance of Italy as a major center for musical development waned. In northern Europe instrumental music in particular had become a matter of great attention and focus, while in Italy instrumental music primarily served the interests of opera. The operas of Rossini, who seemed to arrive on the composing scene in the nick of time, provided a great resurgence to Italian opera.

Austria

Even among child prodigies, **Leopoldine Blahetka** (November 15, 1811, Guntramsdorf, Baden, Austria–January 12, 1887, Boulogne) must have been remarkable. Her father was a journalist and teacher of mathematics and history, and her mother was a brilliant player of the *harmonika*. Her grandfather was the Viennese composer Andreas Traeg.

From an early age Leopoldine was known for her remarkable piano playing. Her debut at age eight placed her firmly in the inner circles of Viennese musical life. Beethoven was so impressed with her playing he recommended she study with Czerny. She became a member of the circle of Schubert's friends and often performed his music. In 1829 Chopin, who was visiting Vienna, was much taken with the eighteen-year-old Leopoldine. When he left Vienna she gave him a composition that she had dedicated to him. They never met again, although later, when she was touring Poland, Chopin offered to perform two-piano music with her.

She stayed in Vienna until about 1840, when she settled in Boulogne. As she concentrated more on her composing and teaching she gradually gave up her performing. Most of her compositions were published during her lifetime. Her only opera was *Die Räuber und der Sänger*. She also wrote orchestral pieces, chamber music, and piano solos.

Opera:

Die Räuber und der Sänger.

Principal source: Norton Grove

Julia von Baroni-Cavalcabo (October 16 or 22, 1813, Lemberg [Lviv], Poland–July 2 or 3, 1887, Graz) studied with Mozart's younger son, Franz Xaver Wolfgang Mozart; she is considered one of his most successful pupils. (At his death she was responsible for having his tombstone made and placed.) In 1835 she traveled with him to Leipzig, where she met Robert Schumann.

His *Humoreske* op. 20 is dedicated to her. In 1839 she married von Webnau and moved to Vienna.

Her first publication was in 1830; subsequently much of her music was published during her lifetime and received critical attention.

One of her best-known works is her piano fantasy op. 25 *L'adieu et le retour*.

Principal source: Norton Grove

We have scanty information about **Elena Asachi** (October 30, 1789, Vienna–May 9, 1877, Iasi, Romania), who was a composer, pianist and singer. She studied first with her father, Anton Teyber, who also was a composer and musician, in Dresden. She next studied with Domenico Donzelli, an opera singer, in Vienna.

She was a professor of music at Iasi Conservatory for many years and had an active career as a pianist, often accompanying foreign musicians on their tours in Romania.

Her husband, Gheorghe Asachi, was a well-known writer. She often collaborated with him.

Her works include several pastoral stage works as well as songs.

Principal source: Norton Grove

We know **Leopoldine Goubau d'Hovorst** (sometimes listed under d'Havorst) by the significant amount of music she wrote for piano, which was published around 1813 in Vienna.

Principal source: WON

Czechoslovakia

The musical precociousness of **Marie Wolowska Szymanowska** (December 14, 1789, Warsaw–July 24, 1831, St. Petersburg) was evident from an early age. Her home was a center for people in the arts, and Marie began performing in concerts at an early age. She had an excellent musical education, studying with Hummel and Cherubini, among others.

Her performing debut was in Warsaw and Paris in 1810, and she soon was regarded as one of Europe's outstanding pianists. That same year, 1810, she married a wealthy landowner, Josef Szymanowska. Josef objected to her having a professional musical career. After ten years they divorced. To support herself and her three children Maria taught, composed and performed extensively throughout Europe.

In 1822 she was appointed court pianist to the Tsar in St. Petersburg, the first female to receive such an appointment in Russia. She continued to tour until 1828, performing throughout Europe and in Russia. Her concerts, which commanded high ticket prices, attracted large audiences. She was known for her beauty and her intellect, and she must have had an attractive personality as well. (She was the inspiration for Goethe's poem *Aussöhnung.* Goethe is said to have been in love with her.) Her salon in St. Petersburg was not only the center of cultural life and a destination for many composers, but it was also a place where Polish émigrés could find assistance and indulge in patriotic conspiracy. Her musical autograph album shows visits from Robert and Clara Schumann, Chopin, Liszt, Beethoven, Rossini, Meyerbeer and Franz Xaver Mozart. She had a strong influence on Chopin.

Most of her compositions are virtuoso piano works. She often utilized folk music and dances in her compositions.

Principal sources: CCH; Grove's

England

The Dussek "family business" continued into the next generation. Although the family originally was from Bohemia, by the late 1700s many family members, including several known women composers, were in England. Among them was **Olivia Dussek Buckley** (September 29, 1799, London–c. 1847, London), the daughter of Jan Ladislav Dussek and Sophia Corri Dussek (see entry). Her mother, who was a composer, taught Olivia piano and harp. Little is known of Olivia's life or her marriage.

Her published compositions include works for harp and piano and teaching pieces.

Principal source: Norton Grove

The family of **Fanny Krumpholtz Pittar** (c. 1785, London?–after 1815) was also musical. Her mother was Anne-Marie Krumpholtz (see entry), a composer and harpist, and her father was Johann Baptiste Krumpholtz, a well-known harpist and Anne-Marie's teacher. Their marriage — and their story (see entry for Anne-Marie Krumpholtz) is rather convoluted. It's perhaps not surprising, then, that when Fanny married Isaac Pittar, a diamond merchant, she received a marriage settlement from the Earl of Hardwicke, thought by some to have been her father.

Fanny was taught by her mother. Her main compositions are works for harp and piano and include waltzes, themes and variations, rondos, and allegrettos. Many of her compositions were published. The British Library has her manuscript book.

Principal source: Norton Grove

Ann Shepard Mounsey [Mrs. Bartholomew] (April 17, 1811, London–June 24, 1891) had a considerable professional career. She began her career at age seventeen when she was appointed organist at Clapton, the first of several positions. The next year she was organist at St. Michael's; then in 1837 she became organist at St. Vedast's.

In 1834 she became an associate of the Philharmonic Society. In 1843 she began an annual series of classical concerts; this continued for six series. Mendelssohn composed the anthem *Hear My Prayer* to premier at one of her series of concerts.

She married William Bartholomew in 1853. He was a musician, painter, chemist and writer. He met Mendelssohn — who was continually in search of an opera to write — after writing him, offering librettos. These proposals never came to fruition musically, but the friendship and working relationship of Bartholomew and Mendelssohn stemmed from that. Bartholomew later served as Mendelssohn's English translator for *Elijah*. Ann, who is known by her maiden name, also became a friend of Mendelssohn.

The same year she married Bartholomew she composed her oratorio "the Nativity," which was performed two years later. She continued to compose and teach and enjoyed a long and successful career. Her publications include a cantata, songs, hymns, lieder, works for piano and works for organ. She and her sister Elizabeth Mounsey [see entry], who also was an organist and composer, collaborated in publishing a collection of sacred music.

Principal sources: Grove's; Norton Grove

Elizabeth Mounsey (1819, London–October 3, 1905, London), like her sister Ann Mounsey (see entry) showed much talent at an early age. She was organist of St. Peter's, Cornhill, in 1834 (she was fourteen at the time), a post she held until 1882. For a time she studied guitar and gave several performances with the guitar in 1833 and 1834.

She became an associate of the Philharmonic Society in 1842.

Elizabeth collaborated with her sister Ann Shepard Mounsey on a collection of sacred music and a collection of hymns. Elizabeth's compositions include works for the organ, the piano and the guitar.

Principal sources: Grove's; Norton Grove

Mary Anne A'Beckett (1817, London–December 11, 1863, London) was the daughter of Joseph Glossop, a friend of George IV. Her husband, Gilbert Abbott A'Beckett (said to be descended from Thomas à Beckett), was known as a writer on the original staff of *Punch* and a producer of plays, including dramatized versions of some of Charles Dickens' writings.

Less is known about Mary.

She wrote three operas, *The Young Pretender*, *Agnes Sorel*, and *Little Red Riding Hood*, the last two produced in London. Although she was invited to conduct the operas herself, she declined to do so. In addition to her operas she wrote songs and two waltzes for piano.

Operas:

The Young Pretender. Three songs were published.
Agnes Sorel, John Braham's St. James's Theatre, London, 1835.
Little Red Riding Hood, Surrey Gardens Theatre, London, 1842.

Principal source: Norton Grove

Although the music of **Mary Linwood** (1755 or 1756, Birmingham–March 2, 1845, Leicester) may have had numerous performances throughout her long life, the first performance we know of is the performance of her oratorio *David's First Victory* in 1840. Her two known operas, *The Kellerin* and *The White Wreath*, were never published.

In addition to being a composer she was an artist in needlework which at that time was a highly developed art form. She was very well known for her skill and renditions and had numerous exhibitions of her work. Her embroidery "paintings" attracted the attention of Napoleon, the British royal family, and Empress Catherine of Russia.

She also ran an educational establishment for women in Leicester and was known for her poetry.

Operas:

The Kellerin.
The White Wreath.

Principal sources: Norton Grove; Charlotte Streifer Rubenstein, "The Early Career of Frances Flora Bond Palmer (1812–1876)," *American Art Journal*, Vol. 17, No. 4, pp. 71–88.

France

Sophie Bawr, Mme. de [Comtesse de Saint-Simon] (October 8, 1773, Paris–December 31, 1860) was a woman of many dimensions: successful author, composer and pianist, and a woman of letters in French society. Her parents, a marquis and opera singer, who were not married, undertook to raise her. However, when she was two her mother left and went to Russia. Her father then raised her and gave her an excellent education. She studied with noted singers and composers including Grétry and Boieldieu, and from an early age she participated in the fashionable salons, often performing her own songs.

As an aristocrat, her father was vulnerable to the Revolution; he was imprisoned and all his property confiscated. Friends, fearing the consequences of their association with Bawr, abandoned them. Sophie and her father survived, somehow, but her father did not live long. On his death Sophie lived with Grétry.

From 1801 to 1802 she was married to Claude Henri de Rouvroy, Comte de Saint-Simon, the social theorist. (Grétry was one of the witnesses at the wedding.) The marriage was brief, and reportedly Saint-Simon entered into it, in part, for the advantage of having her manage a salon for prominent musicians and writers. About seven years later she married Baron de Bawr, a young Russian. When he died about a year later, Sophie was penniless. To support herself she established a musical career that lasted for decades.

She also was a successful writer of novels, plays, history books, stories, and melodramas for which she also composed the music. She wrote about the position of women in society, particularly in the arts, arguing for improvement. She also wrote the first published history of women in music, an article in the *Encylopédie des dames*, 1823. In 1853 she published her memoirs, *Mes souvenirs*.

In addition to the music she composed for *mélodrames*, she wrote an opera *Léon, ou Le château de Montaldi* as well as songs.

Opera:

Léon, ou Le château de Montaldi.

Memoirs:

Mes Souvenirs (Paris: Passard, 1863).

Principal sources: CCH; Norton Grove

Mademoiselle Benaut (var. Benault) (c. 1778, Paris–unknown) was a child prodigy. She lived with her teacher M. Benaut, an abbé, who composed for organ, harpsichord and piano. She is described as a pensioner at the Royal des Dames de Bon Sourcours priory.

Her first two keyboard collections were published when she was nine years old. She also composed organ works.

Principal source: Cohen

Hortense Beauharnais (April 10, 1783, Paris–October 5, 1837, Arenberg) is best known for her connections with the Bonaparte family. Napoleon was her stepfather and his brother, Louis Bonaparte, was her husband.

Her father, the Viscount Alexandre de Beauharnais, was guillotined in 1794. In 1802, she married Louis Bonaparte, who became the king of Holland in 1806. The marriage, which wasn't voluntary, was an unhappy one, and although Hortense came to like much about Holland — she learned painting there and often painted in the countryside — she strongly preferred to live in

France. She and her husband had three sons. When he abdicated the Dutch throne in 1810, Hortense was named regent.

When Paris fell and the Bourbon Restoration took place in 1814, Hortense sought protection from Alexander I, Tsar of Russia. That same year her mother died.

During Napoleon's Hundred Days, Hortense supported Napoleon, which led to her banishment from France after his final defeat. She traveled in Germany and Italy before purchasing a chateau in Switzerland in 1817 where she lived until her death. She is buried next to her mother Josephine in the Saint-Pierre-Saint-Paul church in Rueil-Malmaison.

She was a singer, pianist, harpist, and she played the lyre. Her main compositions are songs, and romances that were based on pseudo-medieval texts.

Her music library is in the Napoleon Museum at Arenberg.

Biography:

Daughter to Napoleon by Constance Wright (New York: Holt, Rinehart and Winston, 1961).

Principal source: Norton Grove

Marie Kiéné de Morognes Bigot (March 3, 1786, Colmar–September 16, 1820, Paris) was better known as a teacher than as a composer. She was Alsatian, but when she was five the family moved to Neuchâtel, Switzerland. She learned to play the piano from her mother.

Her husband, Paul Bigot, whom she married in 1804, was the secretary to Count Andreas Razumovsky, who lived in Vienna. Razumovsky was very musical and played a form of the theorbo. He had a string quartet in residence. (He is best known for commissioning three string quartets from Beethoven.) In this setting Marie met Haydn, Salieri and Beethoven. Marie, who was a very accomplished pianist, often played for the salons.

Beethoven and Haydn in particular were greatly impressed by her playing. When Haydn heard her play, he embraced her and said, "My dear child, that music is not mine; it is yours!" and on the book of music she'd been using he wrote "20 Feb. 1805; this day has Joseph Haydn been happy." When Beethoven heard her play one of his sonatas, he reportedly said, "That is not exactly the reading I should have given, but go on, if it is not quite myself, it is something better." Even if this is apocryphal, it is a good representation of the regard he had for her playing.

She played Beethoven's "Appassionato" Sonata at sight from a handwritten copy, which Beethoven later gave her; he thought she was one of the best interpreters of his music. (This was no small feat; playing from manuscript is difficult enough, and Beethoven's could be remarkably difficult to follow.)

Beethoven makes it clear in his correspondence that they were friends, and he refers to the rivalry between Mme. Bigot and Nanette Streicher (see entry). Meanwhile, Marie was becoming known for her teaching; at that time she gave piano lessons to Schubert, then eight years old.

In 1809 she and her husband moved to Paris, where she met notable composers, musicians and writers. This life of music and salons and culture continued for the next two years. Then, in 1812 during the Russian campaign her husband was captured and lost his position with Count Rasumovsky, and perhaps died during this period. Marie, who then had to fend for herself, spent the rest of her life teaching. The young Felix and Fanny Mendelssohn were her pupils for several months while they were in Paris.

She did not compose very much; her compositions are mainly works for piano including a suite of studies for her pupils.

Principal source: Grove's

There are too many composers for whom the only information we have is performance or publication of her music. **Mlle. Le Senechal de Kerkado** (c. 1786–1805 or later) was the composer of a one-act operetta *La Méprise volontaire ou La double leçon* that was given at the Opéra-Comique in Paris in 1805 when she reportedly was nineteen years old.

Opera:
La Méprise volontaire ou La double leçon, 1805.
Principal source: Norton Grove

The family position of **Louise Angelique Bertin** (February 15, 1805, Les Roches–April 26, 1877, Paris) was both an advantage and a drawback. Her father, Louis Bertin, and her brother Armand, were proprietor and editors of the *Journal des débats*. Louise grew up in the midst of the artistic and literary world of Paris in the early 1800s, but the family's involvement with the newspaper also meant that they were often a controversial factor in the politics of the time. Louise suffered from partial paralysis since birth, and she always felt she had to contend with prejudice arising from her partial paralysis, in addition to prejudice against women.

She was very well educated in the arts and was a composer and musician as well as a painter and a poet. Her first opera was *Guy Mannering,* based on the novel by Sir Walter Scott, a choice that reflected the enormous popularity of his novels. She wrote the libretto herself, and the opera had a private performance in 1825.

Two years later *Le loup-garou,* a one-act opera with a libretto by Eugène Scribe, was produced at the Opéra Comique. Her next opera, *Fausto* in 1831, was a much more substantial and more ambitious opera.

La Esmeralda, in 1836, had a libretto by Victor Hugo and was based on his *Notre-Dame de Paris*, again a choice of an extremely popular writer, but in this case a writer who also wrote the libretto. (He apparently had sketched out a possible opera based on that book.) Berlioz assisted in the preparation of the production. There was — and has been — some suggestion that he composed the music for her, but this was not the case. Unfortunately the opera was produced during a period of public outcry directed towards the Bertin family and their influence, particularly her brother's connections with the opera. *La Esmeralda* was not successful and was heavily criticized. While the opera had some weaknesses, the failure was due to political aspects.

Stung by the failure and the criticism, Louise never composed another opera or any music for public performance.

She increasingly turned her attention to poetry, and she published two volumes of poetry, one of which won a prize from the French Academy.

Operas and stage works:

Guy Mannering, 1825.
Le loup-garou, Opéra Comique, Paris, 1827.
Fausto, Théatre Italien, Paris, 1831.
La Esmeralda, Paris Opéra, Paris, 1836.

Principal source: WWO

Jeanne Louise Dumont Farrenc (May 31, 1804, Paris–September 15, 1875, Paris) was from an artistic and musical background. Members of the Dumont family, including several of the women, had been royal artists for many generations; Louise's brother was Auguste Dumont, the sculptor.

It wasn't unusual for a talented musician to have significant artistic ability as well, but Louise's achievements were notable. From an early age it was clear that both her musical and artistic talent were exceptional. She chose to concentrate on music. By the time she was fifteen she was performing professionally and studying composition and orchestration at the Paris Conservatoire.

In 1821 she married Aristide Farrenc. A music publisher and a scholar, he was interested in early keyboard music, in particular music for harpsichord. He worked for many years finding and publishing the earlier harpsichord music.

Marriage and travel interrupted her music and study briefly, but she soon continued her studies in composition and orchestration with Antoine Reicha, and her compositions began to be published by Farrenc's publishing company.

Among her compositions for piano was a collection of thirty Etudes in which every major and minor key was represented. This received critical acclaim, and in 1845, the Etudes became required in all piano classes at the Conservatoire.

Opera was the passion for much of Paris at that time, and it was generally assumed that a composer would compose opera in addition to other works. Louise was unusual in that she never worked with opera and was more interested in instrumental pieces, particularly the sonata and the symphony. She was particularly drawn to the later sonatas of Beethoven.

One of her most memorable achievements was her appointment as professor of piano at the Paris Conservatoire in 1842, the only woman musician in the 19th century to hold a permanent chair of such a rank at the Conservatoire. She was a distinguished teacher, and many of her pupils won competitions and went on to professional careers. Among her most outstanding pupils was her daughter Victorine (1826–1859), who clearly was destined for an outstanding career in music. Victorine became ill in her twenties and died before she was 33.

After Victorine's death Louise essentially stopped composing and turned her attention to collecting and working with early music. (By then Aristide had dissolved his publishing business and was concentrating on early music.) Louise already had adopted her husband's interest in early keyboard repertoire, and Louise and her pupils had often performed selections from the music. She and Aristide together prepared modern editions of the old manuscripts and prints they collected from all over Europe. The culmination of the research and work was *Le trésor des pianistes* (published 1861–1874) a twenty-three-volume anthology of harpsichord and piano music, which Louise had continued to work on after the death of Aristide. Her own research on early music performance style was ground-breaking and is reflected in the first volume of the publication. Louise is still noted for her work in music history as well as for her composing.

Her chamber music, written primarily between 1840 and 1860, was widely performed and published. In 1861 and 1869 she won the Chartier Prize for her contributions to chamber music. Her two overtures (1834) and three symphonies (1840s) were also performed, although not as widely, but none were published. She also wrote violin sonatas, trios, and works for instrumental combinations. Among her most notable compositions is her Trio, Opus 45 (1857), for flute or violin, cello and piano.

Principal sources: Grove's; Norton Grove

Louise Genevieve La Hye (March 8, 1810, Charenton–November 17, 1838, Paris) was admitted to the Paris Conservatoire at the age of eleven; at that time she was one of the youngest students to be admitted. When she was only twenty, Cherubini, who was then director of the Conservatoire, invited her to teach harmony to a class of young women. The next year her Fantasy for organ and orchestra was performed.

Soon after, she married and moved to Cambrai, giving up her appointment. But by the end of 1834 she was back in Paris and had resumed her teaching. She was often in ill health, and she died very young.

Her published works include a dramatic choral work, variations for piano and string quartet, and a duo for horn and piano. She also wrote some musical settings for her husband's poems. Some of her works were published posthumously.

Principal source: Norton Grove

Louise Puget (February 11, 1810, Paris–November 27, 1889, Pau) received her early music lessons from her mother, who was a singer, and Louise's early training was also as a singer. During her lifetime she was very successful as a composer of *romances* and songs; a good publicist, she often sang them in Paris salons. They were widely published in French and German bilingual editions, in English editions, as piano arrangements, and in illustrated volumes. The French editions were published between 1830 and 1845.

She frequently used texts that were written by the actor Gustave Lemoine, whom she married in 1842. Her success, coupled with her interest in the theater, led her to study with Adolphe Adam and to compose two one-act operettas. The first, *Le Mauvais oeil*, with text by Eugene Scribe, a well-known librettist, and Lemoine was given by the Opéra Comique. Her second, *La veilleuse, ou Les nuits de milady* was performed in 1869. She also composed a few works for piano and a set of quadrilles.

Operas:

Le Mauvais oeil, operetta, Opéra Comique, Paris, 1836.
La veilleuse, ou Les nuits de milady, operetta, Théâtre du Gymnase, Paris, 1869.
Beaucoup de bruit..., operetta.

Principal text: Norton Grove

Many composers had multi-faceted careers, often as artists or writers. **Alda Therese Annette Adrienne Wartel** (July 2, 1814, Paris–November 6, 1865, Paris) was a critic as well as a pianist, composer and teacher. Her father was a violinist at the opera and leader of the Conservatoire orchestra.

When she was a student at the Paris Conservatoire she won prizes in piano and harmony in 1830. A year later she joined the staff as an accompanist and teacher of solfege and remained in that capacity until 1839.

In 1833 she married Pierre François Wartel, a tenor and singing teacher. Her own teaching was interrupted when they lived in Vienna for several years. When she returned to Paris, she was prominent in chamber music circles.

As a critic she is perhaps best known for her review of Louise Farrenc's *Nonet* in 1850, where she commended Farrenc for the significance of her work and compositions, and for not composing frivolous music [*Revue et Gazette musicale de Paris,* March 31, 1850] and for her series of essays on Beethoven's piano sonatas.

She is better known as a critic than as a composer, and there's little information about her composing prior to 1847 when she wrote *Andante Cantibile in F sharp,* which was dedicated to Farrenc. Two works for piano were published in Paris in 1850 and 1851. She was the first woman ever engaged by the Société des Concerts.

Principal sources: Norton Grove; Grove's

Aline Bertrand (1798, Paris–March 13, 1835) studied at the Paris Conservatoire. Following her debut as a harpist in 1820, she toured Europe.

Her compositions include a Fantasy for harp based on themes of Mehul's operas.

Principal source: WON

Germany

Fanny Mendelssohn and **Clara Schumann** are probably the best-known women composers. They are often paired and compared, but their musical lives, particularly their public musical lives, were very different. Although they were close in age, in some respects they seem to be of different generations.

Fanny was born in 1805 and Clara in 1819. Fanny died young, and her family sharply limited her opportunities.

Clara's father was at the other extreme, pushing hard on Clara to compose and perform. Clara was long-lived and her career spanned her entire life. She became a significant figure in music and was somewhat of an icon by the later part of the 1800s, a time when increasing numbers of women were pursuing professional careers in music and composing.

One of the most extraordinary composers was **Fanny Mendelssohn** (November 14, 1805, Hamburg–May 14, 1847, Berlin). She is sometimes listed by "Hensel," her married name, and occasionally by Bartholdy, the name the Mendelssohn family adopted when they converted from Judaism.

She was the oldest of four children; Felix was four years younger. When Fanny was born her mother is reputed to have commented on her "Bach fingers"— and Fanny eventually did play much of the Bach piano repertoire.

Her mother was very well educated as well as being musical. Her father was the son of Moses Mendelssohn, a noted Jewish scholar and writer. On both sides of the family there were strong, independent, well-educated women who were significant role models for Fanny and her younger sister Rebecka.

The youngest child, Paul, eventually entered the family banking business. Both Rebecka and Paul had excellent musical training as well.

The children were all well educated in languages, mathematics, science, drawing, and music. The household was strictly run: lessons began at five in the morning, and everyone was expected to be well occupied every moment of the day.

Fanny's talent as a pianist and composer was evident from a very early age. Her first music lessons — and Felix's — were from their mother, who began them very young with five-minute lessons. She and Felix both received an outstanding musical education; Fanny had the same education as Felix — up to a point. Both began composing early; Fanny's first known composition dates from when she was fourteen.

The Mendelssohns frequently had musicals in their home, and Fanny frequently played. She was a brilliant pianist, and in a different family she would have had an international career as a virtuoso. But the Mendelssohns were very aware of their position and status, and Fanny's role was to be that of a proper wife and mother, a fact her father made abundantly clear in a letter he sent her when she was fifteen. "Perhaps music will be his [Felix's] profession, whereas for you it can and must be but an ornament..."

In 1816 the Mendelssohns converted to Lutheranism and had their children baptized. At that time there were many restrictions on Jewish people that governed where they could live, what work they could do, and where and how they could be educated. With so many opportunities closed to them, many Jewish people converted, a choice that was often more political or pragmatic than religious.

The family took the name Bartholdy, which has been a source of some confusion ever since. The children, particularly Felix, objected strongly to the change of name. Felix refused to use the new name; on programs his music would often be listed as "by Felix B. Mendelssohn," the B. being his only concession. He and his father disagreed sharply about this. Consequently combinations and hyphenations of Mendelssohn and Bartholdy have been used. Today the simple surname "Mendelssohn" is most frequently used for both Fanny and Felix.

Also in 1816 the family went to Paris for several months. While there Fanny and Felix both took piano lessons with Marie Bigot (see entry), who by then was well known as a teacher. Fanny continued to compose and receive training in composition.

She and Felix entered the Berlin Singakademie in 1820. Her parents continued to encourage her composing, but they would not allow her to perform outside the family circle or to publish her music. She specialized in writing lieder and piano pieces.

As she got older her world narrowed; at the same time the world opened up for Felix, with more advanced musical training and travel. Fanny stayed at home.

When she was sixteen she fell in love with a painter, Wilhelm Hensel. He had been attracting attention at the Prussian court and had received several important commissions, as well as the opportunity to study and paint in Italy for several years. The Mendelssohns liked him and found him very congenial, but Fanny's mother thought she was too young to make such an important decision, and Wilhelm was admonished not to press Fanny on the point.

They married in 1829, when Fanny was twenty-four. Wilhelm Hensel probably wouldn't have been the man Fanny's parents would have selected for her — and perhaps that was part of the attraction.

As a married woman Fanny had more independence (which wasn't always the case) than when she was single. The couple had one child, Sebastian, named after Bach, Fanny's favorite composer. Wilhelm strongly encouraged her composing and urged her to publish. Fanny was a prominent figure in the musical life of Berlin, and her salons were well known. She often performed or conducted her own compositions in private performances.

Throughout her life she and Felix were remarkably close. She had a strong influence on his composing, and he usually consulted her about his ideas and compositions as a musical equal. He encouraged her composing but was against publication of her work, as was her father, and of course public performances were out of the question. Her mother and husband were more supportive of her publishing her compositions.

Felix published some of her works under his own name, and at times he performed her music as if it were his own. His attitude is curious and probably complex. There may have been an element of competitiveness involved. One element was the culture of the time. Although Felix is known to have encouraged other women composers to publish and perform their works and apparently saw nothing wrong with their performing in public, this perhaps didn't fit the Mendelssohn concept of a proper young woman of a family of their status and culture.

Fanny's father died in 1835, and soon after she began publishing her music. She finally had some opportunity to travel when the Hensels went to Italy for several months in 1839, a trip Fanny had longed for all her life. They returned to Italy in 1845. She began composing more complex music, including some instrumental chamber works.

In 1847 she died, suddenly, of a stroke. Felix was devastated. Several months later he died, also of a stroke.

Fanny is acknowledged to have been a very talented composer with the potential to handle larger works. The bulk of her compositions (approximately

500) are lieder and vocal works, but she also composed an orchestral work, chamber music, and many pieces for the piano.

Among her most notable works are her Piano Trio op. 11, Prelude in E minor, and the *Oratorium nach den Bildern der Bibel.*

Biographies:

Fanny Mendelssohn by Françoise Tillard, translated by Camille Naish (Portland, OR: Amadeus Press, 1996).

The Letters of Fanny Hensel to Felix Mendelssohn, collected, edited, and translated by Marcia J. Citron (n.p.: Pendragon Press, 1987).

Principal source: Françoise Tillard, *Fanny Mendelssohn,* translated by Camille Naish (Portland, OR: Amadeus Press, 1996).

Many composers had to surmount the difficulty of a father who didn't support their musical ambitions. **Clara Josephine Wieck Schumann** (September 13, 1819, Leipzig–May 20, 1897, Frankfurt-am-Main) had the opposite problem to contend with: her father was all too interested in her musical career.

Her father, Friedrich Wieck, had a music business and taught piano and singing. When Clara was very young he determined that Clara would be a virtuoso pianist, touring, giving concerts and promoting his teaching and the pianos he sold. Her mother was from a family that included professional musicians, and she had performed in the Leipzig Gewandhaus both as a singer and as a solo pianist. There was always music in the household.

When Clara was five her mother left her father and divorced him. By law, in such a case the three oldest children were in the custody of the father.

Clara had no childhood; her life focused on lessons and practicing. At the age of nine, she played in the Gewandhaus, and two years later she made her formal solo debut there. The next year she performed in Paris. Her career was launched, and she would be a most successful woman concert pianist of international renown all of her life. To give Friedrich credit, he was a very good teacher and much sought after.

In an age of prodigies and virtuosos, Clara stood out. Her repertoire was astonishingly mature. Audiences could hardly believe that this slight young girl with the large eyes and slightly melancholy look could play the piano as she did. Her father put together the tours and made all the arrangements, a considerable undertaking given the frequency and extent of Clara's touring. From the first she had a celebrity status that was incredible for the time, with concerts that sold out immediately. And she made money—a lot of money.

Clara had been composing since she was a child; she matured early as a composer, and she often included her own music in her concerts. Friedrich encouraged—or pushed—her to compose; it promoted his teaching and added to the character and uniqueness of her performances.

When she was nine Robert Schumann became her father's pupil. Two years later, in 1830, he moved into the household. (Pupils who were from out of town often boarded with their teachers.) Eventually the two fell in love and decided to marry.

To say that Friedrich, whose temper never was good, opposed this is a considerable understatement. Friedrich may have had some concern about Robert's ability to support Clara, but the real issue was losing control over Clara's career and her performing income. At that time in Germany, a couple wanting to marry had to have the consent of each of their parents, no matter the age of the couple. Clara took the matter to court and also sued for her earnings, which over the years had amounted to a sizeable sum.

Clara and Robert married in 1840. They settled in Leipzig, eventually moving to Dresden and Düsseldorf. As children arrived — eight in all, beginning in 1841 — balancing her career and composing endeavors increasingly became a challenge. Robert supported her composing, but *his* composing took precedence. He was realizing great success as a composer, and Clara frequently included his music in her concerts to make him better known to audiences. She had to schedule her own composing and practicing around his need for quiet while he was working. She wrote primarily for her own concerts.

Robert's deteriorating mental condition was a further complication. In 1854 he tried to commit suicide. He was hospitalized and died in the hospital in 1856.

After Robert's death Clara stopped composing, writing only a march for a friend. She had the children to support, and the best way she could earn money was to continue giving concerts and to teach. The concerts took precedence, being better paying and carrying out her intent to continue promoting Robert's music. She also introduced audiences to Bach, Domenico Scarlatti, Beethoven, and Schubert, composers whose music was no longer performed frequently.

Her celebrity status went beyond her performing; she intersected and knew seemingly everyone in music, and she taught and mentored many of them. She was close friends with many, including Pauline Viardot, Joseph Joachim and Felix Mendelssohn. She became close friends with Brahms and performed his works when he was still unknown.

Her compositions include orchestral and chamber works, much music for piano, and voice. Among her best known are the piano pieces op. 5 and op. 6, her Piano Concerto op. 7, and her Piano Trio op. 17.

Biographies:

Clara Schumann: The Artist and the Woman, by Nancy B. Reich (Ithaca, N.Y.: Cornell University Press, 2001).

The Complete Correspondance of Clara and Robert Schumann, edited by Eva Weiss-
weiler and translated by Hildegard Fritsch. 2 vols. (New York: Peter Lang, 1994).
*The Marriage Diaries of Robert and Clara Schumann: From Their Wedding Day
through the Russia Trip* (Boston: Northeastern University Press, 1993).
Clara Schumann: A Dedicated Spirit, by Joan Chissell (New York: Taplinger, 1983).
Clara Schumann: An Artist's Life, by Berthold Litzmann. 2 vols. (New York: Vienna
House, 1972 [reprint of 1913 ed.].
Letters of Clara Schumann and Johannes Brahms, 1853–1896, edited by Berthold Litz-
mann (New York: Vienna House, 1971).
Concerto: The Glowing Story of Clara Schumann, by Bertita Harding (New York:
Bobbs-Merrill, 1961).
Clara Schumann: A Romantic Biography, by John Burke (New York: Random House,
1940).
   Principal source: Nancy Reich, *Clara Schumann: The Artist and the
Woman* (Ithaca, N.Y.: Cornell University Press, 2001).

   Nanette Streicher (January 2, 1760, Augsburg–January 16, 1833, Vienna)
had a dual involvement in music, initially as a performer and later as an active
participant in the family business of building pianos. Her father, Johann
Andreas Stein, a famous Viennese piano builder, had visions of his daughter
being another *Wunderkind* much like the Mozart children. In 1777 Nanette,
in fact, played for Mozart who thought she was a very good pianist, but he
found her mannerisms silly.
   Her first piano lessons were given by her father. From an early age she
gave concerts, often with another pianist, Nanette von Schaden.
   After her father's death in 1792 she continued the piano business. The
next year she married the musician Johann Andreas Streicher, and in 1794
they moved to Vienna. She also moved her father's business and continued
to operate it with her younger brother Matthias Andreas Stein. Eventually
she, her husband and her brother ran the business as Frére et Soeur Stein.
Beethoven favored "her" pianos, and she was very supportive of Beethoven
and his music.
   She was an excellent pianist and often played in private for friends and
visitors. She organized concerts and focused on offering young artists opportunities to play.
   Her compositions include several chamber pieces and vocal pieces.
   Principal source: New Grove

   Louise Reichardt (April 11, 1779, Berlin–November 17, 1826, Hamburg)
was the daughter of the composer Juliane Reichardt (see entry) and J. F.
Reichardt, also a composer, writer and critic. Her father was also a student
of philosophy, and their home was a gathering place for many of the philoso-
phers and literary figures of her time. Louise sometimes performed her song

settings at these gatherings. Louise made her singing debut in 1794 in Berlin. At one point she was engaged to be married, but shortly before the wedding the gentleman died.

Her father, who had an interesting career himself, moved often, with changes in his positions as well as changes in his political interests. Louise is said to have been with him in many of his moves. In 1809 he moved to Vienna to establish himself in music. Louise's mother was likely dead by then. When her father died in 1814, Louise moved to Hamburg where she supported herself as a singing teacher and composer. The women's chorus that she organized and directed became the nucleus of the Hamburg Singverein. She also became known for her work on the production of Handel oratorios, translating the texts and preparing the choruses for performances.

Her compositions, primarily songs and choruses (both sacred and secular), remained popular for many years.

Principal source: Grove's

One of the more prolific opera composers was **Marie Frederike Amalie, [Amalia] Princess of Saxony** (August 10, 1794, Dresden–September 18, 1870). (She also likely had the longest name of any composer, her full name being a string of at least sixteen names.) She was the sister of King John of Saxony, and she lived in the castle of Pillnitz, Dresden, her entire life. With the unsettled conditions during the Napoleonic Wars the residents of the castle had to flee several times, and her family often had to seek shelter and sleep on straw. She formulated a strong dislike of Napoleon.

At that time Italian opera, which was the rage, was prominent in Dresden, and she modeled her operas on opéra comique and opera buffa. She composed at least fourteen operas under the name Amalie Serena. These were performed for family and within the court. Apparently she had a gift for comedy and comedic characters.

She also composed sacred music, cantatas, songs, music for string quartets and for piano. Her compositions also are under the name Amalie Serena. She stopped composing sometime after 1835 and turned to writing comedies, using the pseudonym Amalie Heiter.

Operas:

Una donna.
Le nozze funeste.
Le tre cinture.
Il prigioniere.
A l'honneur de Nancy.
L'Americana.
Elvira.
Elisa ed Ernesto.

La fedelta alla prova.
Vecchiezza e gioventu.
Der Kanonenschuss.
Il figlio pentito or *Il figlio perduto.*
Il marchesino.
Die Siegesfahne.
La casa disabitata.
   Principal source: Norton Grove

   Two families that frequently appear in accounts of music and art are the Lebrun family and the Danzi family. **Sophie Lebrun** (June 20, 1781, London–July 23, 1863, Munich) was the daughter of L. A. Lebrun, the Munich court oboist and Franziska Danzi Lebrun (see entry), the court soprano. Her father was one of the most noted oboists of the age, and he had license to travel and perform at venues other than the court.
   Sophie was recognized as a pianist from an early age, and she made tours to Switzerland, Italy and Paris. In 1799 she married J. L. Dülken, a Munich court piano maker. Two of her daughters married Munich court musicians; another daughter became a concert singer. Her sister Rosine was a noted soprano.
   Sophie's compositions, primarily sonatas and concertos, weren't published and are now lost.
   Principal sources: Grove's; Norton Grove

   Therese Emilie Henrietta aus dem Winkel (December 20, 1784, Weissenfels–date of death unknown) was a virtuoso harpist. In addition to publishing at least three sonatas for harp and violin, she wrote pamphlets about the construction of the harp.
   Principal source: WON

   Paulowna Maria [also Pawlowna], Grand Duchess of Weimar (February 16, 1786, Russia–June 23, 1859, Weimar), was one of ten children of Tsar Paul I of Russia. She reputedly had a remarkable ability to read orchestral scores on sight.
   She married Charles-Frederick, the Grand Duke of Weimar in 1804. Weimar was a center for learning and the arts, and she soon established herself as a patroness of the arts and of science. The couple had four children.
   Her compositions are works for piano and for voices.
   Principal source: Norton Grove

   Helene Riese Liebmann (1796, Berlin–after 1835) was from a well-to-do family. A child prodigy, both as a pianist and as a composer, when she was ten her concert in Berlin astonished the audience. She soon began publishing her music, and her sonatas, published when she was in her teens, were well received.

She married in 1813 or 1814. She and her husband may have moved to Vienna before moving to London around 1816. She continued composing until 1819, although she no longer performed. No later compositions of hers are known. Her works include sonatas, chamber music, and lieder.

Principal source: Norton Grove

The father of **Emilie Zumsteeg** (December 9, 1796, Stuttgart–August 1, 1857, Stuttgart) was Johann Rudolf Zumsteeg, a composer primarily of lieder; her mother was musical as well. After the death of her father when Emilie was six, her mother opened a music shop. Emilie studied piano and theory from an early age, and she performed as a pianist and a singer when she was growing up. She apparently remained in Stuttgart all her life.

As an adult she taught singing and piano and continued her singing, and for many years she was an important figure in the musical and cultural life of Stuttgart. She helped found the Verein für klassiche Kirchenmusik, the Society for Classical Church Music.

During her lifetime she was well known for her lieder. She also composed sacred choral music and piano works.

Principal source: Norton Grove

The first performance we know of by **Delphine [Adolphine] von Schauroth** (1814, Magdeburg–1887, Charlottenburg?) is a performance in 1823 in Paris of the music of her teacher, Frédéric Kalkbrenner. When she was sixteen she came to the attention of Mendelssohn, who visited Munich while on his way to Italy. Some flirtation and duet playing transpired, and he dedicated several pieces to her. However, nothing came of the relationship. By 1835 she was married to Hill-Handley, an Englishman.

Four years later Fanny Mendelssohn and Wilhelm Hensel, also en route to Italy, visited her in Munich. Fanny liked her as well and admired her playing, in particular her improvisations.

Her compositions are primarily music for piano.

Principal source: Norton Grove

Josephine Köstlin Lang (March 14, 1815, Munich–December 2, 1880, Tübingen) also intersected with the Mendelssohns. Both of her parents were from musical families: her mother's family included noted singers. Josephine, who was sickly as a child, received her first music lessons from her mother. She made her debut as a pianist at age eleven.

Her earliest compositions are from 1828. Not surprisingly, with many family members being singers, she composed mostly lieder. When Mendelssohn met her in 1830, he was impressed with her lieder and her singing. He gave her lessons in theory and recommended she study in Berlin, but her father opposed the idea. Fanny also was enthusiastic about her musical abilities. When Josephine became engaged to Christian Reinhold Köstlin, Felix strongly urged her to stay active as a composer.

However, after her marriage and their move to Tübingen she composed little. Several of her collections were published during the 1840s. The couple had six children.

After her husband's death in 1856, Josephine resumed composing. Friends, particularly Ferdinand Hiller, helped her find publishers for her music. Of her 46 opuses, almost all are lieder; several are piano pieces.

Two years after her death a retrospective of her songs was published. Principal sources: Norton Grove

Greece

Susanna Nerantzi (Zakinthos?–fl. 1830–1840) is the earliest known modern Greek woman composer. Her fantasias were published in 1839 in Milan.
Principal source: Norton Grove

Italy

Katerina Maier (fl. 1800, St. Petersburg) was of Italian parentage, but her father played in the main orchestra at the Russian court and she spent most of her professional life in St. Petersburg.

Her publications include keyboard sonatas and other keyboard works.
Principal source: Norton Grove

Our knowledge of **Carolina Pazzini Uccelli** (1810, Florence–1885, Paris?) consists mainly of dates and performances. The earliest notice of her composing is the performance of her opera *Saul* at the Teatro della Pergola in 1830. She was both librettist and composer. Two years later her melodrama *Anna di Resburgoi* was performed. The next year the overture of her opera *Eufemio da Messina* was performed. Her cantata for orchestra and chorus, *Sulla more di Maria Malibran* honored the famous mezzo-soprano, Maria Malibran, who had died in September 1836. No other works are known.

After being widowed in 1843 Carolina moved to Paris with her daughter, Giulia. She continued to perform, with her daughter, touring in Europe. Operas:

Saul (her libretto), Florence, 1830.
Anna (Emma) di Resburgo Naples, title apparently varied, 1832.
Eufemio da Messina (overture only performed) Milan, 1833.

Principal sources: Norton Grove; Cohen

Adelaide Orsola Appignani, also known as Orsola Aspri (c. 1807–September 30, 1884, Rome), adopted the surname of her stepfather, the violinist Andrea Aspri, and used Orsola as her first name.

She began her career as an opera singer; in 1833 she sang in a performance of Donizetti's *Anna Bolena*. At that time she already was a member of the Roman Accademia Filarmonica. In 1842 she was offered honorary membership of the Accademia di S. Cecilia in Rome.

Known as a singing teacher, she also was a conductor in Rome and Florence. Her works include several melodramas, of which three were performed, as well as a Sinfonia.

Operas and stage works:

Le avventure di una giornata, Melodramma, Rome, Teatro Valle, 1827.
I riti indiani, not performed, 1834.
Francesca da Rimini, not performed, 1835.
I pirati. Melodramma. Rome, Teatro Alibert, 1843.
Clara di Clevers. Melodramma. Bologna, Teatro Nationale, 1876.

Principal source: Norton Grove

Netherlands

Gertrude van den Bergh (baptized January 21, 1793, Cologne–September 10, 1840, The Hague) began her career by having her first composition published by J. J. Hummel when she was nine years old. By the time she was twenty she had moved to The Hague. She had a successful career as a pianist and was particularly known for her interpretation of Beethoven. She also participated in the "revival" of Bach's music.

A woman of firsts, Gertrude was one of the first woman choral conductors in the Netherlands, as well as the first Dutch woman to publish a manual on fundamentals of music theory. Her career was multi-faceted. In addition to her composing, she conducted several choirs and supported herself by teaching. Her pupils included members of the Dutch royal family.

She was made an honorary member of the Maaschappij tot Bevordering der Toonkunst (Association for the Promotion of Music) in 1830. No other woman was awarded the honor until Clara Schumann's election twenty-four years later.

Among her compositions are virtuoso works for the piano, including *Rondeau pour le pianoforte* op. 3, a string quartet, preludes and fugues. Many of her compositions are lost.

Principal source: Norton Grove

Spain

Isidora Zegers (January 1, 1803, Madrid–July 14, 1869) was born into an Andalusian family. She received much of her musical education in Paris where she studied piano, singing, harp, guitar, and composition. When she was nineteen she went to Chile where she, along with Carlos Drewetcke, helped found the Santiago Philharmonic Society in 1827 and the National Conservatory in 1850. She was made honorary director of the Conservatory in 1851. In 1852 she and José Zapiola founded *Seminario musical,* a weekly publication to which she frequently contributed.

Most of her compositions that survive are piano pieces, a set of contradanzas and songs, which date primarily from her time in Paris.

Principal source: Norton Grove

Chapter Six

Romanticism, 1840–1880

Touring virtuosos had been a musical (and commercial) focus for years; certainly the Mozart children and Clara Schumann come to mind. But by the mid–1800s there seemed to be a virtual explosion of virtuosos and touring. There were more performance venues, and there was a large moneyed middle class that could take part in it and also provide an enthusiastic audience. Tours — and the organization of tours — had become an established commercial enterprise.

Increased opportunities for music education provided more opportunities for women to teach, and they began entering the faculties of conservatories.

Large fairs and exhibitions were popular, and they often there had a musical component with competitions and performances. They also provided an effective way for instrument makers to show their wares.

In many places it was a time of political unrest and change, which had a significant effect on music, culture, and opportunities. In Austria the 1848 Revolution of course had a widespread impact in many dimensions. Music became less the provenience of royalty and nobility, and choral societies were founded in cities and towns. Choral singing — male voice — had always been a tradition in Austria, particularly with the frequency of church schools, but now there were many secular choirs as well. At the same time, orchestras began to be made up predominantly of professional musicians rather than amateurs. Austria continued its supremacy in instrumental music. Vienna was still the major center in Austria for music, but other cities and towns had a significant musical life as well.

Germany was a center — *the* center — of musical life and a destination for performers, students, and composers. Women were very much part of this trend. Germany, and particularly Leipzig and the Leipzig Conservatory, was still the destination of choice for aspiring composers and many musicians. In 1856 Clara Kathleen Barnett Rogers was admitted to the Leipzig Conservatory at the age of twelve, the youngest student ever admitted.

The Schumanns, later just Clara Schumann, taught, encouraged, criticized and mentored many of the aspiring and new composers. Friendship with the Schumanns opened doors to important friendships with other composers and musicians. Clara Schumann, who continued to tour and teach, was an important personage in Leipzig.

Symphonic music was undergoing change, particularly with the compositions of Brahms and Bruckner. Both were moving away from the Beethoven tradition, although elements of it remained, but they were moving in different directions, a difference that would increasingly become divisive in the music world.

Richard Wagner, who had been in exile for years, returned to Germany in 1860. His personal life and financial affairs were in a shambles, but he was even more determined to write German opera that would ennoble the German spirit. At that time Italian opera was still the mode, and Germany had not yet developed a national opera "voice."

In France, women were becoming more prominent in the Paris Conservatoire. Some entered at a very young age, and several women were appointed to teaching positions. With increased competition, particularly from Germany, French instrument making and music publishing began to lose their prominence in the market.

In 1889, the centennial of the Revolution was cause for great celebration and creativity: the Eiffel Tower, for example, showed off the skill of French engineering. As part of its commemoration the City of Paris commissioned Augusta Holmes to compose *L'Ode triomphale*, which was performed before an enthusiastic audience of thousands.

Women composers seemed to fare well in Scandinavia; by the end of the century there would be a great proliferation of influential women. Elfrida Andrée, in particular, had a remarkable career: she was the first woman organist in Sweden, the first to compose chamber and orchestral music, and the first woman to conduct a symphony orchestra.

Many Swedish musicians studied abroad, particularly at the Leipzig Conservatory, and when they returned to Sweden they brought back influences from German music. Interactions and exchanges with Danish and Norwegian musicians and composers also influenced Swedish music for several decades. Operas and musical dramas were very popular, and performances of Wagner's works aroused considerable interest and debate.

However, in Norway, until the 1850s music education was available only privately or through military bands. There was no conservatory or professional music school. Musicians studied abroad, with Berlin and the Leipzig Conservatory strongly favored.

The number of professional musicians and organizations increased steadily, and by the 1860s there was an established professional musical life in Norway. Many composers used traditional Norwegian themes and melodies.

Composers in Czechoslovakia continued to utilize traditional music themes and forms. By the 1860s a substantial amount of traditional music had been collected and published. There was a spirit of optimism about Czech music. People felt there was a need for a repertory of historical and comic operas, and in 1861 a competition was established that considered scores and librettos of Czech composers and writers that reflected their Czech heritage.

For many years musical life in Poland had revolved around the churches, large manor houses, and the royal courts, but by the last half of the 19th century musical life was concentrated in the cities. There were many public concerts and programs, with solo performances and small instrumental ensembles. Choral societies were increasingly popular. There were few established orchestras other than opera orchestras. However, there was considerable growth in music publishing and the production of musical instruments throughout the century. Similarly, the amount of writing about music increased, in part bolstered by research on early Polish music, and gave rise to several journals. The rhythms of traditional music and folkdances were written into mazurkas and polonaises as well as sonatas, symphonies, operas, and other classical genres.

The withdrawal of the Turks in the early part of the century was a turning point in Romanian musical life, as musicians and composers turned more toward the west. By the middle of the century Romanian musical life was becoming well established. Several conservatories opened, and there was more theater. The use of folk melodies in music, particularly piano music, had been a significant element of Romanian music from the early part of the century.

In Russia music education and musical life were becoming more professionalized. The Russian Music Society, which was founded in 1859 by Anton Rubinstein with royal patronage, began offering music classes. This was soon followed by the establishment of new music schools that eventually became state conservatories. Anton and Nikolay Rubinstein had given music a more professional standing in Russia, and musicians had a professional, more highly regarded cachet. With this, musical life in St. Petersburg and Moscow underwent a radical shift. Concerts and recitals now began to include music by Russian composers in addition to western European classical music.

Many composers turned their attention to opera, with their music and the stories often reflecting Russian traditions. Unfortunately, this wasn't always commercially successful, as French and Italian opera continued to dominate.

Women composers were continuing to explore other areas of interest in music, often as writers or critics. In addition to her work as a pianist and composer, Ella Georgiyevna Adayevskaya researched the music of ancient

Greece, the Greek Church and Slavonic folksongs. Through her publications she became known as a pioneer in ethnomusicology.

Sacred and operatic music continued to be the focus for Italian composers, although instrumental music was receiving greater attention and more performances. Throughout Europe, opera was continuing to change in significant ways, and Italian operatic composers were having to adapt to Romantic styles and music.

Verdi was on the operatic scene. Although his early operas were subject to great criticism they were very popular, and public acclaim won out over critical carping about his use of instruments and voices and his insistence on using a strong story as the basis for his operas.

The Great Exhibition of 1851 in London was the first of the great international exhibitions — the first world's fair. It was an opportunity for England to show off its substantial prosperity and achievements, and other countries were eager to participate and proclaim their successes as well.

Every accomplished young woman of any substance was expected to have a smattering of knowledge of the arts, including a passing acquaintance with singing or playing the piano. Many women took this much further, establishing themselves as composers and musicians of professional caliber — although often without venues for performance. One woman who pushed the barriers was Elizabeth Stirling, who decided to pursue a BMus at Oxford. In 1856 she submitted a composition on Psalm 130 for five voices and orchestra as part of the requirement for the degree. Since women were not then eligible for degrees at Oxford, the exercise was accepted but not performed.

With the phenomenal success of Gilbert and Sullivan in the late 1870s operettas became all the rage. Women had long been accepted as songwriters, and many women had very successful careers writing songs. England had a tradition of choral music, and being accepted as an accomplished and talented composer of choral music was relatively easier for a woman than with other forms of composing. Operetta seemed a logical step for many women composers. Choral works and choral societies were also very popular in Ireland, perhaps reflecting a long tradition of Irish vocal music.

Spain in the 1860s saw the establishment of several musical societies, and there was more instrumental composing and performing as well as symphonic writing. The salon had always been a popular venue for music, and its popularity continued. The café tradition was gradually giving way to the theater.

Zarzuela and opera were very popular: opera (usually Italian) being considered more for the upper classes, and zarzuela for the people. There was considerable debate about the two genres, with many people firm on the position that zarzuela was Spanish opera.

Opera and operetta by both European composers and Brazilians were tremendously popular in Brazil, and Chiquinha Gonzaga was talented enough to take full advantage of their popularity. She had a remarkable career as a composer of operettas. Luisa Leonardo followed a more traditional path in her study and career, but she also took advantage of the popularity of theater and included incidental music for theater in her range of compositions.

After the Civil War in the United States there was a virtual explosion of interest and involvement in music, and in support particularly for performances of art songs, symphonies, and instrumental solos. Touring companies were bringing music and musical theater of various types to areas of the country that had few musical resources. There was a strong sense of education having an edifying influence, and music was part of that education. In the 1870s John Knowles Paine was made professor of music at Harvard, further solidifying the place of music in education.

This was also an era of involvement in civic life and of societies, associations, leagues, and clubs formed for all sorts of interests and causes, many, again, with a sense of education rather than of furthering the arts. Waves of immigrants brought their traditional music with them, and much of that entered the American music scene in various forms.

Other changes were in the wind.

In 1871 the Vienna Damen Orchestra, led by Josephine Weinlich, performed in the United States. The *New York Times* reported: "The first performance of the Vienna Lady Orchestra was given at Steinway Hall on Monday evening, to the expressed pleasure of a very large and fashionable audience. The spectacle was certainly a novel one.... The view of an organized force of female musicians was, until Monday, never offered in this country" (September 13, 1871).

Austria

The family of **Stephanie Wurmbrand-Stuppach** (December 26, 1849, Pressburg/Bratislava–February 16, 1919, Vienna) was very active in the cultural life of Pressburg, which gave Stephanie the opportunity to meet Brahms and Liszt, as well as Carl Tausig who became her teacher and later her brother-in-law. She herself was a pianist and writer as well as a composer. Her marriage to Count Ernst Wurmbrand-Stuppach brought her to Vienna, where she lived most of her adult life.

Her compositions, which were performed by some of the leading musicians, are primarily virtuoso piano music, but she also composed a violin sonata. She was an early advocate of performances of Béla Bartók's music in Vienna and Manchester.

Her best-known piano compositions include *Die schöne Melusine, Phantasiestückeri* and her *Violin sonata* op. 35.

Anna Pessiak-Schmerlling (1834, Vienna–March 14, 1896, Vienna) taught singing for many years at the Vienna Conservatory.

Her compositions include masses and other large sacred works (which were frequently performed in Vienna), piano pieces, and songs.

Louise Haenal de Cronenthal (June 18, 1836, Naumburg, Austria–March 9, 1896, Paris?) was Austrian but spent most of her life in France. She entered the Paris Conservatoire at age seventeen. She was not only a remarkably prolific composer, but she wrote in a wide variety of genres. Many of her works were performed, particularly in France and Germany, and many were published.

Her compositions include five symphonies, 22 piano sonatas — some of which encompass arrangements made from her symphonies — dance music, a string quartet, nocturnes, and much piano music.

She was also well known for her transcriptions of Chinese music, using music that dated from about 860 B.C. to the 19th century. These transcriptions, which are perhaps her most interesting music, were dedicated to the diplomats who were responsible for the Chinese pavilion at the Paris Exposition of 1867. The transcriptions were awarded an Exhibition medal and were performed every day during the Exhibition.

Pauline Fichtner Oprawill Erdmannsdoerfer (July 28, 1847, Vienna–1916), a pianist, was a student of Liszt. She married Max von Erdmannsdoerfer, a Bavarian conductor.

Her compositions include works for violin, piano and voice, for violin and piano, and songs.

Principal source: WON

Brazil

Chiquinha (Francisca Edwiges Neves) Gonzaga (October 17, 1847, Rio de Janeiro–February 28, 1935, Rio de Janeiro) was a determined woman.

She married at the age of 16, but her husband, who was quite wealthy, disapproved of her musical career. Within four years she separated from him then obtained a divorce, which was unusual for that time in Brazil. She was sharply criticized for her actions and at times ostracized. A few years later she remarried but by the time she was thirty she had (again) separated from him.

To support herself and her children she worked as a piano teacher. She also began composing. The publication of her polka, *Atraente*, in 1877 was a turning point in her career. That same year she also published two waltzes, a tango and another polka. In 1885 her first operetta, *A corte na roça*, was immensely successful, and she became known as "the feminine Offenbach."

That same year she became the first woman to conduct an orchestra in Brazil, when she directed both the theater orchestra and the band of the military police. She was active in the Brazilian movements for the end of slavery and the proclamation of the Republic.

Between 1885 and 1933 she composed seventy-seven stage works, often collaborating with the most famous Brazilian playwrights of the time. Her work was very popular: her three-act operetta *Forrobodó* had over 1500 performances. In addition to operettas, her works include a wide variety of dance music and songs.

Stage works (selective list):

A corte na roça, 1885.
Maria, 1933.
Forrobodó.

Principal source: Norton Grove

The debut of **Luisa Leonardo** (October 22, 1859, Rio de Janeiro–June 12, 1926, Salvador, Bahia Brazil) at age eight, playing in a concert before the Emperor of Brazil, who was both her patron and godfather, set the stage for her remarkable career.

She began her studies at the Paris Conservatoire at age fourteen and remained there for four years, receiving a first prize in piano. Returning to Brazil in 1879 she began a successful career as a performer, but after a year she went to Portugal to be chamber music pianist at court. Two years later she returned to Rio.

In 1885 she left off her career as a pianist to be a touring company actress. She never resumed her career as a pianist, but she did continue to compose, and she often contributed incidental music for the theatrical revues she appeared in. When she retired from the theater in 1901 she moved to Salvador and taught piano and singing.

She composed works for orchestra including *Grande marcha triunfal*, and *Marcha fúnebre*, music for piano, and vocal works.

Principal source: Norton Grove

Czechoslovakia

Agnes Tyrell (September 20, 1846, Brno–April 18, 1883, Brno) was a Moravian composer and pianist. Her father was an English-language teacher in Brno. In 1862 she was studying piano at the Vienna Conservatory. She anticipated having a career as a pianist and gave several concerts, but her poor health eventually prevented her from continuing as a concert pianist. She then began to focus on composing.

Her Symphony in C Major was one of the few symphonic works by a woman at that time. Many of her compositions are vocal works, including songs and song cycles, works for male choruses, female choruses and mixed voice. She also wrote works for piano, chamber groups, and orchestral works in addition to her Symphony in C Major, an opera *Bertran de Born,* which was not performed, and an oratorio "Die Konige in Israel."

Her Etudes, op. 48 and her Grand Sonata, op. 66 are among her most outstanding works.

Opera:

Bertran de Born (unperformed).

Principal source: Norton Grove

England

The mother of **Caroline Orger** (1818, London–March 11, 1892, Tiverton) (sometimes listed under Reinagle) had a career as an actress and an author. Caroline herself had a successful career as a pianist, often playing her own compositions.

In 1843 she performed her Piano Concerto, which is one of the earliest piano concertos by a nineteenth-century Englishwoman. The next year she played her Piano Trio. Performances of various chamber works followed, many of them performed by the Society of British Musicians.

In 1846 she married organist and composer A. R. Reinagle, of the Reinagle family of musicians and composers.

Her works include a piano concerto, chamber music, songs, and music for the piano. Few of her chamber works seem to have survived. Her Piano Sonata is considered "one of the most significant English keyboard works of the 19th century" (Nigel Burton, p. 355, *Norton Grove Dictionary of Women Composers*).

Principal source: Norton Grove

Elizabeth Stirling (February 26, 1819, Greenwich–March 25, 1895, London) had a remarkable career as an organist with well-paid positions in two prominent London churches for a total of forty years. In 1839 she was elected organist of All Saint's, Poplar, an unusual accomplishment for someone at the young age of twenty. She only left the position when she won a competition for a similar position at St. Andrew's Undershaft in 1858. She held that position until 1880.

Elizabeth studied with several distinguished teachers, including George Macfarren. She decided to pursue a BMus at Oxford, and in 1856 she submitted a composition on Psalm 130 for five voices and orchestra to fulfill a requirement for the degree. Since women were not then eligible for degrees at Oxford, the exercise was accepted but not performed.

In 1863 she married F. A. Bridge, an organist.

Elizabeth published original pieces for organ as well as organ arrangements from the works of Handel, Bach and Mozart. She also wrote many partsongs for four voices. Her opera *Bleakmoor for Copsleigh* was performed in a chamber opera company that she and her husband ran.

Opera:

Bleakmoor for Copsleigh.

Principal source: Grove's; CCH

Little is known of **Emma Maria Macfarren** (June 19, 1824, London–November 9, 1895, London) prior to her marriage in 1846 to John Macfarren, brother of the composer George Macfarren. She and her husband spent three years in the United States. She had some renown as a lecturer, and between 1862 and 1873, presumably after their return to England, she toured almost constantly with lecture recitals called "Mornings at the Piano."

She published many piano pieces and fantasias that were usually based on operas. For these publications she used the name Jules Brissac, perhaps not to cause confusion with the Macfarren name. Her songs and a few piano pieces were published using her real name.

Principal source: Norton Grove

Even among very talented and precocious composers **Kate Loder** (August 21, 1825, sometimes given as August 22, 1826, Bath–August 30, 1904, Headley, Surrey) was unusual; she had perfect pitch at the age of three. Her family was musical; she was the cousin of composer Edward Loder, her mother was the piano teacher Fanny Philpot, and her aunt, Lucy Anderson, was pianist to Queen Victoria. Her father was John Loder, professor of violin at the Royal Academy of Music.

Kate began her piano studies at the age of six, working with a Miss Batterbury who assisted her mother. At age 12 she studied with Henry Field; she entered the Royal Academy of Music a year later and studied with her aunt. Kate won the King's Scholarship twice and took part in RAM concerts in 1840.

Four years later she performed Felix Mendelssohn's G minor concerto with Mendelssohn in the audience. Also in 1844 she was appointed professor of harmony at the RAM. By this time she was much sought-after as a teacher. Her chamber music was performed at the Society of British Musicians and reviewed in *The Musical World.*

She married Henry Thompson, a well-known surgeon, in 1851. She fell subject to increasing paralysis about 1871, but she continued to be influential in British music. Brahms's *German Requiem* had its first performance in England at her house.

She had a successful career as a composer in addition to her success as a teacher. In general, her earlier works are more distinguished than her later works; her String Quartet in G minor and the Violin Sonata in E major being particularly well known. Her works include an opera, *L'elisir d'amore,* orchestral and chamber music, and works for piano, organ, and songs.

Opera:

L'elisir d'amore, c. 1850.

Principal source: Norton Grove

Mary Ann Virginia Gabriel (February 7, 1825, Banstead–August 7, 1877, London) had a successful career as a composer of songs, piano works, operettas and cantatas. The daughter of an Irish colonel, she was educated in Italy, and she studied both piano and composition. Little is known about her life apart from her compositions.

Her first publication was a song in 1836; she wrote more than 300 songs altogether. By the late 1850s her composing focus had changed, and her subsequent publications tended to be complex and difficult piano pieces, operatic songs, or English ballads.

Her cantata of Longfellow's poem *Evangeline* had a very successful premiere at the Brighton Festival in 1873. Two years later her cantata *Dreamland* premiered. She wrote a third cantata: *Graziella.* Her operettas, approximately a dozen, were performed by the German Reed Company in London and toured widely. Probably her most successful was *Widows Bewitched.*

In 1874 she married George March, who had written several of her librettos.

Stage works (selective list):

Widows Bewitched, 1865.
Who's the Heir, 1870.
Grass Widows, 1873.
Graziella, 1875.
The Love Tests.
The Shepard of Cournouailles, 1864.

Principal source: Norton Grove

The compositions of **Helene Santa Colona-Sourget** (February 8, 1827, Bordeaux–date of death not known) include a one-act opera, *L'Image*, produced in 1864 and a string trio.

Opera:

L'Image, 1864.

Principal source: WON

Sophia Julia Woolf (1831, London–November 10, 1893, Hampstead) was a three-time King's Scholar at the Royal Academy of Music.

Her published music includes about twenty songs and about twenty piano pieces. These must have been successful, as some of the songs were incorporated into theatrical productions, and several piano pieces were orchestrated for theatrical entr'actes.

Opera:

Carina, Opéra Comique, London, 1888.

Principal source: Norton Grove

Florence May (February 6, 1845, London–June 28, 1923, London) was one of several women who studied with Clara Schumann. Her father — and her first teacher — was Edward Collett May, an organist and teacher.

She was fifteen when she went to Germany to study. Clara introduced Florence to Brahms; she became his pupil and later wrote his biography. She was best known as an interpreter of Brahms and through her concerts helped introduce his work in England.

Her compositions include a Benedictus and Hosanna (performed in Berlin in 1878), songs, and piano pieces.

Principal sources: Grove's; WON

Oliveria Louisa Prescott (September 3, 1942, London–September 9, 1919) was taught by George Macfarren at the Royal Academy of Music. Later, when he became blind, she was his amanuensis. She taught harmony and published a textbook for instrumentalists and for vocalists.

She composed in a variety of forms. She wrote partsongs, songs, and a piano duet that were published, as well as two symphonies, overtures, a, piano concerto, orchestral suite, shorter works for orchestra, *Psalm CXXVI* for voices, music for voice and orchestra, and much chamber music. She also wrote a musical comedy. Many — perhaps most — of her compositions were lost.

Principal sources: Norton Grove; WON

Alice Mary White Smith [Mrs. Meadows-White] (May 19, 1839, London–December 4, 1884, London) also studied with George Macfarren. When she was twenty-one her first Piano Quartet was performed at a trial of new compositions by the London Musical Society. The Quartet attracted considerable attention. Subsequently the Society performed other orchestral works of hers. She married Frederick Meadows White when she was twenty-eight; the same year she was elected Female Professional Associate of the Philharmonic Society.

She was a prolific composer in many genres. Her works include an operetta *Rüdesheim*, two symphonies and other orchestral works, choral works, overtures, fugues and music for chamber groups.

Opera:
Rüdesheim or Gisela, 1865.
Principal source: Norton Grove

Florence Ashton Marshall (March 30, 1843, Rome–March 5, 1922?) was another composer who studied with George Macfarren. She married Julian Marshall who was a collector of a music and a writer. Florence was the author of a biography of Handel and of the *Life and Letters of Mary Wollstonecraft Shelley*, as well as numerous articles. She contributed to the first edition of Grove's *Dictionary of Music and Musicians*, as did her husband.

She conducted the South Hampstead Orchestra, which performed a Brahms symphony and the violin concerto of Saint-Saëns under her direction. Among her honors she was elected an associate of the Philharmonic Society.

Her compositions include choral music, *Nocturne* for clarinet, solo songs, part songs, and educational pieces, a cantata and two operettas.

Stage works:
The Masked Shepherd, operetta, 1879.
Prince Sprite, fairy operetta, 1897.
Principal source: Norton Grove

Elizabeth Annie Nunn (c. 1861–January 7, 1894, Manchester) is one of the many composers of whom we know little or nothing except written music. She wrote a *Mass in C* and other church works.
Principal source: WON

Florence Marian Skinner (fl. 1870s and 1880s) was born in England but worked in Italy. All that is known about her composing is that she wrote two operas.

Operas:
Suocera, Naples, 1877.
Maria Regina di Scozia, St. Remo, Turin, and London, 1883.
Principal source: WON

France

Pauline-Marie-Elisa Thys (c. 1836, Paris–1909) was the daughter of the Opéra Comique composer Alphonse Thys, who had won the Prix de Rome in 1833. She began by composing salon music but soon began composing larger works. From 1857 to 1907 she wrote at least sixteen works for theater including operettas, operas, and *operas comique*, as well as dramas without music. She was both a librettist and composer for many of her works. Many of her works were staged; some had concert performances.

She wrote at least one novel, using the pseudonym Mme. M. Du Coin; she may have used the pseudonym Sebault Ducoin for some compositions.

Operas and stage works:

La pomme de Turquie, operetta, 1857.
L'Heriter sans le savior, operetta, 1858.
Dieu le garde, operetta, 1860.
La Perruque du Bailli, operetta, 1861.
Judith, lyric drama.
Le pays de cocagne, two acts, operetta, 1862.
Manette, operetta, 1865.
Le marriage de Taharin, ou La congiura di Chevreuse, Florence, 1876.
Le cabaret du pot-casse three acts, operetta, 1878.
Nedgeya, Naples, 1880.
La congiura di chevreuse, two acts, opera, 1881.
L'education d'Achille, one act, operetta, 1881.
Le fruit vert, three acts, operetta.
Le roi jaune, operetta, 1887.
Guidetta, three acts, operetta, 1891.

Principal source: Norton Grove

Pauline Michelle Ferdinande Viardot-Garcia (July 18, 1821, Paris–May 18, 1910, Paris) came from a remarkable — and very well-known — musical family.

Her parents, Manuel Garcia and Joaquina Sitches Garcia, were both well-known singers. Manuel trained many accomplished singers, including his children, and his family opera company toured the United States and Mexico from 1825 to 1828.

Pauline also was an accomplished pianist, studying with the leading teachers in Paris, and occasionally with Liszt during his Paris visits. Pauline accompanied the singing lessons her father gave, and she later remarked that she thought she profited more by the lessons than his pupils did.

Her brother Manuel who lived from 1805 to 1906 and was known as the "centenarian of song" was highly regarded for his teaching and for his research into vocal physiology. Maria Malibran, her older sister, is still considered one of the greatest singers of all time. Her death when she was only twenty-eight had a deep and long-lasting impact on Pauline, who was then fifteen.

Pauline was a child prodigy in many aspects. When she was only eight she was accompanying her father. She acquired languages easily and was fluent in Spanish, French, English, German, and Russian. She was skilled in portraiture. She studied composition with Anton Reicha.

When Maria died in 1836, Pauline more or less stepped into her sister's shoes and focused most of her attention on singing. Her mother gave her singing lessons, and a year later, at age sixteen, she made her singing debut in Brussels. Two years later, in 1839, she began her operatic career that nearly matched Maria's. She had an excellent voice and a considerable range; she was a skilled dramatic singer. Her operatic performances were notable both for her singing and acting and they brought her great acclaim. She was without rival in many of her roles.

Pauline was nineteen when she married the writer and critic Louis Viardot. He was a figure in his own right, a theater manager and well connected with the literary and artistic world. He became well known for his translations of *Don Quixote* and of the writings of Ivan Turgenev. They knew "everyone" in Paris, and their home was a center for people in the arts. Pauline was significant in the careers of Saint-Saëns, Gounod, Massenet and Fauré.

In 1843 when she visited Russia, she sang in both Italian and Russian. In turn, she helped open Europe to Russian music.

Finally, in 1863, she retired, and moved to Baden-Baden, although continuing to perform. In 1870 the Franco Prussian War drove her and her husband to London for a year, returning to Paris in 1871. Pauline continued to compose and teach. Not surprisingly, her compositions are primarily vocal music.

She composed four operettas. Turgenev, who was a close friend and spent long periods of time in the Viardot household, wrote the libretto for three of them. She and George Sand collected and transcribed French folksongs; the heroine in Sand's novel *Consuela* was inspired by Viardot. She was also a renowned portraitist. From all accounts she had a colorful and attractive personality.

"She [Pauline Viardot] wrote brilliant operettas in collaboration with Tourgenief [Turgenev], but they were never published and were performed only in private" (Saint Saens, *Musical Memories*, p. 174).

She had four children. Louise Pauline Marie Héritte (see entry), her eldest daughter, was herself a singer, teacher and composer, and taught singing in Europe and Russia.

Her compositions include many works for voices, lieder, chansons, opera and operettas, as well as works for piano and arrangements for voice and piano.

Operas and stage works:

Trop de femmes, operetta, 1867.
L'ogre, 1868.
Le dernier sorcier, Weimar, 1869.
Le conte de fêtes, opéra comique, 1904.
Cendrillon, opera, 1868?

Biography, memoirs:

Pauline Viardot, by Nicole Barry (Paris: Flammarion, 1991).
The Price of Genius, by April Fitzlyon (London: Calder, 1964).
Memoires de Louise Héritte-Viardot, by Louise Héritte de la Tour (Paris, 1923).

Principal sources: Grove's; Norton Grove

Louise Aglae Masson Massart (June 10, 1827, Paris–July 26, 1887, Paris) attended the Paris Conservatoire at the age of eleven and later succeeded Louise Farrenc as professor of piano. Louise and her husband, the violinist Joseph Massart, gave joint concerts for many years.

Her compositions include piano pieces and arrangements for violin and piano.

Principal source: WON

Marie Felicie Clemence de Reiset Grandval (January 21, 1830, Le Mans–January 15, 1907, Paris) began composing in her teens under the guidance of Friedrich Flotow, a family friend. Her education was interrupted when he left Paris. Following her marriage to the Vicomte de Grandval, she studied composition with Saint-Saëns for two years. She took piano lessons from Chopin.

Her one-act operetta, *Le sou de Lise*, premiered in Paris in 1859. That same year it was published under the pseudonym Caroline Blangy. (Throughout her career she published under a range of pseudonyms; interestingly, most of her pseudonyms were women's names.) Between 1850 and 1869 six operas and operettas premiered. She won the Concours Rossini in 1880 for her oratorio *La fille de Jaire*.

Throughout her life she composed and was an active participant in musical life. Her friends included the composers and musicians of her day, and she dedicated many of her works to them.

In addition to her operetta her compositions include three symphonies, two concertos, a concert overture, a ballet, chamber works and piano pieces, a chorale, at least two oratorios, music for solo voices and for choruses, music for orchestra, chamber and solo instruments. She left a manuscript of a grand opera in four acts.

She was regarded as one of the preeminent composers of the time.

Operas and stage works:

Le sou de Lise, operetta, Paris, Théâtre des Bouffes-Parisiens, 1859.
Les fiancés de Rosa, opéra comique, Théâtre Lyrique, 1863.
Il Mugnaio di Marlenac, 1863.
La comtesse Eva, opéra comique, Baden-Baden, 1864.
Donna Maria Infanta di Spagna, opera, 1865.
Le pénitente, opéra comique, Paris, Opéra Comique, 1868.
Piccolino, opera, Paris, Théâtre Italien, 1869.
La forêt, poème lyrique, Paris, 1875.
Atala, poème lyrique, c. 1888.
Mazeppa, opera, Bordeaux, 1892.

Principal sources: Norton Grove

Augusta Mary Anne [Hermann Zenta] Holmes (December 16, 1847, Paris–January 28, 1903, Paris), the daughter of an Irish officer and a Scottish and Irish mother, grew up in France where her parents had settled. She spent much of her childhood in Versailles. Her parents, neither of whom were particularly musical, were well connected with the artistic world of the time, and their home attracted many notable literary, musical and artistic guests. Augusta's godfather was Alfred de Vigny, who may have been her father.

From an early age she showed talent in music, poetry and painting, but her mother discouraged her musical interests. After the death of her mother when Augusta was eleven her father encouraged her musical talents, and Augusta began to take lessons, first on the organ, then in instrumentation. De Vigny was a consistent factor after the death of her mother, acting as mentor and adviser.

She was a strong supporter of Wagner's music and advocated having his works included on the Concerts Populaires. Eventually she met Wagner at his home on Lake Lucerne. She was influenced by him, and perhaps as a result, many of her compositions are on a grander scale. Liszt admired her music, and the two corresponded.

In the 1870s she was part of the circle of friends of César Franck, and she may have studied with him. She was an active participant in the musical life. She was considered a great beauty. Saint-Saëns considered her music over-orchestrated — but that aside, he proposed to her and was rejected.

Also during the 1870s she began composing more seriously. In 1875 she wrote her first opera, *Héro et Léander*, which was not performed; this was followed by *Astarté* and *Lancelot du lac*, also unperformed. However, in 1895, *La montagne noire* was performed at the Paris Opéra.

At the centenary of the French Revolution, the City of Paris commissioned *L'Ode triomphale*, which was performed before an enthusiastic audience of thousands. She was invited to submit a composition for the 1893 World's Columbian Exhibition in Chicago.

She focused on large orchestral works, dramatic symphonies and symphonic poems, but her choral works were more successful. She is probably best known for *Les Argonautes* (1881).

She apparently had a most striking, strong personality, and she dominated the musical and literary scene of her time. She was greatly admired for her beauty and personality. She never married but was the mistress of Catulle Mendès, a French poet and man of letters, with whom she had several children.

Operas:

Héro et Léander, not performed, 1875.
Astarté, not performed.
Lancelot du lac, not performed, c. 1880.
La montagne noire, Paris Opéra, Paris, 1895.

Principal sources: Norton Grove; Grove's

Mélanie Bonis [Mme. Albert Domange] (January 21, 1858, Paris–March 18, 1937, Sarcelles, France) showed great promise with her piano lessons at an early age. In 1876 Professor Maury, who was a family friend, introduced her to César Franck; a year later, at the age of nineteen, she entered the Paris Conservatoire where she studied organ with Franck. Debussy and Pierné were students at the same time. She won prizes in harmony and accompaniment, and she seemed to be destined for a significant career.

Her family had never been in favor of her musical aspirations, and her father arranged a marriage with Albert Domange, who was much older and very well-to-do. After their marriage in 1883 she stopped composing, being more involved with raising her family. She resumed her composing about 1894; this began a rich and prolific time for her. Most of her compositions — more than 300 — were published and most were performed.

She was an ambitious and prolific composer and composed in a variety of genres. Her works include chamber pieces, many piano solos, choral pieces, organ music, and orchestral works. She often used the name Mel to obscure the fact she was a woman.

After her death her children assembled a memoir from her notebooks: *Souvenirs et réflexions.*

Biography, memoirs:

Souvenirs et réflexions de Mel Bonis, extraits de notes autobiographiques et de pensées de Mel Bonis, recuillis par ses petits enfants (Editions du Nant d'Enfer, 1974).

Mel Bonis: Femme et compositeur, by Christine Geliot [great granddaughter of Bonis] (Paris: Editions L'Harmattan, 2000).

Principal source: Norton Grove

One of the members of a pair of mother and daughter composers is **Louise Pauline Viardot Héritte** (December 14, 1841, Paris–January 17, 1918,

Heidelberg), the daughter of Pauline Viardot. Louise was a professor at the Imperial Conservatory at St. Petersburg for four years. She married but left her husband. She then traveled about, seeking out teaching and performing opportunities. Many of her compositions apparently were lost during this period.

Her works include a comic opera, cantatas, string quartets, trios, and piano pieces. Of particular interest are her piano quartets.

Opera:

Lindoro, comic opera, Weimar, 1879.

Memoirs:

Mémoires de Louise Héritte-Viardot : une famille de grands musiciens : notes et souvenirs anecdotiques sur Garcia, Pauline Viardot, La Malibran, Louise Héritte-Viardot et leur entourage (Stock, 1923, Paris).

Principal sources: New Grove; Cohen

Anais, Comtesse de Perriere-Pilt (1836, Paris–December 1878, Paris), a wealthy woman, composed opera and operettas. Her works were performed in her town house where she had a "salle de spectacle" that could accommodate her three-act operas. Her three operettas were publicly performed but weren't well received.

Operas and stage works:

Le sorcier, operetta, Paris, 1866.
Les vacances de l'amour, Paris, (privately produced) comic opera, 1867.
La Dryade, Paris, (privately produced), 1870.
Jaloux de soi, operetta Paris, 1873.
Le talon d'Achille, operetta, 1875.
La Grotto del majo Merlino.

Principal sources: Norton Grove

Marie Trautmann Jaëll (August 17, 1846, Steinseltz, Alsace–February 4, 1925, Paris) was remarkable among prodigies, giving concerts in Germany, Switzerland and France when she was nine and winning the *premier prix* in piano at the Paris Conservatoire at age 16.

She studied composition with Saint-Saëns and Franck. In 1866, at age twenty, she married Alfred Jaëll, a renowned Austrian piano virtuoso; they made numerous concert tours in Europe and Russia.

After her husband's death in 1882 she began spending several weeks a year at Weimar, performing at Liszt's musicales. During the last three years of his life she assisted him with secretarial work.

She taught for many years at the Paris Conservatoire, and her teaching methods became well known. Her most famous student was Albert Schweitzer who went to Paris to study with her. In her later years she performed little, focusing instead on her teaching and on her writing, much of which deals with pedagogy. She was the first to work with the physiology of the hand in improving piano technique, and her exercises, which took into account the hand's anatomy, were a significant departure from the traditional drills. She also wrote articles on piano technique.

She is less well known as a composer than as a pianist and teacher. Her compositions include concertos for cello and violin, piano, symphonic poem, piano pieces, and choral music.

Principal source: Norton Grove

Charlotte Jacques is known to us by her operetta *La Veille*.
Stage work:
La Veille, 1862.
Principal source: WON

Germany

Johanna Mockel Kinkel (July 8, 1810, Bonn–November 15, 1858, London) was one of many composers who were connected with seemingly "everyone" and who, as her life unfolded, was involved with a myriad of issues and achievements. Both writing and music played strong roles in her life. She conducted opera and composed, and her published writings cover a range of genres and topics.

Her father was a teacher at the French lycée in Bonn. At a young age Johanna studied piano and composition. Her early compositions were lieder, duets and stage works for amateur players, which were well received. By then she was conducting opera and writing poetry, political articles and art criticism. She also was a music critic, historian and general writer on music. She married Paul Matthieu, a book dealer, in 1831. They soon separated but weren't divorced until 1839.

Four years after her marriage she traveled to Frankfurt and then moved to Berlin, where she studied composition and piano. Schumann admired her lieder. That same year she met Felix Mendelssohn who became an admirer of her compositions; her friends included Fanny Mendelssohn and Bettina Brentano. (Bettina Brentano von Arnim, Countess of Arnim, was a most accomplished woman in her own right, but she's perhaps best known for her friendships.)

She returned to Bonn in 1839, perhaps in connection with her divorce, and a year later she met Gottfried Kinkel, a theologian, amateur poet, and later an art historian as well as a political leader. They married in 1843; within six years they had four children. Gottfried was becoming increasingly important as a political leader, and Johanna was a newspaper publisher and a writer, often focusing on political topics. In 1849 Gottfried, who had participated in several attempted revolutions, was arrested and sentenced to life imprisonment.

Johanna was vulnerable as well, and she was forced to move to Cologne. She, along with Carl Schurz, engineered Gottfried's escape from Spandau prison, and the family fled to London. Gottfried continued his revolutionary activities, traveling to the United States to raise funds. By then Johanna was finding it impossible to compose. She taught music and was active in the advocacy of women's rights.

Her compositions include stage works, choral music, lieder collections, piano arrangements of folksongs, and pieces for children.

The Kinkel archives are in Bonn.

Stage works:

Die Assassinen, liederspiel.
Die Landpartie, operetta.
Das Malzbier, oder Die Stadt-Bonnsichen Gespenster.
Otto der Shutz, liederspiel.
Themis und Savigny, oder Die Olympien in Berlin, vaudeville.

Principal sources: CCH; Norton Grove

As occurred rather often with women composers, **Emilie Mayer** (May 14, 1821, Friedland–April 10, 1883, Berlin) was an artist as well as a composer. She first studied organ in Friedland, and she soon began composing songs. She moved to Stettin, which at that time was the capital of Pomerania, and took lessons with Carl Loewe, a composer of ballads. She soon was composing chamber music, overtures and symphonies.

In 1847 she moved to Berlin where she studied fugue, counterpoint and orchestration, and she organized private performances of her music in homes. Her first publication was in 1849; a year later she gave the first concert of her own work. Through the years she would give many public and private concerts of her work.

She spent considerable money and energy traveling and on having her music printed and performed. Her tours tended to be successful, and in 1855 after her performances in Munich she was appointed an honorary member of the Munich Philharmonic Society.

Emilie was a prolific composer and her music was widely performed during her lifetime, particularly in Germany, yet most of it has not been performed since her death. In the *Norton Grove Dictionary of Women Composers,* Eva Rieger refers to her as "the most prolific German woman composer of the romantic period" (p. 321).

One of her most successful compositions was her sinfonia in B minor (1852), which had at least eight public performances.

Emilie also worked as a sculptor, creating sculptures out of white bread. She became well known for her sculptures, and some of her works were acquired for royal collections.

Her compositions include sinfonias and other orchestral works, choral music, music for solo voice, chamber works and music for piano.

Principal sources: CCH; Norton Grove

Anna Caroline de Belleville Oury (June 24, 1808, Landshut, Bavaria– July 22, 1880, Munich) was the daughter of the director of the Munich Opera. She grew up in Augsburg. Her first studies were with the cathedral organist, who recommended to her parents that she be taken to Vienna to study with Carl Czerny. Consequently she moved to Vienna in 1816 and began studying under Czerny.

She returned to Munich in 1820. Although she was still very young she gave a few concerts, including one in Vienna in which she played a Hummel concerto with an orchestra. The next year she was in Paris, then returned to Vienna where she studied with Johann Andreas Streicher, husband of Nanette Streicher (see entry). She went on tour in Warsaw and Berlin and made her London debut (with Paganini) in July 1831.

She must have been an excellent pianist. She was compared to Clara Wieck Schumann — by Robert Schumann — who said that she had a better technique than Clara. Chopin also was very impressed with her playing (Schonberg, p. 105).

In October of that year she married Antonio James Oury, the English violinist, and between 1831 and 1839 they toured throughout Europe and in Russia. Eventually they settled in England. In 1847 she and her husband established the Brighton Musical Union, after which she performed less and concentrated on her composing until she retired in 1866.

Her compositions, approximately 180 drawing-room pieces, are primarily dances and fantasies for piano.

Principal sources: Grove's; Harold C. Schonberg, *The Great Pianists from Mozart to the Present* (New York: Simon & Schuster, 1963).

Lina Ramana or **Ramann** (June 24, 1833, Mainstickheim, Bavaria–March 30, 1912, Munich) was an educator and writer as well as a composer. Little is known of her life. In 1865 she became director of a training school for music teachers, a post she held for six years. She then was director of the Nuremberg School of Music from 1865 to 1890. Her two volumes of essays about music stayed in print for many years. Liszt in particular encouraged her writing.

Her compositions are primarily piano music, including sonatas and sonatinas. She also edited Liszt's piano works.

Principal sources: CCH; WON

Caroline Wisender (Brunswick, Germany–August 25, 1868, Brunswick) was one of several composers involved with the blind. Little is known about her life. In 1860 she founded the Wisender School for the Blind. She composed melodramas and two operas.

Operas:
Die Palastdame, 1848.
Das Jubelfest or *Die Drei Gefangenen,* 1849.

Principal source: WON

Ingeborg von Bronsart (August 12/24, 1840, St. Petersburg–June 7, 1913, Munich) was a German composer and pianist, although she was of Swedish parentage. Her parents were living in Russia at the time of her birth.

By the time she was eight she was a remarkable pianist and a composer. She studied in St. Petersburg for two years. Her performing debut was at age twelve. Two years later she attracted attention for her playing of Chopin's *Piano Concerto in E* by memory, most unusual at a time when most pianists played from scores.

In 1858 she moved to Weimar, where she completed her training with Liszt; she was considered one of his most promising pupils. That same year she began her performing career, and for ten years she toured. In her concerts she was often accompanied by Hans Bronsart von Schellendorf, a conductor and pianist — and another pupil of Liszt. The two married in 1861.

Hans was appointed Intendant of the court theatres in Hanover and then in Weimar. Because she had to discontinue her career as a pianist while he served in these two posts (from 1867 to 1895) she turned her focus to composition. In 1895 he retired and they moved to Munich; they died within a few months of each other.

Her most successful composition was the *Kaiser-Wilhelm-Marsch* (1871), which was performed at the opening of the Women's Exhibit at the 1893 World's Columbian Exposition in Chicago. Her singspiel *Jery und Bätely,* which was also very successful, premiered in 1873. *Hiarne,* another success, was performed in 1891. *Die Sühne* (1909) was composed after her husband's retirement and their move to Munich in 1895.

She composed in almost every genre except symphony and oratorio. Much of her music was never published.

Operas and stage works:
Die Göttin von Sais, oder Linas und Llane, idyllische opera, 1867.

Kronprinzliches Palais, Berlin. Lost.
Jery und Bätely operetta, Weimar, 1873.
Hiarne, Berlin, 1891.
Die Sühne, Dessau Hoftheater, 1909.
Principal sources: Grove's; CCH

Auguste Goetze (February 24, 1840, Weimer–April 29, 1908, Leipzig) was a well-known singer of German lieder. (Her father was an operatic tenor.) In 1875 she founded an opera school in Dresden. In 1891 she joined the faculty at Leipzig Conservatory.

Three of her operas, *Susanna Monfort*, *Magdalena* and *Eine Heimfahrt*, were performed frequently; however, *Vittori Accoramboni*, was not performed. She also wrote vocal studies, songs, and material on vocal method.
Operas:
Susanna Monfort.
Magdalena.
Eine Heimfahrt.
Vittori Accoramboni.
Principal source: WON

Among the many who studied with Liszt, **Aline Hundt** (1849–c. 1873?) was reputedly one of his finest pupils.

Her works — and hers was a very short career — include an orchestral march, a work for tenor solo, chorus and orchestra, piano works, songs and choral works, and a symphony that she conducted at its premiere in Berlin in 1871. Amy Fay in *Music Study in Germany* (p. 117) remarked, "Alicia Hund [*sic*] conducting the orchestra in her own symphony ... all the men were highly disgusted because she was allowed to conduct the orchestra herself."
Principal source: WON

Louise Langhans Japha (February 2, 1826, Hamburg–October 13, 1910, Wiesbaden) (sometimes listed under Langhans) was a very successful concert pianist, particularly in Paris. Robert and Clara Schumann were among her teachers. She married the violinist and composer Friedrich Langhans in 1858; they divorced in 1874.

Her works include an opera (or portions of an opera), string quartets, choral works, and piano pieces.
Opera:
One opera (perhaps incomplete).
Principal source: WON

The family of **Luise Adolfa Le Beau** (April 25, 1850, Rastatt, Germany–1927, Baden-Baden) was remarkably supportive of her musical ambitions. She had an uneven career, enjoying successes and winning respect, but in sum, the opposition in Germany at that time defeated her.

Almost all of her education was at home where she was taught by her father, who was with the Baden War Office. She began composing at age fifteen and three years later made her piano debut with the Baden court orchestra. She studied briefly with Clara Schumann. During that time she met Hans von Bülow, who was a lifelong supporter of her work.

In 1874 her family moved to Munich specifically so that she could study with Joseph Rheinberger, who was an outstanding organist and a prolific composer. He had set rules about his teaching including (1) he would never give private lessons, and (2) he would never teach women. He was so impressed with Louise that he broke both his rules.

Most of her great successes occurred during this time: her compositions were favorably reviewed, and she won composition prizes. On her tours she met Liszt and Brahms.

In 1882 her Op. 24 Cello Pieces won an international competition in Hamburg. On the certificates, "Herr," which was printed, had to be crossed out and replaced with a hand-printed "Fraulein." She seemed poised for a long and successful career.

But her professional life included both strong successes and frustrating opposition. She seems to have gotten on the wrong side of people with some frequency. She became estranged from the Rheinberger family, and by the early 1880s her popularity and desirability as a performer in Munich faded. She had trouble getting performances, which she attributed to other musicians' envy of her successes. There were also "political" problems as factions arose over what was seen as the increasing influence of Wagner and his adherents on musical institutions.

Her family moved several times in search of a more amenable venue for her composing — to Wiesbaden where they lived from 1885 to 1890, then to Berlin from 1890 to 1893, then finally to Baden. There she worked as a critic in addition to playing in concerts; her first opera, *Hadumoth*, which she had been trying for several years to have staged in Berlin, was finally performed in Baden in 1894.

She published her memoirs in 1910. In 1925 there was a concert of her work in Baden-Baden to celebrate her 75th birthday.

Her compositions include operas, choral music, orchestral pieces and music for chamber groups and for piano. Among her most notable works are her piano sonata (1879), Symphony in F Minor, op. 41, and cello sonata op. 17. Also of note is the Quartet for piano, violin, viola and cello, op. 28. Performed at the Leipzig Gewandhaus in 1884 it received overwhelming acclaim, and the promoter remarked he could not remember as great as success at the Gewandhaus as hers. The quartet was performed worldwide.

Operas:
Hadumoth, 1894.
Der verzauberte Kalif.
Autobiography:
She reputedly wrote her autobiography in 1910.
Principal sources: CCH; Norton Grove

Sophie Menter (July 29, 1846, Munich–February 23, 1918, near Munich) was the daughter of musicians; her father was a well-known cellist, and her mother a singer. Sophie was best known as a pianist, and she came to be regarded as one of the greatest piano virtuosos of the time. She was very precocious and began studying at the Munich Conservatory at an early age, leaving it when she was thirteen for private lessons.

She began her professional career when she was fifteen, playing Weber's *Konzerstuck* for piano and orchestra. She subsequently toured in Germany and Switzerland. When she was twenty-one her playing of Liszt's piano music at the Leipzig Gewandhaus was highly praised. She was an occasional student of Liszt, who described her as "my only legitimate piano daughter." She also studied with Carl Tausig and Hans von Bülow. In Paris she was described as "l'incarnation de Liszt." Even George Bernard Shaw was immensely impressed with her playing (Schonberg, pp. 246–7).

In 1872 she married David Popper, a cellist. She first performed in England in 1881; two years later she was awarded honorary membership in the Royal Philharmonic Society. That same year, in 1883, she became piano professor at the St. Petersburg Conservatory, but in 1886 she left to continue her concert tours. That same year her marriage with Popper ended.

All of her known works are for piano.
Principal sources: CCH; Grove's

Agnes Marie Jacobina Zimmermann (July 5, 1847, Cologne–November 14, 1925, London) spent most of her life in England, her family having moved there when she was young. At nine she began studying at the Royal Academy of Music. She was one of the many pupils of George Macfarren. She already was composing, and her compositions were often part of the programs at the RAM. She won the King's Scholarship in 1860 and 1862. The next year she made her debut at the Crystal Palace. In 1864 she toured Germany and played at the Leipzig Gewandhaus. She was an accomplished pianist and was well regarded for her technique.

She later made two additional, short tours, but her venue remained England, where she became known for her composing as well as for her performances. In 1868 she and Clara Schumann performed together, playing her

Andante and Variations for two pianos. Throughout her career she was known for her performances of classical music. She edited the sonatas of Beethoven and Mozart, as well as Robert Schumann's piano works.

Her compositions include chamber music, pieces for piano, and vocal works.

Principal sources: Grove's; Norton Grove

Greece

Little is known of **Sophia Dellaporta** (Lixourion, Kefallinia–fl. 2nd half of 19th century) beyond her *Recueil musical*, which is eight compositions that bear the names of heroes of the 1821 Greek War of Independence. This won a prize at the Third Greek Composers' competition, organized in Athens by the 1875 Olympics Exhibition. It was published in Leipzig in 1877.

Principal source: Norton Grove

Ireland

Fanny Arthur Robinson (September 1831–October 31, 1879) had a successful career as a pianist, performing in Dublin, Paris and London. She began her teaching career in London, where she taught for many years. She married Joseph Robinson, an Irish choral conductor. After their marriage they both taught at the Royal Irish Conservatory.

Her compositions include piano pieces and a cantata.

Principal source: WON

Italy

In 1820, when **Mariana Bottini** [née Andreozzi] (November 7, 1802, Lucca, Italy–January 24, 1858, Lucca) was eighteen, two of her compositions, *Stabat Mater* and *Messa de Requiem,* that she had written the year before in memory of her mother earned her admission to the Academia Filarmonica in Bologna as an honorary maestro. Most of her compositions were written when she was in her teens. She did little composing after her marriage in 1823 to Lorenzo Bottini, who was a marquis and prominent in Luccan political life.

Her music includes an opera, cantatas, motets, and other choral music for the orchestra, concerti, two symphonies, music for harp, and numerous dances. On six occasions her music was the only music by a woman used as part of the traditional Luccan festival in honor of St. Cecilia. She also taught harp.

Opera:

Elena e Gerardo, opera, unperformed, 1822.

Principal source: Norton Grove

Felicita Casella (c.1820, Bourges [?]–after 1865) was of French birth but is considered an Italian composer. Her brother was the composer and pianist Louis Lacombe; he was also a music critic. Felicita was a singer as well as a composer. She married Cesare Casella, also a composer and a cellist; the two moved to Oporto.

Her first opera, *Haydée* (or *Haidée*), based on *The Count of Monte Cristo*, was given in Oporto in 1849. A revised form was given in Lisbon in 1853 with Felicita singing the principal role. Her second opera, *Cristoforo Colombo*, was given in Nice in 1865.

She also wrote romances, works for piano including a *Marcia Funebre*, and works for voice and piano.

Operas:

Haydée (or Haidée), (after Dumas' *Count of Monte Cristo*), Oporto, 1849.
Cristoforo Colombo, Nice, 1865.

Principal source: Norton Grove

Teresa Milanollo (1827, Savigliani, Italy–October 25, 1904, Paris) was one of the earlier women — along with her sister Marie, or Maria (1832–1848) — who made a career as a violinist; at that time the violin was considered an unsuitable instrument for women. Her concert tours with Marie were said to rival those of Paganini in artistic and financial success.

She made her debut in 1836 at nine years old; later that year her family moved to France. Also that year she gave a benefit concert in Brussels; throughout her life she performed benefits for the poor and sought ways to help them. The next year the family moved to England but soon returned to France. In 1842 she and Marie toured Europe. There were other European tours and a second tour to London in 1845 where they played at the Philharmonic concerts. The sisters again received brilliant reviews for their playing.

After Marie's early death from TB, Teresa retired for a while, performing only in benefit concerts. She established the Concerts des Pauvres in Lyons, and toured again throughout Europe. In 1857 on the day of her last public concert she married Theodore Parmentier, who was a military engineer, a writer for *Revue et gazette musicale*, and an amateur musician of some note.

Her compositions include opera transcriptions for violin and orchestra,

a choral work titled *Fantasie élégiaque* in memory of her sister, and an Ave Maria for male voices.
Principal sources: Norton Grove; Grove's

Carlotta Ferrari (January 27, 1837, Lodi, Italy–November 23, 1907, Bologna) was known for her poetry as well as her composing. She studied at the Milan Conservatory then moved to Bologna where she was a singer and a teacher. Her poetry tended to be patriotic and dramatic, but she also provided the librettos for her own operas and texts for her songs.

When her first opera was produced (when she was twenty) she had to pay the production expenses of the first performance because of objections that, since she was a woman, the opera would never pay and would be a financial disaster. The performance was a success and her works subsequently were in great demand. The Turin government commissioned her twice: to write a cantata for a deputation at Turin, and for a requiem mass for the anniversary of the death of King Charles Albert. Her writings, both prose and poetry, reflect a wide range of interests; her works include an opera based on Goldsmith's *The Vicar of Wakefield*. She also wrote songs.

Operas:

Ugo, lyrical drama, Milan, 1857.
Sofia, lyrical drama, Lodi, 1866.
Eleonora d'Aroborea, lyrical drama, 1871.

Principal source: WON

Norway

As was the case with many women composers, **Agathe Ursula Backer Grøndahl** (December 1, 1847, Holmestrand, Norway–April 4, 1907, Ormoen, Norway) was exceedingly well educated. Her sister, Harriet Backer, became a well-known and highly regarded artist.

Agathe began composing early, writing small pieces when she was very young. When she was ten her family moved to Christiana, now Oslo, where she began her music studies. In 1865, on the advice of her teacher, she was sent to Berlin where she attended Theodor Kullak's Music Academy (the name by which his school, the Neue Akademie der Tonkunst, was known). The next year she made her performing debut in Oslo. She then went to study with Hans von Bülow in Florence and with Liszt in Weimar. Her sister Harriet often traveled with her. Although Agatha returned to Oslo in 1871 she made frequent concert tours.

In 1875 Agatha married Olaus Andreas Grøndahl. She continued her performing, traveling throughout Norway and remaining professionally active.

She was prominent in Norwegian musical circles; Edvard Grieg was a close friend. Later, as she became almost completely deaf, she was forced to give up performing. She was only fifty-nine when she died. Her son Fridtiof was also a pianist and composer.

She composed two orchestral works while a student in Berlin, choral works, many pieces for piano, and many songs. She often utilized Norwegian folksong arrangements in her compositions and songs.

Principal source: Norton Grove

Poland

Ludmila Jeske-Choinska-Mikorska (1849, Malachów, near Poznan–November 2, 1898, Warsaw) was another of the talented women composers who studied widely. She studied singing in Vienna, Milan, and Frankfurt, and at the Paris Conservatoire she studied orchestration, singing, and composition. As a composer she was known for her songs and comic operas.

In 1877 she began teaching in Poznan; she continued to teach after she moved to Warsaw. Her first operetta, *Zuch dziewczna* [*The Brave Girl*], was performed in Warsaw in 1884, followed by another operetta, *Markiz de Créqui*, in 1892, also performed in Warsaw.

Her operatic overtures and her ballad *Rusalka* earned her a special diploma at the World's Columbian Exposition in Chicago in 1893. In the 1894 exhibition in Amsterdam she was honored with a medal.

A writer as well as a composer, she wrote a novel, *Muzykanci*. She was married to Teodor Choiński.

In addition to her operettas, her compositions include works for orchestra and piano, and songs.

Stage works:

Zuch dziewczna [*The Brave Girl*], operetta, Warsaw, 1884.
Markiz de Créqui, operetta, Warsaw, 1892.

Principal source: Norton Grove

Anna Regan Schimon (September 18, 1841, Aich, Bohemia–April 18, 1902, Munich) studied voice in Florence with her aunt, Caroline Unger, an Austrian opera singer who lived and worked in Italy.

In 1864 she made her stage debut in Siena. Her success encouraged her to continue studying and performing, and from 1864 to 1867 Anna was with the Court Opera in Hanover. She was also chamber singer to Grand Duchess Helena in St. Petersburg; there, her singing engagements included singing at concerts given by Berlioz. In 1869 she visited London where she gave several concerts that were very successful.

In 1872 she married Adolf Schimon, a noted voice teacher and composer. (His father, a painter, was well known for his portraits of composers.) The two toured extensively. After his death she settled in Munich where she taught at the Royal Music School.

Her compositions include two operas and vocal works.

Principal sources: Grove's; WON

Romania

Esmeralda Athanasiu-Gardeev (1834, Galati–1917, Bucharest) began her studies in Bucharest. From there she went to Paris, then to St. Petersburg. She married Vasile Hermeziu, but the marriage lasted only a short time.

She later married the Russian General Gardeev. He was well connected and the marriage provided her entrée to European society; she became acquainted with George Sand, among others. Many of her works are dedicated to royalty and members of the aristocracy. After the Romanian War of Independence (1877–78) she settled in Bucharest and taught piano, guitar and singing. Much of her music was influenced by Romanian folklore.

Principal source: Norton Grove

Russia

Ella Georgiyevna Adayevskaya (née Schultz) (February 10 or 22, 1846, St. Petersburg–July 26 or 29, 1926, Bonn) was an ethnomusicologist as well as a pianist and composer. Her name "Adayevskaya" is a pseudonym.

She began piano lessons when she was eight. At sixteen she entered the St. Petersburg Conservatory where she remained for four years. She then gave concerts in Russia and in Europe. In about 1870 she began composing for the Imperial Chapel choir.

Her major compositions were operas, beginning with *Neprigozhaya* (The Homely girl/*Doch' boyarina* (The Boyar's Daughter). She dedicated her next opera, "The Dawn of Freedom" in 1877 to Alexander II; unfortunately it was rejected by the censor because of its depiction of a peasant uprising. Her final opera, a comic opera named *Solomonida saburova* remained in manuscript form.

She carried out extensive research on the music of ancient Greece and the Greek Church and Slavonic folksongs, and some of her music reflects her research.

She moved to Venice about 1891 and stayed about twenty years before moving to Germany. Her continuing research on folk music resulted in numerous publications on the connection between ancient Greek church music and Slavic folk songs. She is regarded as a pioneer in ethnomusicology.

Operas:

Neprigozhaya (The Homely Girl)/*Doch' boyarina* (The Boyar's Daughter), 1873.
Zarya svogodi (The Dawn of Freedom), 1877.
Solomonida saburova , comic opera, unperformed.

Principal source: Norton Grove

When **Nadezhda Nikolayevna Rimskaya-Korsakova** (October 19 [October 31], 1848, St. Petersburg–May 24, 1919, Petrograd [St. Petersburg]) married Rimsky-Korsakov in 1872, Modest Mussorgsky was the best man.

She studied composition at the St. Petersburg Conservatory and later was Rimsky-Korsakov's pupil in composition and orchestration. In the 1860s and 1870s she frequently performed at music events in private houses, and she composed and wrote transcripts of many pieces by other Russian composers.

After her marriage to Rimsky-Korsakov she stopped composing. There were seven children; the fact that her music was compared unfavorably to her husband's was undoubtedly a factor as well. She had had excellent musical training, and she was a good critic of his work, an aspect that did not escape criticism.

Her compositions include a symphonic tableau and a Scherzo for piano.

Principal source: Norton Grove

When **Valentina Semenova Bergmann Serova** (1846, Moscow–June 24, 1924, Moscow) was sixteen she entered the St. Petersburg Conservatory with a scholarship to study piano with Anton Rubenstein. Reputedly, the reaction of the composer Alexander Serov when he heard her improvisations was "Too bad you're not a boy!" to which she replied "And why can't a girl be a composer?" Subsequently she left the conservatory and studied privately with Serov; in 1863 they married. She and Serov jointly published a book of writings on music that included many of her early writings.

In January 1871, Serov died, leaving his opera *Vrazh'ya sila* (The Power of the Fiend) already in production, although unfinished. The premiere was scheduled for late spring. Serova, with assistance, finished the opera in time. This renewed her interest in composition, with the result that she wrote four operas. The first, *Uriel Acosta*, was performed at the Bolshoi in Moscow. Her compositions also include works for piano, and an orchestral suite.

In addition to her composing she wrote music criticism for more than 50 years. She was a staunch supporter of music education.

Operas:

Uriel Acosta, Bolshoi, Moscow, 1885.
Marie d'Orval, composed during the 1880s, set during the French Revolution. Music is lost.
Khai dievka (The Brandy Drinker), Moscow.
Il'ya Muromets, Moscow, 1899.
Vstrepenulis, relates to political unrest of that time, lost, 1904–05.

Principal source: Norton Grove

Martha von Sabinin (May 30, 1831, Copenhagen–December 14, 1892, in the Crimea) was the daughter of the Eastern Orthodox priest to the Duchess of Weimar, where Martha spent most of her childhood. Her teachers included Robert Schumann, Clara Schumann and Liszt. During that period Martha was also court pianist and a teacher at a prestigious institute for girls in Weimar. For a time she also was court music teacher to the children of Tsar Alexander II. A skillful accompanist, one of her principals was Johanna Wagner, Richard Wagner's niece. She wrote text and music for her choral work *Fanziskus-Lied*; Liszt later used her text.

After 1868 she was a nurse with an order of Sisters of the Annunciation, serving in the field during the Russo Turkish War.

Many of her works reflect ongoing changes in music and genres. Her compositions include melodrama and other dramatic works, impressionistic piano pieces, vocal works, and music for piano.

Principal source: Norton Grove

Spain

As a child, **Soledad Bengoecha de Carmena** (March 21, 1849, Madrid– 1893, Madrid) took part in concerts her father organized at home.

In 1867, when she was only eighteen, her Mass was greeted with enthusiasm by the critics. In 1874 *Flor de los cielos,* and *El gran día,* both zarzuelas, were produced in Madrid. Her third zarzuela, *A la fuerza ahorcan,* 1876, was praised by the critics but only performed twice.

She composed music for orchestra, sacred music, vocal works, and music for the piano. Perhaps her best works were the overture *Sybile,* which was composed in Paris in 1873 and premiered two years later, and the *Marcha triunfal.* Both were performed in Madrid.

Operas:

Flor de los cielos, zarzuela, Madrid, 1874.

El gran día, zarzuela, Madrid, 1874.
A la fuerza ahorcan, zarzuela, 1876.
Principal source: Norton Grove

Sweden

Elfrida Andrée (February 19, 1844, Visby, Sweden–January 11, 1929, Stockholm) was a woman of firsts: the first woman organist in Sweden, the first to compose chamber and orchestral music, and the first woman to conduct a symphony orchestra. (She was also the first woman telegraphist in Sweden.) Her sister was the famous opera singer Fredrika Stenhammer.

Elfrida and her sister first learned music from their father. When Elfrida was fourteen she went to Stockholm, where she passed the examination for being an organist. Initially the school involved in the examination tried to block her from doing this by not allowing her to do the customary preparatory work, and Elfrida had to prepare the examination on her own. She passed the examination, which made her the first woman organist in Sweden. Not surprisingly she was influential in the law being revised so that women could hold the office of organist. In 1861 she was employed as an organist in Stockholm.

She continued her studies, first in Sweden and later in Copenhagen. In 1867 she moved to Göteborg where she held the position of organist at the cathedral until her death. There she organized a series of people's concerts. These "Labor Concerts" were very popular, and she gave about 800 of them. Her motto was "the education of womankind." In 1879 she was made a member of the Swedish Academy of Music.

She was a prolific composer. Her compositions include two symphonies, two organ symphonies, chamber music, choral music, including a mass, and piano pieces. Her opera, *Fritofs saga* (libretto by Selma Lagerlöf), was unperformed. She is perhaps best known for her first Organ Symphony and for her beautiful chamber works.
Opera:
Fritofs saga, libretto by Selma Lagerlöf, unperformed, 1899.
Principal source; Grove's

Laura Aulin (January 9, 1860, Gavle, Sweden–January 11, 1928, Orebro, Sweden) grew up in a very musical family. Her mother was a singer, and her father, an academic, was a well-known amateur violinist. Her older brother was the violinist, composer and conductor Tor Aulin.

She first learned to play the piano from her grandmother, who was a pianist. When she was thirteen she began studying composition, and she soon entered the Stockholm Conservatory, where she remained from 1877 to 1882. She received the Jenny Lind Traveling Fellowship, and in 1885 to 1887 she studied abroad, first in Copenhagen, then in Paris. Jules Massenet was one of her teachers.

Returning to Stockholm, she taught piano and music theory while continuing to compose and give recitals of her own music. She often appeared with her brother and the Aulin Quartet. In the early 1900s she accepted a position playing the organ in Orebro, which is in a provincial setting that was a sharp contrast to Stockholm. It is not clear what led to this decision, but the fact that the Aulin Quartet was performing much less might have been a factor.

Among her best-known pieces are her two string quartets. She also wrote vocal music, an orchestral suite and additional chamber music.

Principal source: Grove's

United States

Constance Fauntleroy Runcie (January 11, 1836, Indianapolis–May 17, 1911, Winnetka, Illinois) was the granddaughter of Robert Owen, who founded New Harmony, Indiana, where she grew up. She was a composer and writer, and she became well known for her work in civic life.

Her parents were both musicians, and her father composed. When her father died in 1852, the family went to Germany, where she stayed for six years. She began by studying piano and harp, but she changed her focus to composition.

In 1861 she married James Runcie, who was an Episcopal minister in New Harmony. Ten years later they moved to St. Joseph, Missouri.

She is considered to be the first American woman to compose large works: a symphony, an opera titled *The Prince of Asturia*, a violin concerto, and a piano concerto. Her works also include a cantata, organ compositions, piano solos, violin solos, and many songs.

She founded the Minerva Club at New Harmony, Indiana, said to be the first women's club in America, and chaired the committee on music and drama at the 1893 World's Columbian Exposition. Her books include a biography of Felix Mendelssohn. Many of her papers and materials are in the Missouri Western State University.

Opera:

The Prince of Asturia.

Principal sources: Missouri Western State University Library web site of her papers; Norton Grove

Clara Kathleen Barnett Rogers (January 14, 1844, Cheltenham–March 8, 1931, Boston) had a successful career as an opera singer, then a career teaching and composing. She came from a musical family. Her father, John Barnett, was a composer, her mother a singer, and her grandfather a cellist. Clara received her first musical training from her parents.

Her family moved to Germany to take advantage of the opportunities in music education for their children. Her initial application to the Leipzig Conservatory was denied, but in view of her musical talent she was admitted when she was twelve, the youngest student ever admitted. She studied piano, harmony and singing. Two of Clara's siblings also attended the Conservatory.

At that time composition classes were not open to women. However, she did compose the first movement of her string quartet at that time. Arthur Sullivan, her classmate, copied the orchestra parts for her, found musicians, and arranged a performance of the piece.

She graduated with honors when she was sixteen. After she left the Conservatory, she continued her studies with Hans von Bülow and took singing lessons. Her debut as an opera singer was in Meyerbeer's *Robert le diable*, performed in Italy in 1863. (Her stage name was Clara Doria.) She toured successfully in Italy then continued her concert career in London for five years. She went to the United States in 1871 and toured for seven years with various opera companies.

In 1878 she married Henry M. Rogers, a Boston lawyer. Boston with its rich cultural life was a good setting; her friends included Amy Beach, Margaret Lang, George Chadwick, Oliver Wendell Holmes, Jr., Amy Lowell, and Henry Wadsworth Longfellow. She held weekly musicales at her home and helped to promote the careers of several of her artistic friends. By the early 1880s, she had begun publishing some of her songs.

In 1888, she helped found the Boston Manuscript Club and was invited by Amy Beach in 1895 to join the Manuscript Club of New York. She joined the faculty of the New England Conservatory in 1902, where she taught voice, and she began to write about music. She wrote several books about singing and her autobiography. Her correspondences and manuscripts are in the Library of Congress.

Her compositions are primarily songs and include two song cycles. She also wrote a violin sonata, string quartet, and music for piano.

Memoirs:

Memories of a Musical Career, by Clara Kathleen Rogers (Clara Doria) (Boston: Little, Brown, 1932).

The Story of Two Lives; Home, Friends, and Travels, Sequence to "Memories of a Musical Career," by Clara Kathleen Rogers (Clara Doria) (Norwood, Mass: Plimpton Press, privately printed, 1932).

Principal sources: Norton Grove; CCH

The musical career of **Abbie Gerrish-Jones** (September 10, 1863, Vallejo, California–February 5, 1929, Seattle) began early and was multidimensional: she was a composer, librettist, and music critic. Born into a musical family, she started composing at twelve and became a church organist when she was fourteen. Her music was first published when she was eighteen.

Little is known of her private life. She married A. Widmore Jones, a naval officer.

She composed eight operas, using her own libretto for five of them. She also wrote songs, piano works, and pieces for teaching. Her Prelude for piano won a prize in 1906 in a competition sponsored by Josef Hofmann. She was also active as a music critic.

Operas:

Priscilla, 1885.
Abon Hassan.
The Milkmaid's Fair.
The Snow Queen, 1917.
The Andalusians.
Two Roses.
Sakura-San.
Aztec Princess.

Principal source: Norton Grove

Although **Celeste de Longpré Heckscher** (February 23, 1860, Philadelphia–February 18, 1928, Philadelphia) was born into an artistic family, her parents objected to her receiving early training in piano and composition. She wrote her first compositions when she was ten.

In 1883 she married Austin Stephen Heckscher. Even with a growing family she continued her studies of composition and orchestration into the 1890s, reputedly studying in Europe.

She gave a concert of some of her works at the Aeolian Hall in New York in 1913. She was president of the Philadelphia Operatic Society for many years.

Her compositions include two operas (performed in Philadelphia), an orchestral suite (also staged as a ballet), piano works, and chamber music.

Operas:

The Flight of Time.
Rose of Destiny, Philadelphia, 1918.

Principal source: Norton Grove

Chapter Seven

Impressionism and Romanticism, 1880–1900

As different musical styles developed and diverged, factionalism and disputes arose. There was controversy over styles of composition and music, most markedly between Impressionism and Romanticism, and there were questions and disagreement about how music should sound. This in turn generated controversy over what should be the structure and sound of an orchestra. The world of opera continued with its own controversies and rifts, primarily over the innovations of Wagner.

There was virtually an explosion of opera and operetta, with seemingly every composer working within those genres. The popularity of Gilbert and Sullivan's operettas triggered enormous public demand for more operettas. Song publishing was at an all-time high.

To some extent women were becoming more of a factor in classical music, but acknowledgment of their abilities and potential was slight, and not without difficulties, prejudice and seemingly insurmountable barriers.

Composers from many countries were professionally active, so that while Germany and Austria might be dominant, there was an increasingly diverse population in classical music.

On May 1, 1893, the Women's Building of the World's Columbian Exposition was dedicated in Chicago. Three large orchestral works by women were among the highlights of the program: *Festival Jubilate* op. 17, by Amy Beach, which had been commissioned for the October 1892 dedication of the Fair but then was rejected from that program; *Dramatic Overture* by Frances Ellicott; and the *Kaiser Wilhelm March* by Ingeborg Bronsart.

Other works by women were performed during the Exposition, including *A Summer Song* by Helen Hood; *Witichis Overture* by Margaret Ruthven Lang; *Titan*, a symphonic sketch by the Russian Grand Duchess Alexandra Josiphovna; and *Irlande* by Augusta Holmes. Jeske-Choinska-Mikorska's operatic overtures and her ballad *Rusalka* earned her a special diploma at the Exposition. A piece by Letitia Vannah was featured. An opera, *Schiava e regina*, that Luisa Casagemas composed when she was in her teens, won a prize in connection with the Exposition. There were performances by women throughout the Exposition, including one by Ruth Deyo who was making her debut as a pianist at the age of nine.

Many of these events and performances took place within the Women's Building, through the efforts of Bertha Palmer and the Board of Lady Managers. While they were an important presence and had some influence, they weren't part of the mainstream of the Exposition.

Women, such as Florence Edith Sutro, were speaking out about their roles as professional musicians and composers. "The dogma that great intellectual effort, strong reasoning, and original production is within the capacity and the proprietary rights of men is a doctrine, which it must be remembered, has been laid down by men" ("Women's Work in Music," *Vocalist*, VIII/5 9 May 1894, 161–165). Sutro was the first woman in the United States to receive the degree of Mus. Doc., granted by the Grand Conservatory, New York, and she was the first student in the women's Law Class of the University of New York.

The availability of music scores from all over the world had a strong impact. Music was more affordable and accessible, and having a location distant from the publishing centers in Europe and the United States was much less of a factor in access. This was a step to opening the classical music world for people outside large cities — and on different continents.

In the earlier years of the nineteenth century, Australian musical life and concerts had been a direct reflection of British tradition. Choral music had been very popular, with every city having its choral society. But later in the century the influence of British music waned as Austria and Germany commanded the center of attention. Australian musicians were more likely to study in Austria or Germany than to study in England. The prevalence of choral societies began to be displaced by the formation of orchestras and symphonies, often in areas outside of large cities. This increase in venues could only help composers.

In the 1890s modernity became the defining factor in Austrian culture. Literature, architecture and the visual arts were perhaps the most noticeable hallmarks of the change — the Viennese Secession movement was founded in 1897 — but there was a similar divide in music as well, as divergences that had arisen earlier in music continued to solidify. On one hand there was Brahms; on the other, Bruckner and Wagner. Mahler was centrally involved, particularly when he became director of the Vienna Hofoper in 1897.

After Belgium became independent in 1830 it immediately established conservatories at Liège and Brussels; other conservatories soon were established. By the latter part of the 1800s, Belgian music, and opera in particular, was becoming much less influenced by the French. Belgium had a long-standing tradition of choral music; symphonic music developed more slowly. In the late 1800s there was a strong emphasis on violinists and violin music.

At that time most Canadian cities had choral societies, often with orchestral ensembles, but it wasn't until the early 1900s that independent orchestras were established. There were many bands; community bands, instrumental groups, and bands sponsored by business groups, often drawing from the numerous regimental bands. Around the 1840s there had been very strong interest in the musical traditions of immigrants, particularly the French settlers. There was a growing sense of national identity, and literary figures and historians began collecting the music more systematically, often drawing on popular songbooks that had been compiled by teachers, nuns and priests.

Cuba attracted foreign musicians, and the prosperity of the sugar cane industry enabled many Cubans to study abroad, particularly in Europe. Musical life in Cuba, particularly Havana, closely followed musical life in European cities. The demand for music scores led to the establishment of several music printing firms in Cuba.

While women in many countries were continuing to knock on doors, some women, like the English composer Ethel Mary Smyth, tended to batter rather than knock. She was one of the first women composers — if not the first — to gain international recognition as an opera composer. Other English composers were gaining recognition as well. Dora Estella Bright was the first woman to win the Charles Lucas Medal for composition in 1888. Liza Lehmann and Maude Valérie White were the preeminent women composers of songs in England at this time — a time when there were many such composers. Maude Valérie White was the first woman to win the Mendelssohn Scholarship. Later, Marie Wurm won the Mendelssohn Scholarship three times in succession.

France was at the heart of the divide between Romanticism and Impressionism in art and music. The new impressionism had come about in French art and the ideas were reflected in much of the contemporary music of that time. There was a split among musicians — as with the artists — in terms of preference for Romanticism or Impressionism.

European music came early to the Hawaiian islands, and the strong European outlook of Kamehameha IV and Kamehameha V nourished (and perpetuated) the culture of Western music. Royal patronage had a strong economic influence on musical life. There were local productions of opera, which were very popular, as well as productions from touring companies.

In Ireland the reconciliation of Irish traditional music and European classical music was a continuing challenge, exacerbated by the political aspects underlying the division.

Opera and stage works continued to be a focus for composers in Italy, although they were much changed and influenced by developments in other areas of Europe. The "new" operettas and other stage genres were widely performed, while more traditional opera productions persevered. As instrumental performances had grown in popularity there also were more diverse opportunities for composers.

The Amsterdam Concertgebouw was finished in 1888, and the Concertgebouw Orchestra was founded the same year. Not only did this provide opportunities for Dutch musicians, but it also was a stimulus to composing. There was resurgence in Dutch art and literature, which also was occurring in many areas of Europe. This rich cultural life attracted musicians and artists.

Church music continued to be a strong element of Norwegian music. In 1883, an organ school was established in Christiana (later Oslo); this became a full conservatory in 1894.

By the late 1800s, the music of Chopin and the substantial number of internationally known performers, particularly pianists, had given Poland a significant presence in music.

Music and musical life in Scotland waxed and waned with the economic and political fortunes of the country. While there had been a flourishing musical life in the 18th century, the earlier part of the 19th century was a low point. Finally, though, toward the end of that century, there was a resurgence of nationalist composers, many of whom were interested in composing larger-scale works.

In Sweden during the late 1800s the establishment of philharmonic societies in several cities and the building of new venues for performance were bringing about more active concert life — and greater opportunity for new compositions to be heard.

European teaching, education, performance, and music continued to have a strong influence on American musical life. Beyond that, however, musicians in the United States were continuing to develop a new classical musical tradition, often influenced by American traditional music — which in turn could have arisen from the traditional music of someone's country of origin, or may have fully developed within the United States.

Music had become accessible to many; seemingly every household had a piano. Every well-brought-up young lady could play the piano to some extent, and music in general was considered part of a well-rounded education.

There was a tremendous efflorescence of women in music in the United States. Inroads, however small, were being made for women entering various careers, professions and trades. It was less uncommon for a woman to own and run her own business. Woman's colleges were becoming a significant factor in academics. And many women were establishing independent lives, with independent careers. Amy Beach — another one of the very few women composers of whom there is some name recognition — was the first American woman to succeed as a composer of large-scale music. Many composers — male and female — benefited by the activities of the American Composers' Concert movement in the 1880s and '90s that actively fostered performances of American works.

In 1893, the same year as the World Columbian Exhibition, Margaret Ruthven Lang became the first woman composer to have her work played by a major orchestra when the Boston Symphony Orchestra premiered her *Dramatic Overture*. Four years later, in 1897, the Boston Symphony performed Amy Beach's *Gaelic Symphony*, the first symphony by a woman composer to be premiered in the United States.

In the 1800s Venezuelan art music was strongly influenced by European romantic style. Several attempts at starting a professional institute or school of music had been unsuccessful. There was only one opera by a Venezuelan composer, and a successful opera company was still out of reach; zarzuelas were very popular, and there were a number of prolific composers of zarzuelas. Teresa Carreño brought international attention to Venezuela and to music in Venezuela. By the end of World War I there was a heightened sense of professionalism in Venezuelan music, musicians and performance.

Australia

Although **Florence Maud Ewart** (November 16, 1864, London–November 8, 1949, Melbourne) spent the first part of her life in England, she is known as an Australian composer. She studied music in Birmingham and London in the 1870s. After earning a diploma in music at the National Training School for Music in London, she studied violin at the Hochschule für Musik in Leipzig. She continued her studies in Berlin. After her return to Birmingham she gave violin recitals and conducted an orchestra until 1894. At that time she was composing lieder and working on her first opera.

She married Alfred James Ewart, a botanist, in 1898. Several years later he was appointed first professor of botany at the University of Melbourne as well as government botanist. Consequently, in 1906, they settled in Australia.

Her success with *Ode to Australia*, which she composed for the 1907 Exhibition of Women's Works, led to other opportunities. She often composed for literary and musical societies. Getting performances of her large-scale works was problematic in Australia, so she traveled to Europe and England trying unsuccessfully to have her larger works performed. She also spent three years in Europe studying composition; Respighi was one of her teachers.

After she and her husband divorced in 1927 she again turned her attention to composing. Her compositions include operas, music for orchestra, chamber music, and vocal music.

Operas and stage work:

Ekkehard, c. 1910, opera, performed in Melbourne at Queen's Hall in 1923.
Audifax and Hadumoth, ballet, Melbourne, unperformed, 1930.
The Courtship of Miles Standish, opera, concert performance, 1930.
Mateo Falconé, opera, unperformed, 1933.
Nala's Wooing, opera, unperformed, 1933.
Pepita's Miracle, opera, unperformed, c. 1945.
A Game of Chess, opera, incomplete, 1949.

Principal source: Norton Grove

Austria

Mathilde Kralik von Mayerswalden (December 3, 1857, Linz–March 8, 1944, Vienna) studied piano with Julius Epstein, the pianist; then, when she was in her early twenties, she studied counterpoint with Anton Bruckner. She studied composition at the Vienna conservatory from 1877 to 1879.

She was very active professionally; her memberships included the Austrian Composers' Union, the Vienna Bach Society, and the Vienna Women's Choral Society.

Most of her compositions are vocal works, many of which use texts written by her brother Richard Kralik. She also wrote operas, melodrama, sacred and secular cantatas, and chamber and orchestral works.

Operas:

Blume und Weissblume.
Der heilige Gral, libretto by Richard Kralik, 1907.

Principal source: Norton Grove

Fannie Bloomfield Zeisler (July 16, 1864, Bielitz, Austria–August 20, 1927, Chicago) was only five when her family came to the United States and settled in Chicago. The family then adopted the name Bloomfield.

She returned to Europe in her teens and studied in Vienna from 1878 to 1883. Following her return to the States she quickly established herself as a pianist and made several successful European tours. In 1885 she married Sigmund Zeisler.

Throughout her career she was particularly interested in promoting music by women composers. Most of her compositions are for the piano.

Her papers are at the Newberry Library in Chicago.

Principal source: Grove's

Belgium

Eva Dell'Acqua (February 25, 1856, Brussels–February 12, 1930, Ixelles), an Italian composer and singer, made her home in Belgium. She was a prolific composer of vocal works; her compositions include about fifteen operettas. Many of her earlier works were performed privately in Brussels and Paris during the 1880s, but at least five of her later works were publicly produced and performed in Belgium.

Stage works:

Le Prince Noir, operetta, 1882.
Le Tresor de l'Emir, operetta, 1884.
Le Feude Paille, operetta, 1888.
Les Fiancailles de Pasquin, operetta, 1888.
Une Passion, operetta, 1888.
Le secret de l'Alcade, operetta, 1888.
L'Oeillet Blanc, operetta, 1889.
La Bachelette, operetta, Brussels, 1896.
Tambour Battant, operetta, Brussels, 1900.
Une Ruse de Pierette, operetta, 1903.
Ziti, operetta, 1906.
Pierrot Menteur, operetta, 1918.
L'Oiseau Bleu.

Principal source: Norton Grove

Henriette van den Boorn-Coclet (January 11, 1866, Liège–March 6, 1945, Liège) attended the Liège Conservatory where she won prizes and medals in solfege, harmony, fugue, and chamber music. Shortly after she left the conservatory she returned as a teacher, a career that lasted from 1892 to 1931.

Her compositions include several symphonies and orchestral works, sonatas and works for piano and strings, and vocal works.

Principal source: Norton Grove

Eugenie-Emilie Juliette Folville (January 5, 1870, Liège–October 28, 1946, Dourgnes or Castres; dates of birth and death vary) was a virtuoso on both piano and violin. She also is known for her work in the revival of harpsichord playing and harpsichord music.

After lessons from her father she studied at the Liège Conservatory where she focused on both violin and piano and studied counterpoint, composition and fugue as well.

She began her performing career when she was about nine, performing on both piano and violin and touring throughout Europe. In conjunction with her interest in harpsichord and its music, she also played the harpsichord in concerts. She taught historical performing practice and piano at the Liège Conservatory from 1879 to 1919.

She composed music for cello and orchestra, concertos for violin and piano, music for theater, a symphonic poem, and three orchestral suites. Her opera *Atala* was performed in Lille and Rouen in 1892 and 1893 and was well received in both cities. Her best-known compositions include the music for the theatrical production *Jean de Chimay*, her symphonic poem *Oceano Nox*, orchestral suites and music for cello and orchestra.

Opera and stage work:

Atala, opera, Lille, 1892; Rouen, 1893.
Jean de Chimay, music for theater, 1905.

Principal source: Norton Grove

Canada

Susie Frances Harrison (February 24, 1859, Toronto–May 5, 1935, Toronto) had several careers. She wrote several volumes of poetry, three novels, and music criticism. She was considered an expert on Canadian folklore and folksongs and she lectured frequently on a variety of topics. She also was an accomplished solo pianist and accompanist and composer.

She utilized several pseudonyms: "Seranus" for her songs and keyboard works that were published in England and the United States and for her music criticism; "Gilbert King" was used for her compositions that were published in England. She was particularly interested in French-Canadian folksongs, which she often arranged for piano, and she utilized them in her opera, *Pipandor*. She also lectured widely on the folksongs.

She wrote music criticism for the Toronto newspaper, and she briefly was editor of the Toronto Conservatory of Music's monthly magazine. She married J. W. F. Harrison, who was an organist and conductor.

Her compositions include a string quartet based on old Irish airs, much French-Canadian music for piano, and an *Address of Welcome to Lord Lansdowne*.

Opera:

Pipandor.

Principal source: Norton Grove

Cuba

Cecilia Arizti (Sobrino) (October 28, 1856, Havana–June 30, 1930, Havana) was one of the finest Cuban composers of her time and she was also a very successful pianist and teacher. She was the daughter of Fernando Arizti, a professor, pianist and composer who had studied in Paris. The family frequently had musical evenings in their house.

Her father was her first teacher. Later, she also studied with Nicolas Ruiz Espadero while continuing harmony and counterpoint with her father.

She traveled to the United States, and in 1896 she performed at Chickering Hall and Carnegie Hall in New York City. A year later several of her early compositions for piano were published in New York. Subsequently, her music was published by some of the best publishers in New York and Europe.

Her compositions include piano works, violin pieces and a piano trio.
Principal source: Norton Grove

Denmark

Tekla Griebel Wandall (1866, Randers–1940, Copenhagen) began piano lessons with her father when she was six. When she was nineteen she decided she would be an opera composer, and she began preparing for the entrance examination for the Kongelige Danske Musikkonservatorium in Copenhagen, where she studied singing, piano and music theory.

When her mother died in 1891 she took over the running of the household, and her opportunities for composing were reduced. Nonetheless she was in Dresden in 1896, studying instrumentation.

In 1902 she married the theologian Frederik Wandall, who was considerably older than she was. They had one child, and she had to support the family by giving music lessons. Henrik Hennings, a music publisher, became her benefactor and published some of her music. He arranged a performance of her opera *Skøn Karen* (*Schön Karin*) in Breslau (Wrocław) in 1894; the opera was also given at the Kongelige Teater in Copenhagen in 1899.

She composed about 115 works, of which about 20 are published. She also wrote several books on music theory as well as poems, short stories, and *Rigmor Vording* (1915), a quasi autobiography.

Operas and stage work:
Don Juan de Marana, opera, 1886.
Skøn Karen, opera, performed with German text, 1894.
I Rosentiden, ballet, 1895.
Principal source: Norton Grove

Hilda Sehested (April 27, 1858, Fyn, Denmark–April 15, 1936, Copenhagen) received some of her early training in Paris; she then returned to Denmark to attend the Kongelige Danske Musikkonservatorium. She graduated in 1901 as an organist, then, for the rest of her life she concentrated on composing. She was an anti-feminist and refused to participate in musical events at the Women's Exhibition in Copenhagen in 1895. However, in 1916 she agreed to write and conduct a cantata for Dansk Kvindesamfund, a Danish women's organization.

Her opera *Agnete og Havmanden* was accepted at the Kongelige Teater in Copenhagen but never performed. She also composed an orchestral suite, chamber music, choral music, and music for piano and songs.

Opera:

Agnete og Havmanden, 1913.

Principal source: Norton Grove

England

Dame Ethel Mary Smyth (April 23, 1858, London–May 9, 1944, Woking, England) was one of the first — if not the first — woman composer to gain international recognition as an opera composer. She also had one of the more vivid personalities among women composers. "Brahms believed everyone resembled a musical instrument. He thought of Smyth as an oboe" (*The Diapason,* June 1997, v. lxxxviii/6, pp. 13–15).

Her family was well-to-do, and she had the traditional upbringing of a Victorian gentlewoman, which also included basic study in music and then more formal training. At age seventeen she became determined to study music at the Leipzig Conservatory. Her family, particularly her father, was against it. After prolonged arguments and tensions with her parents she went on strike.

She entered the conservatory in 1877, but she became dissatisfied with the low standards of the conservatory and left after one year to study privately in Leipzig. During that period she met and came to be friends with "everyone," particularly Brahms and Clara Schumann. Grieg, Dvorak and Tchaikovsky were also students at Leipzig.

Later, Tchaikovsky, after hearing a violin sonata Ethel Smyth had composed, characterized her as a "very serious and gifted composer." Although, he added, her peculiarities and eccentricities include "an incredible, incomprehensible adoration, amounting to a passion, for the enigmatic musical genius of Brahms" (Tchaikovsky, autobiographical account, p. 346).

In 1878 when she submitted her lieder to a publisher, she was told that "no woman composer had ever succeeded, barring Frau Schumann and Fräulein Mendelssohn, whose songs had been published together with those of their husband and brother respectively." Nonetheless, he was willing to publish her songs (Jane A. Bernstein, p. 429, *Norton Grove*).

She continued to study orchestration on her own. Her orchestral debut was a four-movement Serenade that was performed at the Crystal Palace in 1890. Six months later, the premiere of her overture to *Antony and Cleopatra* met with favorable reviews, and she was considered a "promising young composer." Her Mass in D was compared with Beethoven's *Missa solemnis*.

Thereafter she composed only larger-scale music-dramatic works. Her first opera *Fantasio* premiered in Weimar in 1898 but was not well received by critics, who did, however, praise the orchestration. Her second opera, *Der Wald*, was performed by the royal opera in Berlin in 1902, then three months later was produced at Covent Garden. The next year it was the first opera by a woman to be performed at the Metropolitan Opera House in New York.

At that time London was not very receptive to new English opera, so Smyth, like other British composers, composed her operas in German so they could be performed on the continent.

Her third opera, *The Wreckers,* was written in French in hopes of its being premiered in London. Instead, its first two productions in 1906 (in German) were in Leipzig and Prague. She then translated it into English and in 1908 the first two acts were performed in a concert version by the London Symphony Orchestra. The next year Thomas Beecham conducted the full stage production in London. *The Wreckers* is considered to be extremely good and to be her best opera.

The Boatswain's Mate in 1913 was a two-act comedy that utilized English ballad style. About that time she recognized that she was going deaf. She eventually composed two more operas: *Fête galante* (1922) and *Entente cordiale* (1925).

She was very active in the women's suffrage movement. Once, while she was taking part in a protest, she threw a brick through the window of a cabinet minister, for which she served two months in prison. On a more peaceful note, she wrote "March of the Women," which became the anthem of women seeking the vote. She also wrote and spoke out on discrimination against women in music and campaigned for their placement in orchestras.

Increasingly she turned to writing. Many of her ten books are autobiographical, with vivid portrayals of the women she knew, particularly authors, musicians and composers.

She was a prolific composer. In addition to her operas and stage works, she composed lieder, orchestral works, several works for orchestra and chorus, and a variety of chamber and instrumental works.

Many of her autograph manuscripts are at the British Museum.

John Singer Sargent painted a stunning portrait of her.

Operas and stage works:

Fantasio, opera, Weimar, 1898.

Der Wald, opera, Berlin (1902); Covent Garden (1902); Metropolitan Opera House New York (1903).

The Wreckers, lyrical drama, Leipzig, 1906.

The Boatswain's Mate, comedy, London, 1913.

Fête galante, opera, London 1922.

Entente cordiale comedy, London, 1925.

Biography, memoirs:

Ethel Smyth, a biography, by Christopher St. John (London: Longmans, 1959).

Impressions That Remained, by Ethel Smyth (London: Longmans, Green, 1919).

Streaks of Life, by Ethel Smyth (London: Longmans, Green, 1921).

A Three-Legged Tour in Greece, by Ethel Smyth (London: 1927).

A Final Burning of Boats, by Ethel Smyth (London: Longmans, Green, 1928).

Female Pipings in Eden, by Ethel Smyth (London: Peter Davies, 1933).

As Time Went On, by Ethel Smyth (London: Longmans, Green, 1936).

Beecham and Pharaoh, by Ethel Smyth (London: Chapman and Hall, 1935).

Inordinate (?) Affection, by Ethel Smyth (London: Cresset, 1936).

What Happened Next, by Ethel Smyth (London: Longmans, Green, 1940).

Principal sources: Grove's; CCH

Dora Estella Bright [Mrs. Windham Knatchbull] (August 16, 1863, Sheffield–November 16, 1951, Somerset) was the first woman to win the Charles Lucas Medal for composition in 1888. Earlier she had won the Potter Exhibition in 1884.

After studying at the Royal Academy of Music from 1881 to 1888 where she studied with Walter Macfarren (brother of George Macfarren), she began her recital career. Several months later she performed her *Piano Concerto in A Minor* in Dresden, Cologne and Leipzig, then at the Crystal Palace concerts.

In 1892 she became the first woman to have one of her compositions performed by the Philharmonic Society when she played her *Fantasia in G,* which had been specially commissioned. Also in 1892 she gave the first recital of English keyboard music. And, in that same year, 1892, she married Captain Knatchbull. After her marriage she focused on her composing and less on performing.

She wrote three operas, *The Portrait, Quong Lung's Shadow,* and one whose title is not known. She also wrote about a dozen ballets and mime plays, notably the ballet *The Dryad* in 1909 and *La Camargo,* also a ballet. She wrote music for orchestra, variations, chamber music, and music for piano, as well as choral music and songs.

Operas and stage works:

The Portrait.

Quong Lung's Shadow.

Opera: title not known.

Ballets and mime plays, including *The Dryad* in 1909, ballet, and *La Camargo,* ballet.

Principal source: Grove's; Norton Grove

Amanda Ira Aldridge (March 16, 1866, London–March 5, 1956, London) was central to the musical life of the black community in London. Her parents were the famous African American actor Ira Aldridge and Amanda Pauline von Brandt, a Swedish opera singer.

In 1883 she won a scholarship to the Royal College of Music where she was a pupil of Jenny Lind. When severe laryngitis damaged her throat, her successful concert career as a contralto ended. She then began a distinguished career as a teacher; her students included Marian Anderson and Paul Robeson.

She composed under the pseudonym Montague Ring. Her works include piano pieces, art songs, and music for orchestra.

The Aldridge Collection at Northwestern University, Evanston, Illinois, consists of materials relating to her father, Ira Frederick Aldridge (1807–1967) and his children, especially Amanda. The collection includes correspondence, photographs, newspaper clippings, musical manuscripts and scores, personal and legal documents, articles, and memorabilia.

Principal source: Norton Grove

Edith Swepstone (fl. 1885–1930) is one of the many composers about whom we have little information beyond a few professional facts. She studied at the Guildhall School of Music in London. The first performance of her music that we know of was in 1887, when a movement from her Symphony in G minor was first performed at Leyton. In 1895 she was a lecturer on music at the City of London School.

She wrote orchestral pieces including several symphonic poems, many of which were performed with the Bournemouth Municipal Orchestra. In the early part of the 20th century more music of hers was played at Bournemouth than of any other composer. The music has not been located. She set some of Robert Louis Stevenson's "Songs for Children" to music.

Principal source: Norton Grove

As with many composers, **Marie Wurm** (May 18, 1860, Southampton, England–January 21, 1938, Munich) came from a musical family. Her three sisters, who changed the family name to Verne, had careers as pianists.

Initially Marie studied at the Stuttgart Conservatory. Her teachers, who included Clara Schumann, were among the most prominent in Europe. In England her composition teachers included Arthur Sullivan, C.V. Stanford and Frederick Bridge. Remarkably, she won the Mendelssohn Scholarship three times in succession; she then studied composition with Carl Reinecke at Leipzig in 1886.

After her debut as a pianist at Crystal Palace in 1882, she gave concerts in London and in Germany, which was her home and the base of her career for most of the rest of her life. She gave concerts and taught in Hanover, in Berlin from 1911, and in Munich from 1925. In 1898 she established a women's orchestra in Berlin which she conducted and toured with for two years. Her compositions include "Piano Concerto in B minor," sonatas for violin, piano pieces, an opera, a children's operetta, and an overture.

Opera and stage work:

Prinzessin Lisa's Fee, Japanese children's operetta, Lübeck, Stadttheater, 1890.
Die Mitschuldigen, opera, after Goethe, Leipzig, Stadttheater, 1921.

Principal sources: Norton Grove; CCH

Mary Frances Allitsen (December 30, 1848, London–September 30, 1912, London) was the daughter of John Bumpus, the bookseller. Her brothers, John and Edward Bumpus, were music distributors. Allitsen is a pseudonym.

According to Elson, she had a lonely childhood in a little English village and would improvise ballads for her amusement. Her family was hostile to a musical career. Eventually she sent some manuscripts to a teacher at the Guildhall School of Music, and with his encouragement she came to London to study. Her overture "Slavonique" was a success, and "Undine" won a prize. She composed instrumental and orchestral works while a student.

She made her debut as a singer when she was thirty-four, but subsequent problems with her voice turned her focus to composition. She became increasingly interested in musical drama and theatrical presentations. Her compositions include song cycles, songs (some of which were very popular), cantatas, and an opera.

Opera and stage works:

Cleopatra, dramatic cantata, 1904.
For the Queen, musical drama, 1911.
Bindra the Minstrel, opera, published in 1912, unperformed.

Principal source: CCH

Ethel Mary Boyce (October 5, 1863, Chertsey, Surrey, England–date of death not known) was a recipient of various prizes and awards as well as the Lady Goldsmith Scholarship. She seems to have been particularly active in the 1890s.

Her compositions include work for orchestra, for voice and piano, and cantatas.

Principal source: WON

Mary Grant Carmichael (1851, Birkennhead–March 17, 1935, London) attended the Royal Academy of Music. She was widely known as a composer of songs and piano pieces, but she also wrote a Mass in E flat for male voices, and an operetta, *The Frozen Heart,* after Hans Christian Andersen's story. Many of her songs are based on Irish texts and in an Irish idiom.

Stage work:

The Frozen Heart, operetta, 1898.

Principal source: Norton Grove

Teresa Clotilde del Riego (April 7, 1876, London–January 23, 1968, London) wrote and published over 300 songs, many of which were sung by the great singers of her time, including Nellie Melba. She studied piano and composition as well as violin at the West Central College, London, where she won the medal of the Society of Arts for piano.

She composed songs and a song cycle, orchestral works, chamber music, and works for piano.

Principal source: WON

Although **Amy Elsie Horrocks** (February 23, 1867, Rio Grande do Sul, Brazil–after 1915, possibly in Brazil) was born in Brazil and lived there for a number of years, the most visible part of her professional life was spent in England, and she is known as an English composer.

When she was fifteen she entered the Royal Academy of Music, and while there won both the Potter Exhibition and the Sterndale Bennett Prize. In the early 1890s she taught piano in London and gave chamber concerts. She was made a Fellow of the Royal Academy of London in 1895. At some time after 1895 she returned to Brazil.

She wrote an orchestral piece *Undine,* as well as a cello sonata, piano music, piano quartets and other chamber music, cantatas, and vocal music. Much of her work was not published.

Principal source: Norton Grove

Liza Elizabeth Nina Mary Frederica Lehmann (July 11, 1862, London–September 19, 1918, Pinner) began her career as a singer. Her mother, Amelia Lehmann, was well known as a teacher, composer and arranger of songs; her father was a German artist.

Liza was well educated musically; her teachers included Jenny Lind. She had a wide vocal range, but realizing that she lacked the stamina and power for opera, she instead became a recitalist and had a successful career for nine years. During that time she published several songs. She gave a farewell concert in 1894, and retired to marry Herbert Bedford, composer, author (some of his books are about music), and painter of miniatures. After her marriage she turned to composing.

In 1896 she published her song cycle *In a Persian Garden*, based on the Fitzgerald version of the *Rubaiyat of Omar Khayyam*. This fit in with the immense popularity and interest in orientalism at the time, and it was very popular. She continued to write song cycles and musical comedies. In 1910 she made her first tour of the United States, and in 1911 she was the first president of the Society of Women Musicians. She became a professor of singing at the Guildhall School of Music.

Her works include opera and light opera, vocal works with orchestra, and a few chamber and instrumental works in addition to her many songs. She also wrote *The Life of Liza Lehmann, by Herself*, London, 1919.

Few opera premiers have had the unintended drama that Liza Lehman's comic opera *The Vicar of Wakefield* produced. Early in the rehearsal phase it became obvious that the libretto needed significant revision. The librettist declined to undertake the work and gave Liza and the producer carte blanche to do as needed. He would attend the dress rehearsal to put the final touches on the production.

The dress rehearsal so horrified him that he threatened an injunction to block performance. This threat was disregarded, and plans proceeded for the premiere.

The review of the opening by the *Daily Chronicle*, under the headline "Disowned Opera," began: "Not only has the production of the new light opera, *The Vicar of Wakefield*, been marked by the disavowal of authorship by the writer, Mr. Laurence Housman, but it has been rendered unique by an episode which is happily rare in theatrical history — the expulsion of its author from his private box on the first night."

Despite excellent reviews of the music, the opera had a limited run.

Operas and stage works:

Sergeant Brue, musical farce, London, 1904.
The Vicar of Wakefield, romantic light opera, Manchester, 1906.
Everyman, opera, London, 1915.
The Twin Sister, incidental music, unpublished.

Memoirs:

The Life of Liza Lehmann, by Herself (New York: E.P. Dutton, 1919).

Principal sources: Norton Grove; Grove's

Maude Valérie White (June 23, 1855, Dieppe, France–November 2, 1937, London) decided on a career in music at an early age, but her mother was averse to this plan. In 1876 she finally persuaded her mother to let her enter the Royal Academy of Music, where she studied composition with George Macfarren and wrote music to poems that were written in English, German, and French.

In 1879 she was the first woman to win the Mendelssohn Scholarship. However, the death of her mother devastated her and badly affected her health, and she was forced to resign the scholarship. She went to Chile to be with her sister and recuperate.

She returned to London in 1882. Subsequently she studied composition in Vienna for several months, then embarked on her career as a professional musician and composer. She also used her linguistic skills to translate books and plays.

Like many women of her time she traveled in search of suitable climates for her health, but unlike many she did not confine her travel to Europe. She was a gifted songwriter in an era of many songwriters. She also wrote instrumental music, some of which drew on the time she spent in South America.

In her later life she continued to organize concerts to have her compositions performed, and with the help of many patrons, students, performers, and protégés her music became more widely known.

Stage work:

The Enchanted Heart, ballet, incidental music, 1912.

Memoirs:

Friends and Memories, by Maude Valérie White (London: E. Arnold, 1914).
My Indian Summer, by Maude Valérie White (1932).

Principal sources: Norton Grove; Grove's

Rosalind Frances Ellicott (November 14, 1857–April 5, 1924, London) was the daughter of the Bishop of Gloucester. Her father had no interest in music, but her mother was a singer and had been involved with the founding of both London's Handel Society and the Gloucester Philharmonic Society.

Rosalind began her studies at the RAM when she was seventeen, and she remained there for seven years. Her first published composition appeared in 1883. Shortly thereafter, Ellicott began composing ambitious works for chorus and orchestra. At least two cantatas were commissioned for the Gloucester Three Choirs Festival. Her *Dramatic Overture* was performed at the World's Columbian Exposition. In the later 1800s she wrote more chamber works. Much of her work remains unpublished.

She also wrote three overtures, a Fantasia in A minor for piano and orchestra, a cello sonata, and works for violin and string trios.

Apparently little of Ellicott's work has survived.

Stage works:

Elysium, cantata, 1889.
The Birth of Song, cantata, 1892.
Henry of Navarre, cantata.
Radiant Sister of the Dawn, cantata.

Principal sources: Grove's; Norton Grove

Finland

Ida Georgina Moberg (February 13, 1859, Helsinki–August 2, 1947, Helsinki) was one of fourteen children. Her studies in Helsinki included work in composition with Sibelius. She was at the St. Petersburg Conservatory in 1893–94, at the Dresden Conservatory from 1901 to 1905, and at the Dalcroze Institute in Berlin from 1911 to 1912. In 1914 she began teaching at the Helsinki Music Institute.

She conducted orchestras and choirs, often conducting her own works. For many years she worked on an opera based on a poem about Buddha called *Asiens Ijus* ("The Light of Asia"). The opera was never completed, although fragments were performed.

Opera:

Asiens Ijus ("The Light of Asia"), never completed, fragments performed.

Principal source: Norton Grove

France

Cécile Louise-Stéphanie Chaminade (August 8, 1857, Paris–April 18, 1944, Monte Carlo) had an intensely successful career. Almost all of her approximately four hundred compositions were published and many were performed during her lifetime.

She first studied with her mother who was a pianist and a singer. Her father did not approve of her musical ambitions and was opposed to her being a student at the Paris Conservatoire, so Cécile studied privately with various faculty members of the Conservatoire. She began composing while she was very young. When she was eight she played some of her music for Georges Bizet, who was very impressed with her composing ability.

She gave her first concert when she was eighteen, and from then on her reputation as a composer grew steadily. Her work was immediately successful, and by the early 1880s she was becoming established as a composer. In 1882 she wrote a comic opera, *La Sévillane*, that was privately performed. During the 1880s she composed several major works, including *Suite d'orchestre* op. 20, *Ballet symphonique Callirhoë* op. 37, *Concertstück* op. 40 for piano and orchestra, and *Les amazons, a symphonique dramatique*.

While the 1880s were characterized by major instrumental and orchestral works, beginning in the 1890s her compositions were primarily piano works, chamber music, and mélodies. Whether this was due to financial or stylistic considerations is not known. These "smaller" compositions were very popular.

In 1892 Cécile made her debut in England and was an instant success. She toured extensively in England and Europe, often performing her own music. She was a musical celebrity, particularly in England and the United States, where many Chaminade Clubs were formed. Ironically, she was more or less ignored in France. In 1908 she decided to extend her touring to the United States where she appeared in twelve cities. Critical reviews were mixed, but she was very popular, and the tour was a financial success.

She was married to Louis-Mathieu Carbonel, an elderly Marseilles music publisher, from 1901 until his death in 1907. She did not remarry.

She won many prestigious awards including, belatedly, the Légion d'Honneur in 1913, the first given to a woman composer. As the 20th century progressed late–Romantic French music declined in popularity, attention to the music of women composers waned, and her reputation declined sharply.

Her prodigious output includes operas, works for orchestra, chamber works, and many works for piano.

Operas and stage works:
La Sévillane, comic opera, privately performed, 1882.

Biography:
Cécile Chaminade: a bio-bibliography, by Marcie Citron (Westport, Conn.: Greenwood Press, 1988).

Principal sources: Norton Grove; CCH

The **Baroness de Maistre** (date of birth not known–1875) wrote a number of religious works, among them a "Stabat Mater." Of her operas, *Les Roussalkas* in Brussels was most successful.

Operas:
Les Roussalkas, opera, Brussels, 1870.
Ninive.
Cleopatre, c. 1870.
Sarandapale, 4 acts, c. 1870.

Principal source: WON

Marguerite Olagnier (dates of birth and death not known) is known to us by her opera *Sais.*

Operas:
Sais, opera, 1881.
Le Persan.

Principal source: WON

Amanda Courtaux, O.P. (October 27, 1856, Port Louis, Mauritius Island–April 21, 1941, Sinsinawa, Wisconsin) had a remarkable life in music, beginning as a young composer and teacher. When she was 62 she entered the religious life of the Sinsinawa Dominican Sisters and took the name Sister Mary Amanda.

Her father, Endore Courtaux, was stationed at Mauritius as a representative of the French government. Her mother, Amanda Riviere, was a school teacher. After the family returned to France, Mathilde, as she was then named, entered the Paris Conservatoire in 1879. When she graduated she was awarded the First Medal, the highest award of the institution. At that time she already was teaching piano and composing, and her compositions had attracted the attention of a publisher, who continued to publish much of her music.

At age 51 she was awarded the rosette of Officer of the Academy of Fine Arts, which was presented to her by the Minister of Public Instruction of the Fine Arts and Culture of the Republic of France. This was a remarkable honor for her.

During World War I she taught in Fribourg, Switzerland, where she lived with the Sinsinawa Dominicans at Villa des Fougeres, a residence for college students during their junior year abroad and for Sinsinawa Sisters who were attending the university. It was then she made her life-changing decision, and she inquired about becoming a Sinsinawa Dominican herself. She continued to teach piano for eighteen more years at Sinsinawa locations, including Rosary College in River Forest, Illinois, and at Fribourg.

Her compositions include a gavotte, scherzo, and many works for piano. She is perhaps best known for her "Priere De Sainte Cecile."

Her manuscripts and papers are at the Sinsinawa Dominican archives in Sinsinawa, Wisconsin.

Principal source: personal research: Dominican University archives; API (Alliance Publications, Inc.)

Berthe Marx (July 28, 1859, Paris–date of death unknown) entered the Paris Conservatoire at the age of nine without having to complete the usual examinations required for admission. She won numerous prizes, including the First Prize when she was fifteen.

She then began her concert career, touring throughout Europe. Her husband, Otto Goldschmidt, a composer and critic, was the former husband of Jenny Lind. Berthe toured frequently, alone and with the violinist Pablo de Sarasate.

Her compositions include salon pieces for piano and several Rhapsodies Espagnoles.

Principal source: WON

Henriette Renie (September 28, 1875, Paris–March 1, 1956, Paris) also entered the Paris Conservatoire at a young age, where she won prizes for harp when she was eleven. She won additional awards for harmony and composition when she was older.

Her compositions include works for harp, a concerto for harp and orchestra, and music for piano and cello.

Principal source: WON

Hedwige (Gennaro) Chrétien (1859–1944) won first prize in harmony and in fugue at the Paris Conservatoire when she was twenty-two. She later became a professor at the Conservatoire. Her music brought her fame in England and the United States, but little is known of her life.

Her 150 compositions include two comic operas, a successful ballet, chamber and orchestral works, piano pieces and songs.

Operas and stage work:
Ballet oriental, Paris, Théâtre National de l'Opéra, Paris.
Le menuet de l'impératrice, comic opera, 1889.
La cinquantaine, comic opera, Paris, 1911.

Principal source: Norton Grove

Mlle. Gignoux is known to us by her opera *La Vision de Jeanne d'Arc.*

Opera:
La Vision de Jeanne d'Arc, 1890.

Germany

Little is known about **Hendrika van Tussenbroeck** (December 2, 1854, Utrecht–June 22, 1935). She composed vocal and instrumental works and both the libretto and music for a children's opera *Three Little Lute Players,* as well as several miniature operas.

Operas:
Three Little Lute Players, children's opera.
Miniature operas.

Principal source: WON

Elise Schmezer is known by her opera, *Otto der Schütz,* and her compositions *Twelve Songs* and *Two Songs.*

Opera:
Otto der Schütz

Principal source: WON

Hawaii

Lili'uokalani, Queen of Hawaii (September 2, 1838, Honolulu–November 11, 1917, Honolulu) was skilled in both western European and Hawaiian music, and she was perhaps the first person of Hawaiian ancestry to combine those skills. Many of her songs attempt to synthesize the two styles. She played a number of instruments including piano, organ, and several plucked string instruments, and for a time she was a church choir director.

She began her musical training at the Chiefs' Children's School. Her first published piece, *He mele lāhui Hawai'i*, 1866, was the Hawaiian national anthem for ten years.

In 1877 she was designated heir apparent by her brother King David Kalakaua, at which time she received the name Lili'uokalani. She reigned from 1891 until 1893 when she was deposed.

She wrote mostly songs, including the well-known "Aloha 'oe." She also composed a portion of *Mohailani*, a three-act comic opera (using the name Mme. Aorena), taking her theme from Hawaiian history.

Opera:

Mohailani, three-act comic opera (using the name Mme. Aorena), incomplete.

Principal source: Norton Grove

Ireland

Adela Maddison (December 15, 1866–June 12, 1929, Ealing) was an Irish composer. Little is known of her early life. In the late 1890s she moved from London to Paris to further her career. There she studied, gave concerts and hosted gatherings of musicians and composers, and people influential in music. Debussy, Fauré, Delius, and the Princesse de Polignac who was a significant patron of music, were among her friends; she was a pupil of Fauré. She spent several years in Germany. In 1910 her opera *Der Talisman* was performed at the Leizig Stadttheater and received enthusiastic reviews. During World War I she returned to England where she later became involved with the Glastonbury Festivals.

Her compositions include three operas, instrumental works, and songs. Little has survived.

Operas:

Der Talisman, 1910.
The Children of Lir, 1920.
Ippolita in the Hills, 1920s.

Principal source: Oxford

Annie Wilson Patterson (October 27, 1868, Lurgan, Ireland–January 16, 1934, Cork) is best known for her work with traditional Irish music. After receiving her BMus, and DMus at the Royal University of Ireland — she was the first woman to earn and receive the DMus — she became an organist, conductor, and music examiner in Dublin.

She was involved in collecting, arranging and publishing Irish music. In 1897 she was one of the organizers and founders of the Feis Ceoil, Irish Musical Festival, which continues today. She frequently lectured on Irish music, gave radio talks, and wrote articles and books on music appreciation. She wrote numerous books on music, including *Chats with Music Lovers, The Story of Oratorio, The Profession of Music, Schumann,* and *How to Listen to an Orchestra.* In 1924 she was appointed lecturer in music (specializing in Irish music) at University College in Cork. She also edited music "advice" columns in several periodicals. In 1897 she founded the Irish National Music Festival in Feis Ceoil.

She composed in many forms, including songs and choral works, cantatas, and symphonic poems. She is said to have composed two operas, *The High-King's Daughter* and *Oisin.*

Operas: (unverified)
The High-King's Daughter.
Oisin.

Books:
The Story of Oratorio, by Annie Wilson Patterson (London: Walter Scott, 1902).
Schumann (Master Musician Series), by Annie Wilson Patterson (London: J. M. Dent, 1903).
Chats with Music Lovers, by Annie Wilson Patterson (London: T. W. Laurie, 1907).
How to Listen to an Orchestra, by Annie Wilson Patterson (London: Hutchinson, 1913).
The Profession of Music, by Annie Wilson Patterson (London: W. Gardner, Darton, 1926).

Principal sources: Grove's; Norton Grove

Italy

Gabriella Ferrari (September 14, 1851, Paris–July 4, 1921, Paris) studied at the Conservatory of Naples and the Conservatory of Milan. After she married Francesco Ferrari, an Italian correspondent for *La Figaro*, she studied in Paris.

She had a successful career as a pianist, but Gounod encouraged her composing. After his death in 1893 she studied at the Leipzig Conservatory, then returned to Paris. She then focused solely on composition.

She wrote at least eight operas, five of which were performed in Paris. Several were unfinished orchestral pieces and works for piano.

Operas:

Sous le masque, 1874.
Le dernier amour, comic opera, one act, 1895.
L'âme en peine, 1896.
Le tartare, a *tableau musical,* 1896.
Le Cobzar, lyrical drama, one act, Monte Carlo, 1909.
Le captif, incomplete.
Lorenzo Salvieri, incomplete.
Le corregidor, incomplete.

Principal source: Norton Grove

Gilda Ruta (October 13, 1856, Naples–1932?, New York) enjoyed considerable fame as a pianist. She also was an opera singer. Her mother was an English singer, and her father, composer Michele Ruta, was co-director of the Naples Conservatory.

After first studying with her father, she studied with Liszt in Rome. Her debut in Naples launched her career as a concert pianist, and she toured and performed extensively, including a tour to New York.

She won a gold medal for her orchestral and vocal works at the 1890 International Exhibition in Florence. Six years later she settled in New York, where she composed and taught piano.

She's perhaps best known for her Piano Concerto, works for piano and strings, and Violin Sonata.

Opera:

The Fire Worshippers.

Principal source: Norton Grove

Vincenza Garelli della Morea, Countess de Cardenas, listed under "Garelli" (1859, Valeggio, Pavia–after 1924, Rome?) often used the pseudonym Centa della Morea. Her principal study was in Turin. After she married the Count de Cardenas she lived in Milan. In 1888 she moved to Rome.

Her works include several operettas and other stage works, which were all performed, as well as orchestral music for pantomimes and ballet, and music for piano and string quartet.

Stage works:

Incantesimo, operetta, Teatro Garibaldi, Padua, 1915.
Il viaggio dei Perrichon, operetta, Teatro Alfieri, Turin, 1916.
Le nozze di Leporello, commedia, Teatro social, Bbrescia, 1924.

Principal source: Norton Grove

Virginia Mariani Campolieti (December 4, 1869, Genoa–1941 Mila) was well known for *Apoteosi di Rossini,* her cantata for soloists, chorus and orchestra, which won the Bodoi Prize. She also composed a three-act melodrama as well as chamber music and songs.

Stage works:

Apoteosi di Rossini, cantata.
Dal sogno alla vita, melodrama, Vercelli, 1898.

Principal source: Norton Grove

Elisabetta Oddone Sulli-Rao (August 13, 1878, Milan–date of death not known) had a strong interest in Italian folksongs and did much to bring them to public notice. She was a student at the Milan conservatory.

Her compositions include chamber music, operas, and two volumes of children's songs.

Operas and stage works:

A gara colle rondini.
La capanna ardente, three acts, 1920.
Paraventa e fuoco, children's operetta, one act, 1925.
La commedia di Pinocchio, children's operetta, five acts, 1927.
Petruccio e il cavalo cappuccino, children's operetta.

Principal source: WON

Mary Rosselli-Nissim (June 9, 1864, Florence–September 26, 1937, Viareggio) was a sculptor and painter as well as a composer. Her drawing-room songs were her first compositions to receive wide attention. In 1896 her first opera, *Hephta,* which she had composed in 1891, received honorable mention at the Vienna Steiner Contest. Two years later her second opera, *Max,* was performed in Florence.

She then turned her focus to painting, sculpture and industrial design. In 1911 she was awarded first prize at the Turin International Exhibition. However, she continued to compose operas: *Fiamme,* completed in 1915, and *Andrea del Sarto,* performed in 1931.

Operas:

Nephta, one-act, 1891.
Max, 1898.
Fiamme, 1915.
Andrea del Sarto, 1931.

Principal source: Norton Grove

All that is known of **Gisella Delle Grazie**, listed under Delle, (June 17, 1868, Trieste–fl. 1894–95) is that she wrote operas including: *Atala,* performed in 1894 in Turin, and *La trecciaiuola di Firenze,* performed in 1895 in Trieste.

Operas:
Atala, Turin, 1894 (under a pseudonym).
La trecciaiuola di Firenze Trieste, 1895.
Il Passaporto del Droghiere or *Passaporto*, opera.
Principal source: Cohen

Adolfa Galloni (c. 1861, fl. 1890s) is known to us by her opera *I Quattro Rustici*. She also composed vocal and instrumental music.
Opera:
I Quattro Rustici, 1891.
Principal source: WON

Netherlands

Cornélie van Oosterzee (August 16, 1863, Batavia [now Jakarta], Java–August 12, 1943, Berlin) was one of the first Dutch women to write orchestral works. She studied theory in The Hague and then went to Berlin to study composition and instrumentation. Although she remained in Berlin for the rest of her life, she continued to conduct Dutch orchestras and she was a music correspondent for a Dutch newspaper.

In 1898 her cantata for women's choir, soloists and orchestra was part of the opening ceremony of the National Exhibition on Women's Work in The Hague. Some of her works were performed by the Berlin Philharmonic Orchestra. She was awarded the Order of Orange Nassau.

Her orchestral works include a symphony and an overture (based on Tennyson's *Idylls of the King*), choral works, other orchestral works and an opera. Much of her work was probably lost in Berlin during World War II.
Opera:
Das Gelöbnis, music drama.
Principal sources: Norton Grove, WON

Catherina van Rennes (August 2, 1858, Utrecht–November 23, 1940, Amsterdam) was well known for her songs and pedagogy. Initially she had a career as a soloist, primarily in operas and oratorios, but her true calling was as a music educator and composer. She was very popular in the Netherlands, in part because of her children's songs and cantatas, which she composed to Dutch texts.

In 1887 she founded her own music school, and she taught for over forty years.

Her composition *Oranje-Nassau Cantate* op. 33 (with a choir of 1800 children and an orchestra) was performed at the coronation of Queen Wilhelmina in 1898. She also composed vocal music and children's songs. She composed little instrumental music.

Primary sources: Grove's; Norton Grove

Norway

Borghild Holmsen (October 22, 1865, Christiania (Oslo)–December 6, 1938, Bergen) studied with several notable teachers, including Agathe Grondahl in Oslo, Carl Reinecke in Leipzig and the composer Albert Becker in Berlin.

After her studies she returned to Christiania and made her debut as a pianist in 1898, then gave concerts throughout Scandinavia, in England and in the United States. She taught many of the next generation of Norwegian composers. She also was a music critic. Her works were published between 1900 and 1911.

Her compositions include music for band, violin, piano, and songs.

Primary source: Norton Grove

Poland

Natalie Janotha (June 8, 1856, Warsaw–June 9, 1932, The Hague) was regarded as one of the finest pianists of her time and she performed throughout Europe. She was an enthusiastic and flamboyant pianist. Reportedly, she never gave a concert without her dog — as long as he was alive. Prince White Heather had to be on stage within her view. She also would place a prayer book on the piano (Schonberg, p. 334).

She first studied with her father, who was director of the conservatory in Warsaw. Her first public performance was at age eight. She later studied with Brahms and Clara Schumann. In 1885 she was appointed court pianist in Berlin. She received a diploma from the St. Cecilia Academy in Rome, and the Academies at Cracow, London and Rome made her an honorary member.

She lived in London for many years. Because of political problems (according to the Grove Dictionary of Music and Musicians), she was suspected of being an enemy alien and she was arrested and deported in 1916. She then moved to The Hague. Subsequently she gave few public performances and then usually as accompanist to the dancer Angele Sydow, who had choreographed some of her piano pieces.

Chopin's music was a strong influence in her life, and she was known for her interpretations of Chopin. Through a friendship with his relations (her mother was said to be a good friend of Chopin's sister) she had access to unpublished Chopin material. She translated several books about Chopin that were written in Polish. Not surprisingly many — if not most — of her 400 piano works show the influence of Chopin.

Her compositions also include works for piano and orchestra and music for organ and choir.

Principal sources: CCH; Grove's

Halina Krzyzanowska (1860, Paris–1937, Rennes(?) won the *prix d'honneur* at the Paris Conservatoire when she was seventeen. A pianist as well as a composer, she performed throughout Europe. In 1896 she was made *officier* of the Academie de France; four years later she was appointed professor of piano at Rennes Conservatory.

She composed music for orchestra, a symphony, string quartet and chamber works, incidental music to a play, an opera, *Magdusia*, and an oratorio. Her music received much acclaim during her life.

Opera:

Magdusia, opera.

Principal source: Norton Grove

Romania

Maria Chefaliady-Taban (November 4, 1863, Iasi–June 11, 1932, Bucharest) made her debut as a pianist when she was seventeen in 1880. She studied at the Iasi Conservatory from 1881 to 1883, then for two years at Vienna. She taught in Iasi and Bucharest.

Her compositions include instrumental music, choral music, and songs.

Principal source: Norton Grove

Scotland

Christina W. Morison (1840–date of death not known) was the first Scottish woman to compose an opera. She also composed piano pieces and songs.

Opera:

The Uhlans, Dublin, 1884; Glasgow, 1885.

Principal source: WON

Sweden

Helena Munktell (November 24, 1852, Brycksbo, Sweden–September 10, 1919, Stockholm) followed a familiar pattern: she studied first in Sweden then continued her studies in Paris. Her parents were well educated and wealthy. Her father, Henrik Munktell, was a very talented musical personality. He died in 1861.

Helena spent two years in Paris where her teachers included Vincent d'Indy. She returned to Sweden, and for the next thirty years she spent winters in Paris and summers in Sweden.

In 1885 she gave a program in Stockholm that included some of her own songs, establishing herself as a composer. The next fifteen years were particularly busy and productive; she continued to perform but her main focus was composing. She became a Member of the Swedish Musical Academy in 1915.

Her compositions include an opera, orchestral works, works for violin, and vocal music. Perhaps her best-known work is the Violin Sonata op. 21, composed in 1905.

Opera:

I Firenze, opéra comique, Paris, 1889.

Principal source: Norton Grove

Although **Laura Constance Netzel** (March 11 1839, Rantasalmi, Finland–February 10, 1927, Stockholm) was born in Finland, she spent most of her professional life in Sweden. Much of her energy went to helping others, particularly homeless women and children. She made her debut as a pianist when she was seventeen. During the 1860s she studied piano and singing in Stockholm. In 1866 she married Professor W. Netzel, who was a doctor and scientist.

She was in Paris in the 1880s, studying composition. She also began composing, thinking to use her income for hospitals for homeless women and children. She organized "cheap concerts for workers" in Stockholm during the 1890s and 1900s.

She performed for many years.

Her compositions, which total about 70 works, include piano trios, choral works, and works for violin and piano. She used the pseudonym Lago for her compositions.

Her manuscripts are in the Kungliga Musikaliska Akademien in Stockholm.

Principal source: Norton Grove

Sara Wennerberg-Reuter (February 11, 1875, Otterstad, Skaraborgs lan, Sweden–March 29, 1959, Stockholm) was the niece of Gunner Wennerberg, the famous Swedish composer, poet and politician.

Her early musical training was in Göteborg, where she studied organ and harmony with Elfrida Andrée (see entry). She then studied at the Stockholm Conservatory, qualifying to be an organist and choral director. She was at the Leipzig Conservatory from 1896 to 1898, and at the Berlin Hochschule für Musik from 1901 to 1902. In 1907 she married Hugo Reuter.

For many years she was the only woman in the Swedish composer society. In 1931 she was awarded the Litteris et Artibus for outstanding service to the arts.

Her works include cantatas — which were very popular — orchestral works, choral works, and many songs.

Principal sources: Grove's; Norton Grove

United States

Amy Marcy Cheney Beach (September 5, 1867, Heniker, New Hampshire–December 27, 1944, New York City) was recognized during her life as the foremost woman composer of the United States. She was the first American woman to succeed as a composer of large-scale music. Today, she is the best-known American woman composer.

Her musical talent was exceptional, even among prodigies. When she was two she could sing a large number of songs, on pitch and correctly (and she had absolute pitch). She began playing the piano when she was four; she also began composing when she was four. She began lessons when she was six; her mother was her first teacher. When she was seven she had her first public recital, playing music by Handel, Beethoven and Chopin along with her own works.

In 1875 the family (she was an only child) moved to Boston. Her parents were opposed to her studying in Europe, so she had private instruction at home. She also was largely self-taught, particularly in orchestration and fugue. She had one year of formal training in composition, harmony and counterpoint with Junius Welsh Hill in 1881–1882.

She made many successful appearances in recitals, often to an audience that included Henry Wadsworth Longfellow, Percy Goetschius, Oliver Wendell Holmes, William Mason, and Henry Harris Beach, a physician. Her public debut was in 1883. Several months later she played her first solo recital in Chickering Hall. She then made her debut with the Boston Symphony Orchestra and with the Theodore Thomas Orchestra.

That same year she married Dr. Beach. She was nineteen; he was more than twice her age. He preferred that she give only limited public performances. She acceded and turned her focus to composing, which he encouraged. She composed steadily for the next twenty-five years. Most of her works were for piano, voice and chorus.

The *Festival Jubilate* was commissioned for the dedication of the Women's Building of the World's Columbian Exposition in Chicago. The next year she began composing her *Gaelic Symphony*. She continued to give annual recitals with orchestral, choral, and chamber groups that featured her works,

After her husband's death in 1910 she traveled to Europe to promote herself as a performer and composer. She was much acclaimed in Europe. She returned to the United States at the onset of World War I and gave concerts throughout the East and Midwest. After the war she made several trips to Europe. She was active professionally and headed several organizations. In 1925 she co-founded (with Mary Howe; see entry) the Society of American Women Composers and served as its first president.

A prolific composer, she composed in virtually every genre. Her most notable works include the Mass in E flat op. 5, the Symphony op. 32, and the Piano Concerto op. 45.

Opera:

Cabildo, performed, 1932.

Principal source: CCH

Helen Hopekirk (May 20, 1856, Edinburgh, Scotland–November 19, 1945, Cambridge, Massachusetts) was considered one of the great concert pianists of her generation, and she performed and toured extensively. She also had a successful career as a composer. The major part of her professional life was spent in the United States.

After studying in Edinburgh she attended the Leipzig Conservatory where she studied both piano and composition. One of her fellow pupils was George Chadwick. Her debut at the Leipzig Gewandaus in 1878 was followed by a debut performance at the Crystal Palace in 1879, after which she toured England and Scotland.

In 1882 she married William A. Wilson, a music critic, painter and businessman who acted as her manager. After a successful American debut with the Boston Symphony Orchestra in 1883, she toured the United States for three years. She then went to Vienna (with William) for further study, after which they moved to Paris so she could have more training in composition.

William was badly injured in a traffic accident in 1896; in the aftermath Helen decided to seek a different direction for her career. George Chadwick, who was now director of the New England Conservatory, offered her a teaching post at the conservatory. After four years of teaching at the conservatory she decided to teach privately.

She was very involved in music in Boston and continued to perform and compose. She worked as an active promoter of new works, particularly Edward MacDowell's piano works, as well as works by Fauré, Debussy and d'Indy. She performed until 1939, often with her own work comprising much of the program. She was also active in the suffragette movement.

Her works include orchestral and vocal music, two piano concertos, violin sonatas, and instrumental pieces; she frequently made use of Scottish folk tunes in her music.

The Helen Hopekirk Collection at the Library of Congress has her original music manuscripts, biographical material, and five scrapbooks of press clippings and programs. Some of her papers, primarily letters, are at Arizona State University.

Principal sources: CCH; Norton Grove

Emma Roberta Steiner (1850, Baltimore(?)–February 27, 1928, New York) was largely self-taught. Although her mother was an excellent pianist, Emma was not encouraged to study music. She went to Chicago in the 1870s to pursue a career in music.

She began as a singer in the chorus of an opera company, then, with the encouragement of Edward Everett Rice, became a conductor of his opera company. She was one of the first women in the United States to have a career as a conductor. She conducted for more than thirty years, and she is said to have conducted 6000 performances of more than 50 operas and operettas.

She conducted the company of Heinrich Conried before he became manager of the Metropolitan Opera in 1903. He held her conducting in high esteem. As manager of the Metropolitan Opera it is said that he wanted to hire her but couldn't because of protests about her gender.

Four of her works were selected to be performed at the World's Columbian Exposition in 1893. Following that, she conducted several concerts of her own work in New York.

In the early 1900s misfortune struck. Much of her music was destroyed in a warehouse fire, There were family problems when her father, who had remarried after her mother's death, left Emma out of his will in preference to his stepdaughter, and Emma brought suit. Illness affected her eyesight.

Emma left off her musical career and went to Alaska, where she was a prospector, often going to areas well off the usual paths. (She discovered several important tin deposits.) After about ten years she returned to the United States and resumed her musical career. She helped found a home for musicians who were elderly or in need of care. In 1925 the Metropolitan

Opera had a special performance of her works; no woman conducted there again until 1976.

Her compositions include light operas, overtures, and piano music. She also prepared orchestrations.

Operas and stage works:

Fleurette, San Francisco, 1877.
Brigands, 1894.
Day Dreams, 1894.
The Man from Paris, 1900.
The Burra Pundit, 1907.
The Alchemist, operetta.
La belle Marguerite.
Little Hussar.

Principal source: Norton Grove

Letitia Katherine Vannah (October 27, 1855, Gardiner, Maine–October 11, 1933), who went by Kate, received the Mus.Doc degree from St. Joseph's College in Emmetsburg, Maryland. After graduation she lived in London for about two years.

She returned to Gardiner where she was a church organist and performed in many public concerts. Most of her compositions are songs, but she wrote several works for orchestra and instrumental works. One of her pieces was featured in the 1893 World's Columbian Exposition in Chicago. She also collaborated with Elinore C. Bartlett on an opera, *Heligoland.*

Operas and stage works:

Heligoland.

Principal source: WOM

Emma Marcy Raymond (March 16, 1856, New York–November 1913) was a pupil of Louis Gottschalk. She's best known for her song writing and piano music, but she also wrote an opera, *Dovetta.*

Opera:

Dovetta, 1889.

Principal source: WON

Mary Knight Wood (April 7, 1857, Easthampton, Massachusetts–December 20, 1944, Florence) was active in many of Boston's musical organizations, and she frequently performed in recitals. She studied piano and composition in Boston then in New York. After her marriage to A. B. Mason she lived in Florence, Italy.

Her compositions include chamber works, a piano trio, and songs.

Principal source: Norton Grove

Stella Prince Stocker (April 3, 1858, Jacksonville, Illinois–1925) began her studies at the Jacksonville Conservatory, then continued her studies at the University of Michigan. After graduation she attended Wellesley College and the Sorbonne, followed by study in Berlin and New York.

She was particularly interested in Native American music and legends, and she lectured on those topics in the United States and other countries. She often used Native American melodies in her music.

Her compositions include music for a play and a pantomime, four operettas and music for piano.

Stage works:

Beulah, operetta.
Queen of Hearts, operetta.
Ganymede, operetta.
Raoul, operetta.

Principal source: WON

Florence Edith Clinton Sutro (May 1, 1865, England–April 29, 1906, New York City) was another woman of firsts: she was founder and first president of the National Music Clubs and Societies; the first woman in the United States to receive the degree of Mus.Doc., granted by the Grand Conservatory, New York; the first student in the women's Law Class of the University of New York, where she was the valedictorian.

Her compositions include a fugue, piano works and songs.

Principal source: WON

Laura Sedgwick Collins (1859? Poughkeepsie, New York–1927, New York) was probably the first American woman to study with Dvorak in New York. He praised her compositions as "real American music — creative, not imitative." She was also a graduate of the Lyceum School of Acting and had a wide-ranging acting career that included a one-person show in New York, *Sarah Tarbox MA* by Charles Barnard, in which Collins performed all eleven characters and used her own songs.

Her works include many songs, incidental music for plays, an operetta, a cantata and chamber works.

Principal source: Norton Grove

Helen Hood (June 28, 1863, Chelsea, Massachusetts–January 22, 1949, Brookline, Massachusetts) was one of the many women composers involved in the World's Columbian Exposition in Chicago, where she received a diploma and a medal.

After her initial studies in Boston, she studied in Berlin. She returned to Boston where she performed as a pianist and taught for over 40 years. She began composing at an early age and was still composing in the 1930s.

Although she's best noted for her songs, her compositions include a piano trio, works for solo piano, and an opera, *Die Bekehrte*.

Some of her papers are in the papers of George Henry Hood (her father) at Duke University library.

Opera:

Die Bekehrte.

Principal source: Norton Grove

Although **Elizabeth Sprague Coolidge** (October 30, 1864, Chicago–November 4, 1953, Cambridge, Massachusetts) is best known as a music patron and benefactor, she was an accomplished composer. She grew up in Chicago's "gold coast." She was serious about her piano study and wanted to be a pianist: Theresa Carreno and Fanny Bloomfield Zeisler were family friends. However, a career was not a consideration for a woman in her family's level of society.

Among her many contributions and endowments, she created the Elizabeth Sprague Coolidge foundation at the Library of Congress in 1925. Income from the trust was paid to the library to enable the Music Division of the library to hold festivals, award prizes for first performances of compositions at festivals, and generally to further musicology.

She began her composing in the 1890s; eventually composing became a refuge from her increasing deafness.

Principal sources: Cyrilla Barr, "The Musicological Legacy of Elizabeth Sprague Coolidge," *Journal of Musicology*, vol. 11, No. 2, pp. 250–268; Grove's.

Clara Anna Korn (January 30, 1866, Berlin–July 14, 1940, New York) came to the United States when she was three. Initially she intended a career as a concert pianist. However, while Tchaikovsky was visiting New York he happened to see some manuscripts of her composition; he wrote her and urged her to compose. In 1891 she won a scholarship to the National Conservatory in New York; she studied composing with Dvorak, Horatio Parker, and Bruno Klein. She later taught at the conservatory for about five years.

She was a founder of the National Federation of Music Clubs, the Women's Philharmonic Society and the Manuscript Society of New York. She wrote for music journals and often spoke out about the difficulty women composers have getting their orchestral work performed, and she encouraged women composers not to isolate themselves.

In a letter to the editor of *Musical Courier* (August 7, 1907, p. 26), she wrote:

How can any woman produce a successful orchestral work under existing conditions? You write a song, and some accommodating singer will sing it for you and give you the chance to correct mistakes; the same with a solo piece, or any other solo composition. But where is the orchestra that will "try" a manuscript orchestral selection, especially if it is not at all certain that it is worth trying?

Her works include an opera, orchestral works, chamber music and piano works.

Operas and stage works:
Their Last War.
Principal source: Norton Grove

Margaret Ruthven Lang (November 27, 1867, Boston–May 30, 1972, Boston) began her studies in piano and composition with her father, Benjamin Lang, who remained her teacher and mentor for many years. He was active in the musical life of Boston and conductor for the Cecilia and Apollo Clubs. He often included her works in their programs.

In 1887 the first public performance of her work, five songs, received favorable reviews. Two years later, the performance of her song *Ojala* at the Trocadero during the Paris Exposition of 1889 established her reputation. (The next year the song was part of the dedication of the Lincoln Concert Hall in Washington.) Her songs were in demand by many of the prominent singers, and there were concerts solely of her work. In 1893 the Boston Symphony Orchestra premiered her *Dramatic Overture*, the first work by a woman composer to be played by a major orchestra. That same year *Witchis* (now lost) was chosen for an American Composers' Concert at the World's Columbian Exposition and was performed three times. Orchestras continued to perform her works for many years, even by the Boston Symphony Orchestra, which was notorious for ignoring women composers.

Her last work appeared in 1919, but she remained interested in new music and attended concerts throughout her life. The Boston Symphony Orchestra gave a concert in honor of her 100th birthday.

Unfortunately, her orchestral compositions are all lost. Her choral works, chamber music, songs and works for piano remain.
Principal source: CCH

Florence Newell Barbour (August 4, 1867, Providence, Rhode Island–July 24, 1946, Providence) was trained as a pianist.

Her compositions include piano suites, songs, anthems, works for strings and piano, and works for women's voices.
Principal source: WON

Patty Stair (November 12, 1869, Cleveland–April 26, 1926, Cleveland) began studying at the Cleveland School of Music in 1882 and joined the faculty in 1889. Three years later she became organist at the University School and also began teaching there. She taught at both institutions throughout her life. She also conducted many women's choral groups. She was the first woman from Ohio to be a Fellow of the American Guild of Organists.

Her compositions include two light operas, solo and part songs, anthems, works for organ, and *Woodland Scene* for an orchestral of toy instruments.

Stage works:

The Fair Brigade, operetta, three acts.
An Interrupted Serenade.

Principal sources: Norton Grove; WON

Isabella Beaton (1870, Grinnell, Iowa–January 19, 1929, Mt. Pleasant, Iowa) first studied at the Iowa Conservatory, graduating in 1890. She then went to Berlin where she studied piano, composition, and the history of music. She held a variety of teaching positions: at Iowa College from 1892 to 1893, and in Berlin from 1893 to 1897. After receiving her M.A. and PhD from Western Reserve University in Ohio, she founded the Beaton School of Music in Cleveland.

Her works include a string quartet, piano sonata, a *Scherzo* for orchestra, and music for piano, violin and organ.

Principal source: WON

Venezuela

Teresa Carreño (December 12, 1853, Caracas–June 12, 1917, New York) was a noted piano virtuoso and an internationally known opera singer and piano virtuoso. Her father was finance minister and an organist; her mother's family was closely linked to Simon Bolivar.

She was one of those people who was larger than life. Schonberg relates that she was called "The Walküre of the Piano." He went on to say: "Carreño had overpowering personality, overpowering talent, overpowering physical strength, overpowering technique. And on top of that she was one of the most beautiful women of her time, and an Amazonian sort of way. In short, she was overpowering in every direction, and there seemed nothing she could not do" (328).

By the time she was six Teresa was composing polkas and waltzes, and it was apparent that musically she was very gifted. In 1862 the family moved to New York City where Teresa met Louis Moreau Gottschalk, who became her teacher. Teresa toured throughout North America, and in 1863 she played for Lincoln in the White House (where she complained about the piano).

In 1866 the family went to Europe where Teresa made a strong impression on many composers and singers. Rossini introduced her to the musical notables of Paris, and Liszt foresaw a brilliant career for her. He wanted to have her as a pupil, but her father did not permit this. Liszt advised Teresa not to become just an imitator of other performers. She never did but instead carved out her own very successful career. Her performing career lasted throughout her life. She had a lovely voice as well and could have had an outstanding career as a singer.

Teresa married four times, which earned her (and to some extent women performers in general) a certain notoriety. Her husbands were violinist Emile Sauret, baritone Giovanni Tagliapietra, pianist Eugen d'Albert, and last, Arturo Tagliapietra, Giovanni's brother.

Once, in Caracas when the opera conductor abandoned the company she took over and conducted the opera for two weeks, which added to her colorful reputation.

Her compositions are primarily works for piano, many of which she wrote between the ages of six and fifteen. She also composed a string quartet, a piece for string orchestra, and at least two choral works with orchestra. Her music incorporates elements of European rhythms, Viennese waltzes, and Latin and North American folk melodies.

Biography:

Teresa Carreño: "By the Grace of God" by Marta Milinowski (New York: Da Capo Press, 1977 [c. 1940]). Reprint of the edition published by Yale University Press, New Haven.

Principal sources: CCH; Schonberg; Norton Grove

Chapter Eight

Into the 20th Century

Women increasingly were becoming part of professional musical life in many countries. But change was slow and at times seemed insignificant in the context of the professional lives of male composers. But, as a few doors and barriers were pried open — often with extreme reluctance — there were more opportunities for education and performance.

Many women studied internationally, often attending several conservatories, and frequently they spent time with one teacher and then moved on to study with a different teacher. Some had international careers. They held professional posts in the conservatories, and an increasing number of women composers were music critics.

Competitions and prizes proliferated in the later 1800s and the 1900s, and women entered the ranks of winners of the prestigious awards. In France, Lili Boulanger became the first woman to be awarded the Prix de Rome, in 1913, with her cantata *Faust et Helene*. Catherine Murphy Urner was the first winner of the George Ladd Prix de Paris, which allowed her to go to Paris in 1920 to study composition with Charles Koechlin for a year. Elizabeth Kuyper was the first woman to win the Mendelssohn Prize for composition in 1905. She was also the first woman to teach theory and composition at the Berlin Hochschule für Musik. Ina Boyle's orchestral piece, *The Magic Harp*, won a Carnegie award in 1920.

Florence Beatrice Price, the first African American woman to be recognized as a symphonic composer, won two prestigious Wanamaker Awards in 1932: one for her Symphony in E Minor and one for a piano sonata. In 1933 the Chicago Symphony Orchestra performed her Symphony in E Minor, which made Florence the first black woman composer in history to have a symphonic work performed by a major American orchestra. Her music was featured in a program at the 1933–34 Chicago World's Fair, the Century of Progress Exposition.

While conservatories were still the main education venue, more colleges and universities were offering formal music study. Institutions could be reluctant — if not resistant — to granting degrees to women, however. The experience of Elizabeth Stirling when she decided to pursue a BMus degree at Oxford in 1856, a time when women were not eligible for degrees at Oxford, persisted far too long. (When she submitted a composition as part of the requirement for the degree, the exercise was accepted but not performed.) For decades, the Leipzig Conservatory had a two-tier system of certain classes (theory being one), one for men and a much diluted course of study for women.

Even well into the 1900s women were not entering the conservatories in great numbers. When Frida Kern graduated from the Vienna Music Academy in 1927, she was the only woman to have completed studies in composition and conducting at the Academy.

Six years later, in 1933, Marian Ursula Arkwright, who had graduated *magna cum laude* from Radcliffe in 1900, was awarded an honorary M.A. degree from Tufts College. In 1939 Boston University awarded her a Doctor of Music Degree.

As the granting of honorary degrees in general became more widespread, a few of the earlier women composers were recognized for their achievements in music. Chapman College, where Mary Carr Moore was professor of theory and of composition, awarded her the honorary DMus in 1936. Mary Howe received an honorary doctorate from George Washington University in 1961. Margaret Sutherland was awarded an honorary doctorate of Music from the University of Melbourne in 1969 in recognition of her contribution to Australian music.

Barbara Giuranna was represented at the Venice Biennale in 1936, the first Italian woman composer to be so honored.

The persona and teaching of Nadia Boulanger had a major impact on music well into the twentieth century, and she was highly sought out as a teacher. She was long-lived and professionally active all her life. Many composers, including many of the women in this book, studied with her. With such a full list of students, it is easy to get the impression that her studio was open to anyone. It wasn't. Nadia knew the worth of her abilities, and she was a very demanding teacher. Being admitted to her studio, to have her as a teacher, was a significant credential for composers and musicians.

Recognition could occur in different ways. For some it was on a collegial basis, as women moved more in professional music circles. Germaine Tailleferre was the only female member of the French group of composers known as Les Six.

For others it was national recognition. After the death of Mexican composer Maria Grever, her bust was placed in the composers' gallery in Chapultepec Park in Mexico City.

Performing with professional orchestras (never mind having their music played) remained a formidable barrier for women throughout almost the entire century. Rebecca Clarke was among the first women who were full members of a professional London orchestra, as part of Wood's New Queen's Hall Orchestra, from 1912 to 1914. The conductor, Sir Henry Wood, was the first conductor to admit women in his orchestra. Katharine Emily Eggar was the first English woman to perform her own chamber works at a London public concert. In 1921 Helen Eugenia Hagan was the first black woman to give a solo concert recital in a New York concert hall.

Conducting was, and still is, an enormous barrier for women. Susan Spain-Dunk conducted her own music at Queen's Hall Promenade Concerts for four years and was invited by Sir Henry Wood to write a work for that venue. Marguerite Canal was the first woman to conduct orchestral concerts in France, in 1917. Martha Linz was the first woman accepted as a conducting pupil at the Berlin Hochschule für Musik. In the 1930s she traveled with the Berlin Philharmonic as a violinist and conductor. When Ethel [Liggins] Leginska's opera *Gale* premiered at the Chicago City Opera in 1935, she conducted. She also conducted orchestras in Munich, Paris, London and Berlin. In 1937 Nadia Boulanger became the first woman to conduct a symphony orchestra at a Royal Philharmonic Society concert in London. But these are rarities.

To address the problem of the lack of opportunities for women to conduct, perform, and to have their music played, women's symphony orchestras were formed, particularly in the 1920s and 1930s. These orchestras had varying degrees of success and duration. However fine their quality, they never approached a significant level of acceptance and renown.

Opera remained a difficult world to enter. Leginska's opera *Gale* was one of several entries by women composers into the operatic world. *Narcissa*, by Mary Carr Moore, is considered by many to have a claim to being the first major "American" opera.

Composers often were influenced by traditional music of their country, music of other countries, and indigenous music. American composers often were influenced by Native American music. The compositions and writing of Lily Strickland, who was well traveled, reflect her study of music from a variety of cultures, including Native American music and music from India. Some composers, like Marguerite Beclard d'Harcourt, worked in ethnomusicology. She and her ethnologist husband, Raoul d'Harcourt, studied and traveled in South America, and together they wrote a book on the music of the Incas. Mirrie (Irma) Hill worked with the music of indigenous Australians.

Various music-based institutions came into existence in the earlier part of the twentieth century. The Society of Women Musicians was formed in

Britain in 1911, with Liza Lehmann the first president. In the United States the Society of American Women Composers was founded in the 1920s. Amy Beach was its first president.

Also in the United States, the MacDowell Colony was founded. It had long been the dream of Edward MacDowell, a composer, and Marian Mac-Dowell, who was a pianist, to establish a community for artists on their property in New Hampshire. In 1908 this dream began to come to fruition. The MacDowell Colony, which continues today, would be a major resource and influence for many composers in the twentieth century.

Increasingly women were speaking out on their own behalf. "The conventions of music must be challenged.... We believe in a great future for Women Composers" (Katherine Emily Eggar, at the inaugural meeting in 1911 of the Society of Women Musicians which she helped found).

Men weren't necessarily silent.

It has, then, taken men whole centuries to learn music. They do not yet seem able to write it well in isolated communities without the benefits of association with old and new masters, and the chance for the publishing of ambitious work to a competent audience. America, through pilgrimage to Europe, is only now giving hope of a national school of music. Women have been, as a sex, just such an isolated community [Rupert Hughes, "Women Composers," *Century Magazine* LV/5 (March 1898) 768–769].

The lack of newspaper coverage and publicity for works by women composers was an ongoing concern, particularly when it seemed that a performance of anything a man composed would be covered. Amy Fay's comments in "Musical Courier" on the imbalance elicited several letters from readers, including the following rather sardonic statement:

As women composers are justly entitled to receive mention in these publications [New York newspapers], just the same as prize fighters, murderers, and applicants for decrees of divorce, I cannot understand why their just claims for recognition have been so completely ignored. [Berenice Thompson, *Musical Courier*, July 8, 1903].

Musical life was in a state of flux. In many regions and for many people, utilizing traditional, nationalist music became even more important.

Change seemed universal.

Austria continued to be a lightning rod for change. Schoenberg's determination to change the tonality and harmonics, which began to take active form around 1908, made him increasingly the center of controversy.

The early 1900s were an immensely creative time in Czech musical life. Much Czech music was influenced by impressionism and modernism with its rhythms and harmonies and often using traditional themes. After World War I music tended to follow this established style, but composers were experimenting with the new music and tonal systems. The onset of the communist regime in the 1950s had a smothering influence on Czech music and creativity, as it did in many countries.

Croatia had long had a robust musical tradition, with remarkable composers, many of whom worked abroad. There had been a low point in the mid–1800s, due to political reasons, but that had been followed by a resurgence of energy and activity. The work of many composers was influenced by traditional music, and in the later 1800s there was increased attention to ethnomusicology and the musical history of Croatia. The 1900s saw an explosion of creativity that had a strong influence on Croatian music. Composers shaped both the form and characteristics of Croatian music, and their work opened up new possibilities for Croatian composers.

In Hungary, German Romanticism had long influenced Hungarian composers, and not surprisingly, many of the teachers in the Budapest Academy that Liszt had co-founded, were German. But change was setting in, brought about in part by increased usage of Hungarian folk melodies and traditional music, and recognition that Hungarian music wasn't compatible with Romanticism.

The opening of the Philharmonic Hall in Warsaw in 1901 meant the city finally had a full symphony orchestra. Polish music at that time was in a lull, and several young musicians took it on themselves to actively connect with the European mainstream of music. Poland's independence in 1918 brought about new interest in Polish folk music and its exotic elements. Not everyone's attention was on modernism, however. Wanda Landowska and her husband were intensely involved in the heritage of the harpsichord and the preservation of harpsichord music.

George Enescu expanded the use of Romanian traditional folk music in classical genres, breathing new stimulus into the musical life of his country.

In pre–Revolutionary twentieth-century Russia, the period from 1900 to 1917, the musical center shifted markedly from St. Petersburg to Moscow, although St. Petersburg remained a presence in musical life. Music and opera increasingly reflected the new modes of harmony and rhythm.

The Soviet era changed everything in Russia, including music. Decisions about the composition, writing, and performance of music and drama became state matters, with very little, if any, initiative left to the individual creators and performers.

In Italy instrumental music finally was beginning to flourish, and there was increased interest in incorporating traditional music or using it as the basis for compositions. Puccini gave a new freshness to Italian opera.

The Athens Conservatory, founded in the late 1800s, followed the European tradition and leaned heavily toward Germanic influences and to some extent French. In the early years of the conservatory, traditional Greek music and Greek composers were virtually ignored, giving rise to factions and divisions among musicians in the early 1900s.

In France, the Prix de Rome loomed large early in the century, with Lili Boulanger being the first woman to win the coveted prize. Her sister Nadia had tried for it several times without success. During the twentieth century, however, the significance of the Prix de Rome diminished until it finally was discontinued in 1969.

In Ireland the divide between traditional music and European art music continued, and attempts to reconcile the two elements into one Irish music were unsuccessful. Music became uncomfortably politicized.

Music in Denmark was flourishing in the early part of the 20th century, with opportunities for education and performances becoming more widespread. Copenhagen continued to be the center of cultural life, but much musical life was decentralized.

Swiss music continued to strongly reflect regional differences, particularly in the French and the German areas. In some respects Switzerland was a microcosm of the major stylistic differences and tensions between French and German music.

In Spain the zarzuela remained very popular, as did opera, and many composers were turning to Spanish opera. Piano music increasingly featured Spanish traditions of rhythm and harmony. The use of the guitar as a solo instrument received increased attention, with more salon and concert music written for guitar or featuring the guitar.

There were a great number of Dutch women composers at this time; their various careers reflect much opportunity and the changing times.

In England women were becoming more prominent as professionals. With Ethel Smyth, it finally seemed possible that a woman might have a fully international career as an opera composer, but this was not to happen.

The United States came of age musically in the early twentieth century. Increasingly it became a destination for European musicians, many of whom came for reasons other than the touring and performance opportunities.

Dvorak, in 1893, set the tone when he came to the United States to be director of the National Conservatory of Music. He and his music were strongly influenced by his Czech roots, and he recognized very clearly the rich diversity and heritage of music in the United States. He called attention to the vast resources of melody, rhythms, themes and subject matter for composers. And composers increasingly were utilizing these resources, adapting them and blending them with traditional classical music forms.

Women in the United States in the early part of the century were finding—or making—opportunities for themselves. In the 1890s when Carrie

Jacobs Bond met with little success trying to get more of her songs published, she formed her own publishing company: Carrie Jacobs, later Bond & Son. The business grew, and she had to move it eight times in Chicago to keep up with its growth. She finally moved the business to Hollywood in 1920.

There was still a sense that European music and training were superior to that in the United States, but that conviction was diminishing. Increasingly the United States was becoming a destination for music study. Jazz electrified much of the musical world, and jazz elements began to enter classical forms. The disruption of World War I and the rise of totalitarian governments brought many European artists to the United States, further enriching its musical artistic life and culture and adding to its diversity.

The first independent orchestras in Canada were formed in Quebec and Toronto just after the turn of the century. Opera, provided by touring companies, had long been popular, and in 1891 the Vancouver Opera House had opened. Other opera companies formed in the early 1900s and struggled to establish themselves; it would be several decades before additional opera companies could be sustained.

In Chile prior to the early 1900s, musical performances were provided by international touring companies or musicians and were sporadic at best. There likely would have been private musicales, of course, but permanent ensembles for public performance were only formed after 1910.

Cuban operas, symphonies, art songs, and piano music were heavily influenced by European styles, but by the early 1900s many composers were using traditional elements in their music. It is interesting how Maria de las Mercedes Adam de Arostegui, although long resident in Spain, maintained her musical ties with Cuba.

The Mexican Revolution in 1910 had a strong impact on the arts in Mexico. Much music became more nationalistic and drew heavily on traditional music.

In Uruguay, the latter part of the 1800s had been a particularly fruitful time in music, with the establishment of the first Uruguayan opera, the first symphony, and a string quartet. Early in the twentieth century composers began to include more nationalist music in their compositions.

Experimentation and development were the norm, seemingly in every aspect: tonality, scales, harmony, instruments, rhythms, and musical forms. Composers in every country were grappling with changes, resisting new forms, and adapting the changes to accommodate their own composing. Mildred Couper was one of the first musicians to experiment with quarter-tone music. The music world was in a considerable state of flux. Much seemed possible.

After World War I there was a strong sense of rejecting the old — the 19th century — and creating the new. Seemingly everything was affected, including social mores and styles. In music this took the form of a complete rejection of Romanticism in favor of new forms and harmonies. Jazz became a strong focus. The music of many composers whose works had been standards for performance now were considered old-fashioned, and their music was heard less frequently.

The Great Depression diminished opportunities for everyone. Women lost much of the ground they had gained in every profession.

In some areas of Europe, World War II decimated an entire generation of composers and musicians. Those who survived often had to negotiate living and creating in a repressive, totalitarian regime that lasted long after the war, or they were forced to deal with having to forge a new life in exile.

In the aftermath as the world tried to adjust and come to some equilibrium, there was a return to the "familiar" classical music. Contemporary music faced a strong barrier of rejection. What was wanted was music by composers whose names were household words. Audiences and listeners wanted familiarity; seemingly no one was interested in the tapestry of music history. Music by 19th century male composers whose names were unfamiliar, or who were perceived as second rank, disappeared from programs. Music by composers of "other" countries, and music by women was rejected and there was no consideration that their music might be worth listening to and considering.

Today, tastes have begun to broaden a little, particularly with respect to a wider acceptance of male composers, both contemporary and historic. Music programming reflects a slightly broader spectrum of choice and is more likely to include music by composers from Middle Europe, Spain, and Scandinavia. But overall, music programming remains narrow, and historic composers generally fare better than contemporary composers. The masterpieces "sell."

And music by women has not entered the repertoire.

Australia

Two remarkable women, **Mirrie Hill** and **Margaret Sutherland**, each championed Australian music and new music.

Mirrie (Irma) Hill (December 1, 1892, Sydney–May 1, 1986, Sydney) had her first major composition, Rhapsody for Piano and Full Orchestra, performed by the forerunner of the Sydney Symphony Orchestra before she was twenty.

She was fifteen when she began composing. When the Conservatorium of Music in Sydney opened in 1916, she was one of the first students having won a scholarship for composition, chamber music, and interpretation of piano music. Shortly after her graduation in 1919 she began teaching at the conservatory. She had an active interest in music education, and she worked with the Australian Music Examination Board, both as an examiner and as a composer of educational music.

In 1921 she married Alfred Hill, a composer and her former teacher. After his death in 1960 she established the Alfred Hill Award, an annual award in composition for a student at the Conservatorium.

She often used texts of Australian poets in her songs, and some of her compositions incorporate aboriginal themes and rhythms. She became interested in the music of Australian Aboriginals when anthropologist Charles Mountford suggested she write the score for a documentary film about Aboriginal life. Through him she had access to many recordings of indigenous Australian song performances.

She composed throughout her life, in a variety of genres. Her works include a children's operetta, music for orchestra, and instrumental and vocal music. The *Arnhem Land Symphony* (1954) and the five orchestral pieces *The Little Dream* (1930) are among her most notable works. Her last piece, written when she was eighty-seven, was a string quartet, a form that she maintained was the most difficult test of a composer. It was her first string quartet.

A documentary film about her was produced for the Australia Council Archives. In 1980 she was awarded the OBE for services to music.

Stage work:

Old Mr. Sundown, children's operetta, 1935.

Principal sources: Australian Music Centre (website); Norton Grove

Margaret Sutherland (November 20, 1897, Adelaide–August 12, 1984, Melbourne) came from a family of writers, musicians, artists, scientists and academics. When she was four her family moved to Melbourne, Victoria.

She won a scholarship to study piano and composition at the Marshall Hall Conservatorium, now the Melb Conservatorium. She then attended the Melbourne University Conservatorium. When she was nineteen she was a solo pianist in concerts with the New South Wales State Orchestra.

She performed and taught theory and piano until 1923, when she left Australia to study composition, orchestration and conducting in Europe, first in London, where she studied with Arnold Bax, then in Vienna. Her first published works appeared while she was in London. She then returned to Australia.

Between 1925 and 1935 she didn't compose or perform. When she resumed her musical career she became active in the music and cultural life of Australia. She worked hard to make the works of Australian composers better known. Ironically, her own work went largely unrecognized for many years.

During World War II she arranged midday chamber music concerts for the Red Cross. She was also active with the Council for Education, Music and the Arts. After the war she was a member of the Australian advisory committee for UNESCO. She was active in many civic and professional organizations throughout her life.

Her opera, *The Young Kabbarli*, composed in 1964, is based on an incident in the life of Daisy Bates, the civil rights activist and writer. It was honored as the first Australian opera recorded in Australia.

In 1969 she was awarded an honorary doctorate of music from the University of Melbourne in recognition of her contribution to Australian music. In 1970 she was made an OBE.

Her compositions include an opera, ballets, orchestral music, choral music, songs, music for chamber groups and solo instruments. Her orchestral work, *Haunted Hills*, was choreographed by Graeme Murphy in the award-winning *Glimpses*. Her Concerto grosso, 1955, is considered one of the finest of her works.

Opera:

The Young Kabbarli, one-act chamber opera, Hobart, 1965.

Principal source: Norton Grove

Austria

In 1958 **Grete von Zieritz** (March 10, 1899, Vienna–date of death not known) was the first woman to receive the title of honorary professor from the Austrian president, preceding that awarded to Frida Kern by two years.

From 1912 to 1917 she studied at the Graz Conservatory. She then moved to Berlin to continue her studies; in 1919 she began teaching at the Stern Conservatory. Her first success as a composer was in 1921 when the performance of her Japanese songs for Soprano and Piano attracted much notice. Five years later she began studying at the Berlin Hochschule für Musik. In 1928 she was awarded both the Mendelssohn Prize for composition and the Schubert Grant from the Columbia Phonograph Company.

She toured widely and often included her own pieces in her performance. For her 89th birthday in 1988 her *Zigeunerkonzert* was played at a concert given by the Moscow Philharmonic Orchestra.

A prolific composer, she composed many chamber works, a substantial number of orchestral pieces, chamber works for solo and combined instruments, choral works, and vocal works with orchestra, with piano, and with other instruments.

Principal source: Norton Grove

When she graduated from the Vienna Music Academy in 1927, **Frida Kern** (March 9, 1891, Munich–December 23, 1988, Linz) was the only woman to have completed studies in composition and conducting at the academy.

Her family moved to Linz when she was five. She began her study of music with private piano lessons, then entered the Linz Music Academy.

In 1909 she married Max Kern. Two years later she began writing music, but she didn't enter the Vienna Academy until 1923. After her graduation four years later, she went on to establish a woman's orchestra, which toured in Europe and North Africa.

Her early compositions are primarily chamber music for strings, but by 1937 she was composing orchestral works. She was awarded the composition prize of the city of Linz in 1942. From 1943 to 1945 she was a lecturer in music theory at the University of Vienna; after leaving that position she focused exclusively on composing. In 1960 the Austrian president awarded her an honorary professorship.

Many of her compositions are for chamber ensembles, but she also composed large orchestral works, vocal works and works for piano.

Principal source: Norton Grove

Irma von Halácsy (December 31, 1880, Vienna–March 7, 1953, Vienna) studied at the Vienna Conservatory, after which she toured as a concert violinist. In about 1912 she gave up her performing career to focus on teaching and composing.

Among her compositions are six operas, none of which have been performed in a complete form. She also wrote a Violin Concerto in 3 minor, op. 1, a String Quartet in F, op. 4, a violin sonata and a ballet. For years many of her manuscripts were thought to be lost, but they were rediscovered in 1986 and are now in a private collection.

Operas:

Antinoos, 1909.
Abbé Mouret, 1921.
Der Puppenspieler, 1922.
Herz atout, 1923.
Schelmenerbschaft, 1943.
Salambo, 1948.

Principal source: Norton Grove

Johanna Müller-Hermann (January 15, 1878, Vienna–April 19, 1941, Vienna) was professor of composition at the Neues Konservatorium in Vienna, succeeding J. B. Forester, with whom she had studied.

Her father was an Austrian state official; her mother was a very talented singer and instrumentalist. Johanna began composing as a child. Her formal music instruction was in Vienna with a series of well-known instructors, ending with Forester.

She wrote songs, music for piano and chamber works, but her most significant works were the larger forms. For her oratorio, *In Memoriam*, she used text by Walt Whitman. She also composed a symphonic fantasy on *Brand* by Ibsen.

Principal sources: Grove's

Although **Alma Maria Mahler** (Werfel) (August 31, 1879, Vienna–December 11, 1964, New York) wrote few compositions, the legendary aspects of her life are plentiful.

Her father, Emil Schindler, the Viennese landscape painter, died when Alma was thirteen. Alma had composition lessons with Alexander Zemlinsky; there was strong consideration of marriage. However, once she met Gustav Mahler, who was forty-one at the time, marriage with Zemlinsky was no longer a consideration. She and Mahler married in 1902; prior to the marriage she had to agree to give up any composing ambitions. Their marriage was not an easy one and was complex and often unhappy. In 1910 when Gustav selected five of Alma's songs and had them published, marital problems were a factor — Gustav had learned of Alma's affair with the architect Walter Gropius and this caused some consternation. Gustav died in 1911.

She then married Gropius, by whom she had a daughter. She later divorced him, and in 1929 she married the poet and novelist Franz Werfel. They fled Germany and eventually settled in California, where she played a significant role as hostess (not without controversy) to the émigré community. When Werfel died in 1945, she moved to New York.

Alma made herself a legend. Her two autobiographical works, one detailing her life with Mahler, the other a more general autobiography, were widely read and controversial on several levels. Not only were they unusually candid for the time, but the political aspects were very problematic, presenting her in sympathy with Mussolini and certain German fascists, although not Hitler, and having at least an affectation of anti–Semitism.

Her known works are songs published in the collections of 1910, 1915, and 1924.

Books and biography:

Gustav Mahler: Memories and Letters, by Alma Mahler, translated by Basil Creighton (London: Murray, 1968).

The Diaries, 1898–1902, selected and translated by Antony Beaumont (London: Faber and Faber, 1998).

The Bride of the Wind: The Life and Times of Alma Mahler-Werfel, by Susanne Keegan (New York: Viking, 1992).

Principal sources: CCH; Norton Grove

Vally Weigl (September 11, 1890, Vienna–December 25, 1982, New York) was one of many composers who married her teacher, in this case it was her composition teacher Karl Weigl, who was a well-known composer in Europe. She worked with him at the Musicological Institute of Vienna University.

In 1938, with the help of the Quaker Society of Friends, they moved to New York where she continued to compose and teach. She set many poems to music for chorus, for solo voice, and for instrumental chamber ensembles. After receiving a grant from the National Endowment for the Arts, she composed and recorded *Natures Moods, New England Suite,* and four song cycles.

When she was in her fifties she had a serious shoulder injury. Following that, she received her master's degree in music therapy from Columbia University in 1955. She then became chief music therapist at the New York Medical College and taught at Roosevelt Cerebral Palsy School. She also directed research projects at Mount Sinai Hospital's psychiatric division and the Hebrew Home for the Aged, and lectured both in the United States and in Europe. She became very active in presenting programs of music, dance, poetry, and art designed to promote the cause of peace and understanding. After her husband's death she focused on preserving Karl's music and making it better known, particularly in the United States.

Her compositions include instrumental pieces and chamber music, choral music, and vocal-chamber works.

Principal source: Norton Grove

Belgium

The career of Lucie Vellère says much about the century, with its increased professional opportunities for women. The upheavals of the two World Wars are undoubtedly reflected in her life as well, but our information is unfortunately scanty

Not all composers took the traditional path of music study, then a career in music. **Lucie Vellère** (December 23, 1896, Brussels–October 12, 1966, Brussels) was a pharmacist. Her rich musical life was outside the mainstream musical establishment.

She composed over a period of forty-five years. Her compositions won several prizes and awards, including first prize in the Comité National de Propagande de la Musique Belge competition in 1935 and the Brabant prize in 1957.

Her works include orchestral works, chamber music, vocal music, *Air de Syrinx,* an unaccompanied choral work, and works for piano.

Principal source: Norton Grove

Canada

Gena Branscombe (November 4, 1881, Picton, Ontario–July 26, 1977, New York) was born in Canada but spent much of her professional life in the United States. She lived and worked in the United States for more than 75 years, although she had many ties to Canada and often visited. Her piano pieces, songs, and choral and orchestral works were published in both the United States and Canada.

She studied at the Chicago Musical College, where she twice won the gold medal for composition. From 1903 to 1907 she taught piano in Chicago. She then moved to Whitman College in Walla Walla, Washington, where she was director of the piano department. Subsequently she studied in Germany with Engelbert Humperdinck for a year. In 1910 she moved to New York.

She was choral conductor for the Branscombe Choral, for which she composed and arranged many works. The Choral also commissioned works by other women composers.

She was involved with and active in an astonishing number of organizations, particularly women's arts organizations, and she was a strong advocate of American music, women composers, and contemporary music. She often drew on historical events for her songs and choral works. *Pilgrims of Destiny,* 1928, won the annual prize of the League of American Pen Women for the best work produced by a woman composer. Although she is best known for her choral works and her orchestral works, she also wrote chamber music.

Quebec Suite, from her opera *The Bells of Circumstance,* is one of her best-known orchestral works. She wrote the text to the opera, concerned with the first French settlers in Canada. Her *Introit, Prayer Response and Amen,* written when she was in her nineties, premiered in 1973.

Opera:

The Bells of Circumstance, opera, 1920s.

Principal sources: Norton Grove; Grove's

Anne Catherine Roberta Geddes-Harvey (December 25, 1849, Hamilton, Ontario–April 22, 1930, Guelph, Ontario) graduated from the University of Toronto with a BMus in 1899. Prior to that, in 1876, she was appointed organist and choirmaster at St George's Anglican Church in Guelph, a position she held for 50 years.

Her opera *La terre bonne,* also known as *The Land of the Maple Leaf,* was first performed in Guelph at the Royal Opera House in 1903. Only one song from her opera is known to exist. *Salvator,* an oratorio, premiered in Guelph in 1907 and was later published. She also wrote anthems, hymns, songs, and several instrumental pieces.

Opera and stage work:

La terre bonne, also known as *The Land of the Maple Leaf,* opera, Royal Opera House, Guelph, 1903.

Salvator, oratorio, Boston, 1907.

Principal source: Norton Grove

Sophie-Carmen Eckhardt-Gramatté (December 25, 1898 or January 6, 1899, Moscow–December 2, 1974, Stuttgart) was a Canadian composer, pianist and violinist, of Russian and French parentage. Even among prodigies she was unusual.

Her mother, Catherina de Kochevskaya, was a pupil of Anton and Nicholas Rubinstein and a music instructor in the household of Tolstoy. She was married to Nicolas de Fridman but separated from him before Sophie-Carmen was born. Fridman was not Sophie's father, but until 1920 she was known professionally as Sonia Fridman.

Her mother sent the infant Sophie to England, where she spent four years with foster parents in an expatriate Tolstoian colony, Whiteway. She was then reunited with her mother who took her to Paris, where her musical education began. A precocious student, she entered the Paris Conservatoire in 1908 as a violin student and a piano student. When she was eleven she was giving solo concerts in Paris, Geneva and Berlin, as pianist and as violinist. Her *Étude de Concert* was published in Paris in 1910.

In 1913 she left the Conservatoire and early the next year moved to Berlin with her mother and sister, whom she supported by playing in cafés. The daughter-in-law of violinist Joseph Joachim arranged for a scholarship from the banker Franz von Mendelssohn (of the banking branch of the Mendelssohn family) for Sophie to study violin. Sophie soon began playing in recitals and private concerts; she continued performing for six years. Increasingly, though, she wanted to devote her time to composing. By 1920 she was composing larger works, including *Ziganka*, a pantomime ballet.

She married the German expressionist painter Walter Gramatté in 1920 and from 1922 until 1929 used Sonia Fridman-Gramatté as her professional name. Later she used only Gramatté. She and her husband lived in Barcelona from 1924 to 1926, where Sonia met and was mentored by Pablo Casals.

In 1926 she returned to Berlin, where she continued performing. After the death of her husband she toured more widely. She gave a concert of her own works with the Philadelphia Orchestra under Leopold Stokowski and with the Chicago Symphony Orchestra under Frederick Stock. In 1930 she gave up her performing career.

In 1934 she married Ferdinand Eckhardt, an Austrian art historian living in Berlin, who had been interested in the graphics of her late husband. In

1939 the couple moved to Vienna, and she adopted the professional name S. C. Eckhardt-Gramatté.

When her husband became director of the Winnipeg Art Gallery in 1953 they moved to Canada. She continued her composing, although she again did some performing and a little teaching. She received numerous commissions and honors.

For several years she had planned to organize a competition that would encourage young musicians to play works of contemporary composers, but she died before she could bring this to fruition. However, in 1976 the first competition for the S. C. Eckhardt-Gramatté competition for the Performance of Canadian Music took place.

Ferdinand Eckhardt completed a catalogue of his wife's compositions in 1980, which was published in volume 1 of the 23-volume *S. C. Eckhardt-Gramatté: Selected Works* (Winnipeg 1980–4), a limited edition reproduction of the manuscripts of virtually all the composer's works. His biographical study, published in 1985 as *Music from Within*, is a detailed personal account of her extraordinary life. He also established the Eckhardt-Gramatté Foundation in Winnipeg to provide assistance in the performances of her works.

Biography:

Music from Within: A Biography of the Composer S. C. Eckhardt-Gramatté, by Ferdinand Eckhardt (Winnipeg, Manitoba: The University of Manitoba Press, 1985).

Principal sources: Norton Grove; Grove's

Chile

Although the life spans of Marta Canales and Carmela Mackenna overlapped and they both lived in Santiago, their music lives and composing seem to have had few intersections. Obviously they would have known each other, and they may have been friends and talked about their music and composing.

Carmela Mackenna (July 31, 1879, Santiago, Chile–January 30, 1962, Santiago) first studied in Chile then moved to Berlin to continue her education. She continued to use Europe as her musical base, and the majority of her compositions were written and published in Europe, and many were also first performed there. In 1936 her Mass for unaccompanied voices won second prize in the International Religious Music Competition in Frankfurt.

She wrote pieces for orchestra, many chamber works, and works for solo piano. Some of her works for solo voice use texts by Pablo Neruda and Paul Verlaine.

Principal source: Norton Grove

Marta (Pizarro) Canales (July 17, 1893, Santiago, Chile–December 6, 1986, Santiago) grew up in a home that was a center for musical gatherings. It also was the first venue for her conducting and composing.

Most of her compositions are sacred choral music. In 1933 and again in 1947 she formed a woman's choir for the performance of sacred polyphony. Her work as a composer earned her first prize at the Latin-American Exhibition in Seville in 1929–1930.

Her unaccompanied choral works include *Madrigales Teresianos* (1933) and *Misa gregoriana* (1937). She also composed works for chorus and orchestra.

Principal source: Norton Grove

Croatia

Although **Dora Pejačević** (September 10, 1885, Budapest–March 5, 1923, Munich) was a Croatian composer, her works were most frequently performed outside Croatia.

Her parents were Count Teodor Pejačević and the Hungarian Baroness Lilla Vay de Vaya, who was an accomplished musician and gave Dora her first lessons. She also was an actress and a patron of the arts. Although Dora studied at the Croatian Music Institute in Zagreb, and privately in Dresden and Munich, she was largely self-taught.

She divided her time between her ancestral home, where she did most of her composing, and the European cities that were cultural centers. In 1921 she married Ottomar von Lumbe, after which she made Munich her primary home.

She played a significant role in shaping Croatian music at that time, introducing the orchestral song to Croatian music and utilizing subtle differences in expression, all while retaining the rich characteristics of Croatian music. In Croatia her work was considered as being aligned with the modern movement in literature and the Secessionist movement in the visual arts.

She excelled in large works but composed in a variety of genres, including works for orchestra, lieder, chamber works, and works for piano. Among her best works are *Drei Gesänge* for voice and piano, her late piano miniatures, her Symphony in F Minor, and the Piano Concerto.

Principal source: Norton Grove

Cuba

Maria de las Mercedes Adam de Aróstegui, listed under "Adam" (September 24, 1873, Camaguey, Cuba–October 20, 1957, Madrid), was nine when her family moved to Spain, where she spent most of her life.

She began her musical training in Spain, first with private lessons then at the Conservatorio Real in Madrid, where she received first prize for piano. In Paris she studied with Jules Massenet (instrumentation and composition), Vincent d'Indy and Louis Diémer, who was a well-known pianist. Much of her music was performed in Paris. She performed in recitals and in chamber concerts with Pablo Casals in Spain.

She maintained professional and personal ties with Cuba. Several of her works were performed in Cuba by the Havana Symphony Orchestra and the Havana Philharmonic Orchestra.

She was a prolific composer, particularly in the 1930s. Her orchestral works include *The Serenata Española, La pereginación de Childe Harold. La vida es sueño*, her only opera, is based on Pedro Calderón's play. She drew on a variety of texts and authors, including Sir Walter Scott for the *Ballade guerrière écoissaise*. She also wrote songs and music for voice and cello.

Opera:

La vida es sueño, based on Pedro Calderón's play.

Principal source: Norton Grove

Czechoslovakia

Julie Reisserová (October 9, 1888, Prague–February 25, 1938, Prague) was one of Nadia Boulanger's many pupils. She first studied composition in Prague then continued her studies in Berne. Moving to Paris, she studied with Albert Roussel and with Boulanger.

Her husband was a Czech diplomat and musicologist, and Reisserová took it upon herself to make Czech music more widely known outside of Czechoslovakia, utilizing her husband's travels to various capitals in Europe, particularly Berne, Belgrade, and Copenhagen.

Many of her works were performed by eminent performers. Most of her compositions are vocal works, but she also composed several orchestral works, including *Pastorale Maritime*.

Principal source: Grove's; Norton Grove

The career of **Sláva Vorlová** (March 15, 1894, Nachod, Czechoslovakia– August 24, 1973, Prague) spans many changes in her life. She came from a musical family; her mother was a pianist and singer, and her father founded a small community orchestra.

She was interested in composing by the time she was eight. After her initial education, she studied at the Vienna Conservatory, focusing on singing and piano. Unfortunately she lost her voice and did not finish her training.

However, in 1918 she passed the state examinations and qualified as a teacher. She married in 1919, and there was a hiatus of thirteen years before she returned to systematic study and resumed composing. The next year she composed her opus 1 string quartet, which had a successful performance. The continuing performances and successes encouraged her and gave her recognition.

During World War II she wrote several pieces that contributed to the war resistance, and her chamber works gained recognition. After the war she continued her studies in composition at the Prague Conservatory, graduating in 1948. Her graduation piece was JM op. 18, dedicated to Jan Masaryk.

The takeover of the communist regime in the 1950s brought drastic changes, and her artistic opportunities and social standing were ruined. To help deal with the doctrine of mass culture, she used folksongs and historical themes in her compositions. She used a pseudonym for her compositions that utilized a jazz style; these were never performed. In some of her compositions she utilized her own method for a seven-tone serial system.

Her works also include three operas written in the late 1940s and early 1950s.

Operas:

Zlaté ptáče [*The Golden Bird*], fairy-tale opera, 1949.
Rozmarýnka, folk opera, 1952.
Náchodská kasace, historical opera, 1955.
Dva Světy, 1958.

Principal sources: Norton Grove; Grove's

Denmark

Nancy Dalberg (July 6, 1881, Bodstrup, Denmark–September 28, 1949, Copenhagen) grew up on the island of Fyn, where she knew the composer Hilda Sehested (see entry) from childhood. Nancy planned to have a career as a pianist, but her hopes were thwarted when she injured her arm. Subsequently she focused on music theory and composition. She wanted to go the conservatory in Copenhagen, but her father, a wealthy industrialist, felt that places in public institutions such as the conservatory should be held for students who could not afford private lessons. She studied first with Johan Svendsen who was a well-known composer, violinist and conductor, then, beginning in 1913, with Carl Nielsen. She assisted him in orchestrating and copying some of his compositions.

Her compositions include orchestral works, chamber works, and songs, some of which were set to texts by Selma Lagerlöf.

The Royal Library of Denmark has a collection of about sixty music manuscripts of her orchestral works, chamber music and vocal music.

Principal source: Norton Grove

Benna Moe (January 14, 1897, Copenhagen–May 30, 1983, Copenhagen) earned a degree in organ playing in Copenhagen in 1915. Her organ concerts were particularly successful in Sweden. In the 1940s she stayed for long periods of time in Stockholm and in Mora, where she was a music teacher and town composer.

She was cinema organist in Copenhagen from 1948 to 1950. Although she gave church concerts, particularly in her later years, she never held a post as church organist.

Her compositions include both serious and light music. She wrote a ballet *Hybris,* but did not orchestrate it. In addition she composed music for chamber and solo instruments, much vocal music, and dance music.

The Royal Library of Denmark holds a collection of her music manuscripts and boxes of her papers.

Stage work:

Hybris, ballet.

Principal source: Norton Grove

England

Rebecca Clarke (August 17, 1990, Harrow, England–October 13, 1979, New York) was distinguished as both a composer and a viola player. She was among the first women who were full members of a professional London orchestra, in her case Wood's New Queen's Hall Orchestra, from 1912 to 1914.

Her father, who was rather a tyrant, insisted that all four of his children learn to play an instrument so that he could have chamber music on demand. It fell to Rebecca to copy out many of the scores, which gave her insight into the construction of the compositions and allowed her to focus on theory and composition.

She began her studies in violin at the Royal Academy of Music but in the third year her father withdrew her from the academy after a professor proposed marriage to her. She then studied at the Royal College of Music. At that time she began to focus more on composition. She also changed her focus from violin to viola on advice from her instructor, Sir Charles Villiers Stanford, who told her that playing the viola, in the middle of the strings and the orchestra as it were, allowed greater insight into the structure of an orchestral work.

Her father disapproved of her having a career. Consequently, when she left the RCM in 1910 she was on her own. She supported herself as a violist, playing with various orchestras and ensembles. She was particularly successful at playing chamber music. In 1912 she became a member of the Queen's Hall

Orchestra whose conductor, Sir Henry Wood, was the first conductor to admit women in his orchestra.

In 1916 she made her first visit to the United States, performing as a soloist; she played her composition *Morpheus* at Carnegie Hall. She lived in the United States from 1916 to 1918, then toured the Hawaiian Islands and went on a world tour of British colonies with the cellist May Muklé, a lifelong friend.

In 1921 she entered her Viola Sonata in a juried competition sponsored by Elizabeth Sprague Coolidge. Entrants were by pseudonym. Her Sonata tied for first place with a piece by Ernest Bloch. There could only be one winner, so the jury asked Mrs. Coolidge to cast the deciding vote. Her vote was for Mr. Bloch's piece, making Clarke's Violin Sonata the second-place winner. The jury insisted on learning the name of the other winner. Mrs. Coolidge wrote, "You should have seen the faces of the jury when it was revealed the composer was a woman."

Rebecca divided her time between Britain and the United States. During World War II she was unable to return to England and had to remain in the United States. In 1944, she married the pianist James Friskin, a friend from college whom she had re-encountered by chance in New York. She settled in New York and was active as a teacher, lecturer and writer, but did less composing and playing.

Her 90th birthday in 1976 brought renewed attention to her music, thanks in part to a radio program of her music.

Many of her compositions are for violin and other string instruments; she also composed a substantial number of songs and vocal pieces. Among her most notable compositions is her 1921 piano trio, which won second place at the Berkshire Festival in 1921 and was performed in London and New York to great acclaim. Her Rhapsody for Cello and Piano in 1923 was commissioned by Elizabeth Coolidge and was premiered at the Berkshire Festival.

Principal sources: CCH; New Grove

Ethel [Liggins] Leginska (April 13, 1886, Hull, England–February 26, 1970, Los Angeles) was born with the name "Liggins" but adopted the name Leginska because of the Polish sound of it — that being a time when Polish pianists and musicians were attracting much attention. A virtuoso pianist, she was known as the "Paderewski of women pianists."

When she was a young child her exceptional skill as a pianist attracted the attention of Arthur and Mary Smith Wilson, a Hull shipping magnate and his wife. Their patronage enabled her to study at the Hoch Conservatory in Frankfurt, then in Vienna for three years, and finally in Berlin. When she was sixteen she made her debut with the Queen's Hall Orchestra in London then made several concert tours in Europe.

In 1907 she married the composer Roy Emerson Whithorne.

She made her first tour in the United States in 1913, to great acclaim. She was a great favorite with the public, and she was not afraid to break with tradition to some extent: she might play an entire Chopin program without an interval or wear a tailored ("practical") dress rather than the typical glamorous dress.

She studied composing in New York, but continued her performing. In 1926, she retired from performing, in part because of health, but also to devote more time to composing and conducting. She directed major orchestras in Munich, Paris, London and Berlin. In the United States she conducted the Boston Women's Symphony Orchestra and the Chicago Women's Symphony Orchestra. She also conducted at leading European opera houses. Her conducting career peaked when her opera *Gale* premiered at the Chicago City Opera in 1935, with her conducting. Eventually the number of her conducting engagements decreased, possibly because she was less of a novelty.

She moved to Los Angeles in 1940 and taught piano. In 1957 she conducted her opera *The Rose and the Ring*, which had been composed in 1932.

Most of her composing was done prior to the late 1920s. In addition to her operas she wrote symphonic poems and music for piano and orchestra.

Operas:

The Rose and the Ring, 1932.
Gale, one-act opera, 1935.

Biography:

Leginska: Forgotten Genius of Music, by Marguerite and Terry Broadbent (The North West Piano Player Association, Wilmslow, Cheshire: 2002).

Principal sources: ANB; Norton Grove

Marian Ursula Arkwright (January 25, 1853, Norwich–March 23, 1922, Highclere, England) was awarded both a MusB (1895) and MusD (1913) from Durham University. She helped found the English Ladies' Orchestral Union.

Winds of the World, her symphonic suite, was awarded a prize from the magazine *The Gentlewoman* for an orchestral work composed by a woman. Her Suite for strings, written for the Australian Exhibition of Women's Work at Melbourne in 1907, received good critical notice.

Her brother Godfrey Arkwright was a well-known musicologist.

Her works also include a Requiem and chamber music, but she was best known for her pieces for children, including *The Water-Babies*, an operetta based on Charles Kingsley's book. She was one of the few women members of the Society of British Composers.

Stage work:

The Water Babies, operetta.

Principal source: Grove's; Norton Grove

When **Ethel Barns** (1880 [sometimes given as 1874], London–December 31, 1948, Maidenhead, England) made her debut at the Crystal Palace in 1896, it was probably as a violinist, although she was talented enough to have made her debut as a pianist, and could have had a career as either — or both. Prior to her debut she studied at the Royal Academy of Music. She then toured England and the United States.

In 1899 she married the baritone Charles Phillips, and together they held Barns-Phillips Chamber Concerts at Bechstein Hall. This was a good venue for her violin compositions, and the concerts often encouraged other violinists to perform her compositions. She served on the first council of the Society of Women Musicians and was active with the organization.

Her compositions, which include music for orchestra, chamber music (particularly for violin), and music for piano were widely performed. She was perhaps best known for her *Fantaisie trio*, and *Concertstück*. Her songs have a strong sentimental aspect.

Principal source: Norton Grove

Although **Ellen Coleman** (c. 1886, London–February 5, 1973, London) was composing sonatas when she was 14, she didn't begin formally studying composition until 1921, when she was in her 30s. She became friends with many musicians, including Wanda Landowska (see entry). In 1937 and 1938 she presented three concerts in Paris that featured her own works.

One of her two operas, *The Walled Garden,* was broadcast twice by the BBC. She wrote two masses, one of which was performed at Fribourg Cathedral, a cello sonata, chamber music, a song cycle, many songs, and many piano pieces. Her most notable works include the Cello Sonata in A minor, *Swansong*, a cycle of five songs, and *Poems and Pictures* for piano.

Operas:

The Walled Garden, one act.
One other opera, title not known, possibly *Masses.*

Principal source: Norton Grove

Louisa Emily Lomax (June 22, 1873, Brighton–August 29, 1963, Brighton) was one of many women who studied at the Royal Academy of Music where she won several medals. As a student she wrote stage works with music, librettos and special effects that singled her out.

Several years after her graduation, she was appointed as professor of composition at the RAM, a position she held from 1918 to 1938.

In spite of her promising start with stage works, her opera *The Marsh of Vervais* was never fully performed. She wrote some works for production in a toy theatre, a venue she used in her later career.

She also wrote two cantatas, orchestral works and music for piano as well as solos and partsongs.

Opera and stage works:

The Marsh of Vervais.
The House of Shadows, 1905.
The Wolf, 1906.
The Brownie and the Piano-tuner, 1907.

Principal source: Norton Grove

As a student at the Royal Academy of Music, **Susan Spain-Dunk** [Mrs. Henry Gibson] (February 22, 1880, Folkestone, England–January 1, 1962) won several prizes for her compositions, including the Cobbett Prize for chamber music. She had a very successful musical career.

Several years after her studies at the RAM she returned as a professor, a position she held for many years. She was violist of the Winifred Small Quartet, well known for presenting programs of music "anthologies" of chamber music, featuring movements of different works, hoping to attract the attention of people not very familiar with classical music. These were usually given at dinners. Her chamber music initially attracted attention to her as a composer.

She conducted her own music at Queen's Hall Promenade Concerts for four years and was invited by Sir Henry Wood to write a work for that venue; the piece was *Idyll for Strings*. She also conducted at other venues, including Bournemouth, where she conducted her piece *Stonehenge*. She was the first woman to conduct a military orchestra in England in March 1932.

Her compositions include works for chamber music, symphonic poems and overtures for military band. Among her best-known works are her *Suite for Strings*, *Idyll for Strings*, *Romantic Piece for Flute and Strings*, the Kentish Downs Overture in 1926, and *The Phantasy Quartet*.

Principal source: *Who Was Who* (London: A. & C. Black).

Katharine Emily Eggar (January 5, 1874, London–August 15, 1961, London) was the first English woman to perform her own chamber works at a London public concert. She studied in Berlin, Brussels and at the Royal Academy of Music in London.

One of the three founding members of the Society of Women Musicians — the others being Marion Scott who spearheaded the effort and Gertrude Eaton — Katharine spoke at the inaugural meeting in 1911: "The conventions of music must be challenged. Women are already challenging conventions in all kinds of ways.... We believe in a great future for Women composers."

She wrote articles for musical periodicals and lectured to the Royal Musical Association. Her compositions are mainly chamber works, songs, music for piano, and songs with instrumental accompaniment.

Principal sources: Norton Grove; Grove's

Llewella Davies (late 19th century, Brecon, South Wales–date of death not known) won numerous prizes for performance and composition as well as several scholarships during her studies at the Royal Academy in London. She made her debut in November 1897. Later, she toured extensively with Nellie Melba.

Her works include sketches for orchestra, a violin sonata, string quartet, and many songs.

Principal source: WON

Mary Lucas (May 24, 1882, London–January 14, 1952, London) studied piano at the Dresden Conservatory and in London. After her marriage in 1903 she ceased her musical activities for a while, but soon began to study composition.

Performances by the Bournemouth Municipal Orchestra of her *Rhapsody* in 1928 and her *Fugue for Strings* in 1929 brought her considerable attention. In the 1930s she gained notice for her chamber music and ballets. She also composed choral works and part songs.

Stage works:

The Book of Thel, masque, 1935.
Cupid and Death, ballet, 1936.
Undine, ballet, 1936.
Sawdust, ballet, 1941.

Principal source: Norton Grove

Mary Louisa White (September 2, 1886, Sheffield, England–1935) was best known for her fairy operettas. She taught music and developed the letterless style of music instruction. Her compositions also include work for piano and part-songs.

Some of her papers are at the University of London.

Stage works:

The Babes in the Woods, 1898.
Beauty and the Beast.

Principal source: WON

Some artists, composers, and writers are so self-critical that they destroy large portions of what they produce. **Dorothy Gow** (1893, London–November 1, 1982, London) was such a composer. When she was in her thirties she studied composition with Ralph Vaughan Williams at the Royal College of Music.

In 1932 she won the Octavia Traveling Scholarship to study in Vienna. Her chamber music was regularly performed during the 1930s, particularly at the Macnaghten-Lemare concerts, and her Prelude and Fugue for orchestra was broadcast by the BBC in 1931. Her works were given few performances in her later years.

She composed chamber music. The *String Quartet in One Movement* (1947) is perhaps her best-known work.

Principal source: Norton Grove

Dorothy Howell (February 25, 1898, Handsworth, England–January 12, 1982, Malvern, England) began her studies at the Royal Academy of Music in 1914, where she stayed for five years. In 1924 she returned as professor of harmony and counterpoint, a teaching career that lasted for forty-six years, until her retirement in 1970.

As a composer she focused on piano music. In 1919 her symphonic poem *Lamia* premiered at the Promenade Concerts and was performed four more times that season. In 1921 her *Phantasy in G Minor* for violin and piano won the Cobett Prize. In 1971 she was elected a member of the Royal Philharmonic Society.

In addition to piano music, she composed orchestral works; *Christmas Eve*, a suite either for string orchestra or string quartet; choral and vocal works; and music for piano and for violin.

The British Library holds a catalogue of her works, compiled by Celia Mike.

Principal source: Norton Grove

Ethel Scarborough (January 10, 1880, Crouch End, London–December 9, 1956, Graffham, Sussex) studied harmony both in Berlin and at the Royal Academy of Music (1900–1903).

She was a prolific composer in her earlier years. After 1925 she left off composing and became increasingly involved in Labour politics.

Her works include piano music, a symphony, orchestral works including *Aspiration,* an orchestral fantasy, choral works, piano concertos and song cycles. She often conducted her own works, particularly at Bournemouth. Her song cycles were broadcast in the 1930s.

Principal source: Norton Grove

France

Nadia Boulanger (September 16, 1887, Paris–October 22, 1979, Paris) was a remarkable teacher as well as a composer, and her influence extended well into the twentieth century.

She had a very regimented non-childhood. From early on she was carefully groomed to be a virtuoso pianist and an important composer. Her father, Ernest Boulanger (1815–1900), who had won the Prix de Rome in 1835, taught at the Paris Conservatoire, as did her grandfather. Her mother had been a student of Ernest Boulanger. Nadia and her younger sister Lili (see entry) grew up with composers and musicians.

The fact that her father was seventy-two when Nadia was born was a significant factor in her life. It was made clear from early on that Nadia eventually would be responsible for the support of her younger sister Lili and her mother. Lili, whose health was never very good, suffered from what later came to be known as Crohn's disease.

Nadia entered the Conservatoire when she was ten, studying harmony, organ and composition. The death of her father in 1900 was a blow to the family, as he did not leave the family well off. Under French law at that time, the widow had few rights, could not have sole custody of the children, or have complete control of her financial affairs. However, Nadia was able to continue her studies at the Conservatoire. When her mother took Lili to various spas in attempts to find a cure, or at least some relief, for Lili, Nadia lived with relatives.

In addition to her classes at the Conservatoire, Nadia studied organ privately, and in 1903 she performed in a public recital. She was under pressure to win every possible prize at the Conservatoire and to perform which would help with the family finances, although taking paying positions was against the rules of the Conservatoire.

She entered the competition for the Prix de Rome in 1906 and 1907, but it wasn't until 1908 that she placed significantly. That year she entered an instrumental fugue instead of the required vocal fugue in the preliminary submission, which caused considerable controversy. However, the fact that she placed second in the competition with *La sirène* was considered a significant achievement for a woman. She entered again in 1909 and again won a significant prize, but not the Prix de Rome.

Nadia oversaw the musical education of Lili, who showed remarkable promise as a composer, and Nadia always considered Lili to be the more talented of the two. Lili decided that she would enter the Prix de Rome competition. She had studied music for years but had not had the intensive training and education that Nadia had. Lili's plan was to spend two or three years getting the education and training she needed for the competition. She entered the 1912 competition but did not have the stamina to complete it and had to drop out.

The next year, in 1913, she entered and won the Prix de Rome by a decisive margin of 33 out of 36 votes. There's an intense irony to this. Nadia had studied virtually all her life and had made several attempts for the Prix. Lili acquired the technical knowledge in a few years, went after the Prix de Rome and won it. (One wonders how Nadia felt about this.) Lili appeared launched for a brilliant career in composing, but there was the overriding issue of her health.

Nadia came under the mentorship of Raoul Pugno, who was a well-regarded concert pianist. He saw to it that she had a place on his programs, and they made concert tours together. The reviews of her performances tended to be positive at best but not enthusiastic. Reviews of her compositions were similarly lukewarm.

Lili's death in 1918 affected Nadia profoundly. She continued to perform and compose, but increasingly she taught, and it was this that was her gift. She was highly sought out as a teacher; students from all over wanted to be part of her teaching studio. True to her character, she was strict and precise in her teaching. She taught in France and the United States, and she knew "everyone" in classical music — and had taught many of the pianists. Many of her students became well-known composers and musicians.

In 1937 she became the first woman to conduct a symphony orchestra at a Royal Philharmonic Society concert in London.

Her known compositions include orchestral pieces, choral works, vocal works, and instrumental pieces. *Rhapsodie variée* for piano and orchestra, 1912?, is one of her best-known works. Reportedly she was working on an opera with Raoul Pugno at the time of his death in 1914.

Principal source: *Nadia Boulanger: A Life in Music* by Leonie Rosenstiel (New York: W.W. Norton, 1982).

When you hear the music that **Lili Juliette Marie Olga Boulanger** (August 21, 1893, Paris–March 15, 1918, Mazy, France) composed in her very short life, you wonder what she would have gone on to compose, and you know it could have been brilliant.

Her father was an opera composer who won the Prix de Rome in 1835 and subsequently taught at the Paris Conservatoire. Her mother had been one of his pupils. Her older sister, Nadia, also talented musically, oversaw the early part of her musical career.

Lili contracted bronchial pneumonia in 1895, which damaged her immune system. She was often ill and was susceptible to what became known as Crohn's disease. As a result she could work only sporadically. When she was sixteen she determined to focus on composing and winning the Prix de Rome. She studied harmony and counterpoint, then entered the Paris Conservatoire in January 1912. A year and half later, in July 1913, she became the first woman to be awarded the Prix de Rome with her cantata *Faust et Helene*.

Her subsequent publishing contract with Ricordi included the composition of two full-length operas, and there was a recording contract as well. In 1914 and 1916 she spent about six months at the Villa Medici, but her studies were interrupted with work on the war effort. She founded and organized the Comité Franco–Américain du Conservatoire National, working to keep musicians in touch and help their families. She concentrated on composing as much as possible when she was able.

In 1916 she began work on *La Princesse Maleine* as part of her publishing contract. She almost finished the opera, but only one complete scene survives. She was growing increasingly weaker, and by early 1918 she was dictating her composition *Pie Jesu* from her bed.

She wrote primarily choral music, much of it large choral and orchestral works, but she also composed instrumental works and piano music. Much of her music is lost or was destroyed.

Opera:

La Princesse Maleine, opera, nearly complete. One scene remains.

Principal source: *Nadia Boulanger: A Life in Music*, by Leonie Rosenstiel (New York: W.W. Norton, 1982).

Jane Vieu (1871–April 8, 1955, Paris), like many composers, had her first music lessons from her mother, who was well trained in music. By the age of eleven Jane was composing.

In 1902 her fairy musical, *La Belle au bois dormant* was performed. After 1907 her compositions were published by Maurice Vieu, who was probably her husband. They later formed the publishing house Maurice Vieu and Jane Vieu.

She composed a wide variety of works, about 100 in all, at times using the pseudonym Pierre Valette. Her compositions include orchestral works, works for stage, and vocal work. Her operetta *Arlette* premiered in Brussels in 1904. She also wrote a solfege manual for use at the Paris Conservatoire.

Stage work:

Arlette, operetta, Théâtre Royal des Galeries St Hubert, Brussels, 1904.

Principal source: Norton Grove

Germaine Tailleferre (April 19, 1892, Pau-St.-Maur, France–November 7, 1983, Paris) entered the Paris Conservatoire at the age of twelve. Her father was strongly opposed to her attending the Conservatoire, so Germaine gave piano lessons to pay her professors and support herself. She was a prodigy at the piano and had a remarkable memory. Not surprisingly she was awarded numerous prizes.

In 1917 her two-piano piece *Jeux de plein air* so impressed Erik Satie that he christened her his "musical daughter." Satie was a strong influence in her career, and her inclusion in his group of Nouveaux Jeunes brought her public attention. Nouveaux Jeunes was formed during student days at the Conservatoire and was the forerunner of Les Six, which formed in 1920. Germaine was the only female member of Les Six, which included Arthur Honneger, Darius Milhaud, Georges Auric, Francis Poulenc and Louis Durey.

Les Six was created as a "political reply" to the Russian composers known as The Five, who wanted to focus on producing a specifically Russian kind of art music. The five included Mily Balakirev (the leader), César Cui, Modest Mussorgsky, Nikolai Rimsky-Korsakov, and Alexander Borodin.

In contrast, Les Six was never a cohesive group. They didn't have a fixed agenda as a group, and the members remained autonomous in their work. However they did collaborate on *Les Mariés de la tour Eiffel*, a ballet with two speaking voices with text and choreography by Jean Cocteau, which premiered in 1921. They also made an album of piano pieces.

In many respects the 1920s marked the peak of Germaine's career. Although she was a prolific composer and composed throughout her life, she never regained the acclaim she had when she was younger, particularly as a member of Les Six.

She made two unhappy marriages — to caricaturist Ralph Barton in 1926, and to the lawyer Jean Lageat in 1931. These drained much of her creative energies. Continuing financial problems led her to accept commissions as rapidly as possible, which resulted in works that were hastily written and on the ordinary side. She did compose concertos in the 1930s that were well received and successful, as was her *Cantate de Narcissei* in 1938. Her film music was skillfully done and in much demand.

She spent 1942 to 1946 in the United States, after which she produced the second violin sonata. She then turned her attention to opera, primarily opera bouffé, and composed ten operas and stage works in the 1950s.

Her compositions also include orchestral pieces, works for piano and for various instruments, chamber music, ballets, choral music and songs. Among her most notable works are *Jeux de Plein Air* for two pianos (1922), *Pastorale* for flute and piano, and *Image* for piano, flute, clarinet, string quartet, and celesta.

Her skill in art is said to have rivaled her talent in music.

Operas and stage works:

Zoulaina, opera, Opéra Comique, Paris, 1930.
Le marin du Bolivar, Paris Exhibition, 1937.
Dolores, operetta, Opéra Comique, Paris, 1950.
Il était un petit navire, satire lyrique, Opéra Comique, Paris, 1951.
Parfums, comedie musicale, Monte Carlo Opera, Monte Carlo, 1951.
La fille d'opéra, Radiodiffusion-Télévision Français, 1955.
La bel ambitieux, Radiodiffusion-Télévision Français, 1955.

Monsieur Petitpos achete un chateau, Radiodiffusion-Télévision Français, 1955.
La pauvre Eugénie, Radiodiffusion-Télévision Français, 1955.
Memoires d'une bergere, Radiodiffusion-Télévision Français, 1959.
Le maître, chamber opera, Radiodiffusion-Télévision Français, 1960.
La petite sirene, opera, Radiodiffusion-Télévision Français, 1960.
Principal sources: CCH; Norton Grove

There is sketchy information about **Cécile Gauthiez** (March 8, 1873, Paris–date of death not known). In 1920 she became professor of harmony at the Schola Cantorum, where she had studied.

She composed a mass, choral works, piano music, other church music, and chamber music.
Principal source: WON

Marguerite Beclard d'Harcourt (February 24, 1884, Paris–August 2, 1964, Paris) was an ethnologist as well as a composer. Her earlier studies in music gave her a strong background in Gregorian chant, ancient Greece and folksong. She accompanied her ethnologist husband, Raoul d'Harcourt, on at least two trips to South America, in 1912 and 1918. Together they wrote a book on the music of the Incas. She studied French songs in America and edited books of Canadian songs, as well as books of Indian melodies. She utilized some indigenous and traditional melodies in her own music.

She wrote an opera, *Lindoro,* songs, and music for orchestra and chamber orchestra.
Opera:
Lindoro.
Principal source: Norton Grove

Marguerite Canal (January 29, 1890, Toulouse, France–January 27, 1978 near Toulouse) was the first woman to conduct orchestral concerts in France, at the Palais de Glace, in 1917. Born into a musical family, she was an excellent student at the Paris Conservatoire, taking first prize in harmony, piano accompaniment, and fugue.

She conducted at the Palais de Glace in 1917 and 1918. The next year she was appointed to the faculty of the Conservatoire, to teach solfege for singers.

In 1920 she won the Prix de Rome, with *Don Juan.* To take advantage of the residence at the Villa Medici she left the Conservatoire. She didn't return until 1932 but then stayed until her retirement. She married Maxime Jamin, who published some of her earlier works. They later divorced, and she had to sue for the rights to the catalog of her works.

Her works include an opera (incomplete), a Requiem whose revision never materialized, works for orchestra and chorus, songs, and a violin sonata.

Opera:
Tlass Atka ("Le pays blanc"), begun 1922.
Principal source: Norton Grove

Like so many young Frenchwomen, **Simone Plé-Caussade** (August 14, 1897, Paris–August 6, 1985, Bagneres-de-Bigorre, France) studied at the Paris Conservatoire. She was married to composer Georges Caussade, one of her teachers at the Conservatoire, who was twenty-four years older than she was. She became a professor of harmony and counterpoint at the Conservatoire in 1928, possibly succeeding her husband in the position.
    Her works include music for organ, piano, and orchestra.
    Principal source: Cohen

Jeanne Leleu (December 29, 1898, St. Mihiel, France–March 11, 1979, Paris) began studying at the Paris Conservatoire when she was nine. Both of her parents were musicians: her father was a bandmaster and her mother was a piano teacher. At age eleven she was one of the two children who premiered Ravel's *Mother Goose Suite*. She remained at the Conservatoire for many years, winning several firsts: for piano in 1913 when she was fifteen, in 1918 for harmony, in 1919 for score-reading, and in 1922 for composition.
    She won the Prix de Rome in 1923, for her cantata *Beatrix*. It was the first of the important prizes and awards she was to receive that included the Georges Bizet prize and Monbinne Prize, in addition to being honored by the Institut de France.
    Her two ballets, *Un jour d'été* (1940) and *Nautéos* (1947) had considerable success. In 1947 she became professor of sight-reading at the Paris Conservatoire.
    In addition to the ballets, her works include orchestral music, incidental music to *Le cyclope* (text of Euripides) 1928, and work for piano.
    Stage works:
Le cyclope (text of Euripides), incidental music, 1928.
Un jour d'été, ballet, 1940.
Nautéos, ballet, 1947.
    Principal sources: Grove's; Norton Grove

Marcelle de Manziarly (October 1 [October1/13], 1899, Kharkiv–May 12, 1989, Ojai, California) had a diversified career in both occupations and locations. She was a student of Nadia Boulanger, who promoted her music in Paris. (Nadia, at her 1934 debut as a conductor in Paris, conducted Manziarly's *Triptyque pour une madame de Lorenzo d'Alessandro*.) Following her studies with Boulanger, she took courses in conducting in Basel and piano in New York.

She divided her time and career between France and the United States: she conducted, performed as a pianist and taught in the United States, and she taught in Paris. She was the pianist for the premiere of her Piano Concerto with the Concertgebouw in 1933 at the ISCM (International Society for Contemporary Music) Festival. In 1944, her orchestral piece *Sonate pour Notre-Dame de Paris*, for the liberation of Paris, gained wide attention.

Her compositions include a chamber opera, works for orchestra, chamber groups, and piano, and vocal music.

Opera:

La femme en fleche, chamber opera, 1954.

Principal source: Norton Grove

Germany

In her mid-teens **Johanna Senfter** (November 27, 1879, Oppenheim, Germany–August 11, 1961, Oppenheim) entered the Hoch Conservatory in Frankfurt to study piano, violin, organ, and composition. Following that she went to the Royal Conservatory in Leipzig to study with Max Reger, where she won the Nikisch prize for composition in 1910.

She became very active professionally after 1916; she composed many works and gave numerous concerts. She founded the Oppenheim Music Society in 1921 and organized her own concert series, performing her own works. In 1923 she founded the Oppenheim Bach Society.

She was a prolific composer. Her works include nine symphonies, concertos, vocal and choral music, works for string quartets and chamber groups.

Principal source: Norton Grove

Ilse Fromm-Michaels (December 30, 1888, Hamburg–January 22, 1986, Detmold, Germany) first studied at the Hochschule für Musik in Berlin from 1902 to 1905, then at the Sternsches Konservatorium from 1905 to 1908. In 1911 she began study at the Rheinische Musikschule in Cologne.

Her musical interests cover a wide range. Although she was an accomplished pianist, most of her works are instrumental and for voice. She was devoted to the music of Mozart and composed cadenzas for his concertos, and she promoted contemporary music and often included it in her performances. When her husband was classified by the Nazis as Jewish, she curtailed her concert giving. In 1946 she began teaching piano at the Hochschule für Musik in Hamburg and taught there until 1969.

She composed throughout her life but she was not a prolific composer. Being of a critical mode, she destroyed some of her works because she was dissatisfied with their quality. She won first prize for her *Symphony in C minor* at the Third International Competition for Women Composers in 1961.

In addition to the *Symphony in C minor,* her works include vocal works, and work for chamber orchestras.

Principal source: Norton Grove

Evelyn Faltis (February 20, 1890, Trautenau, Germany–May 13, 1937, Vienna) was the first woman to coach solo singers at Bayreuth in 1914.

After her initial schooling in Paris she attended the Vienna Music Academy. Later, at the Dresden Hochschule für Musik her *Phantastische Sinfonie* won a prize. She also studied with Sophie Menter (see entry) in Munich. In 1924 she began work at the Städdtische Oper in Berlin. Throughout her life she worked with theater and opera.

Her compositions include a symphonic poem *Hamlet,* a piano concerto, chamber works, and a Mass.

Principal source: Norton Grove

Greece

Eleni Lambiri (1882 or 1883, Athens–March 30, 1960, Athens) was the first modern Greek woman composer known to have had a full professional career. Her father was the composer Georgios Lambiris.

She first studied at the Athens Conservatory, where she won a bronze medal. In 1908 she began four years of study at the Leipzig Conservatory.

She returned to Athens. Eventually she moved to Milan for ten years, after working as a conductor. By 1925 she had returned to Greece and was director of the Patras Conservatory, until retiring in 1953.

Her compositions include melodramas (music for performance against a spoken text) that were performed in Italy, a symphony, string quartet, and piano music.

Stage works:
To apokeriatko oneiro, 1913
Isolma, 1915
Principal source: Norton Grove

Hungary

Martha (or Marta) **Linz** (December 21, 1898, Budapest–date of death not known) was the first woman accepted as a conducting pupil at the Berlin

Hochschule für Musik. She also graduated from masters classes. At some point she studied composition with Zoltan Kodaly as well. She lived in Berlin after 1924. In the 1930s she traveled with the Berlin Philharmonic as a violinist and conductor. She married Dr. Kalman von Kriegner, who was a musicologist and a jurist.

Her compositions include orchestral and vocal works, chamber music, and piano pieces.

Principal source: Cohen

Ireland

Ina Boyle (March 8, 1889, Enniskerry, Co. Wicklow–March 10, 1967, Enniskerry) studied violin, cello, and composition in Dublin. Charles Wood, her cousin, gave her composition lessons by correspondence.

Although she was a prolific composer, she had infrequent opportunities for performance. In 1920 the performance of *Soldiers at Peace,* for chorus and orchestra, was a great success. That same year *The Magic Harp,* an orchestral piece, won a Carnegie award. She was one of six winners out of fifty-two; the award, open to British composers, was publication of the music. In 1928 she went to London and studied in London with Ralph Vaughan Williams. He took great interest in her music and career, and wrote letters of introduction for her. Ina soon returned to Ireland, but during the next few years she would return to London periodically to have lessons.

In addition to *Soldiers at Peace* and *The Magic Harp,* she wrote choral works, part-songs, solo song cycles, a string quartet, as well as a number of larger works and concertos for orchestra, or for chorus and orchestra — and three ballets. Her last big work was a pastoral opera, *Maudlin of Paplewick.*

A Spanish Pastoral, a choral piece using words by St. Teresa of the 16th century, premiered. *The Musical Times* in December 1935, noted, "The music graciously and with an individual touch paints the scene of the annunciation to the shepherds."

Opera:

Maudlin of Paplewick.

Principal source: Norton Grove

Italy

Lucia Contini Anselmi (October 15, 1876, Vercelli, Italy–date of death not known) studied piano and composition at the Rome Conservatory then went on to a successful career as a concert pianist. She performed both in Italy and abroad. *Ludentia*, a composition for piano, was awarded a gold medal at the International Composers' Competition in Perugia in 1913.

Her compositions include works for string orchestra, for piano (some arranged for orchestra), violin and piano and for cello and piano. Perhaps her best-known works are *Preludio*, *Gavotta*, and *Minuetto* for string orchestra, piano Sonata in C minor, and *Sibylla Cumaea* for piano, also arranged for two pianos and for orchestra.

Principal source: Norton Grove

The compositions of **Giulia Recli** (December 4, 1890, Milan–December 19, 1970 Milan) attracted the attention of both La Scala in Milan and the Metropolitan Opera in New York. She was the recipient of numerous important awards and honors, including the "Arti" prize of Trieste. She was the first Italian woman composer whose work entered the symphonic repertory.

Her education was broad; she studied piano, singing and the humanities. In addition to composing widely and in many genres, she was a music critic and an officer of the Sindacato Musicisti.

Her many compositions include an opera, a ballet, symphonic works, violin pieces and many songs. Perhaps her most significant works are her opera *Cento ducati e Bellauccia* and the ballet *Piume d'oro*.

Opera and stage work:

Cento ducati e Bellauccia, opera.
Piume d'oro, ballet.

Principal source: Norton Grove

Little is known about the life of **Eugenia Calosso** (April 21, 1878, Turin–after 1914). She studied in Turin and began her career as a conductor at San Remo, making numerous concert tours throughout Europe until 1914. She also conducted at other European venues.

Her compositions include orchestral suites, pieces for piano, lieder, madrigals, pieces for violin and piano, and the opera *Vespero*.

Opera:

Vespero.

Principal source: Norton Grove

Emilia Gubitosi (February 3, 1887, Naples–January 17, 1972, Naples) had an active and varied career: composing, teaching at the Naples Conservatory from 1914 to 1957, performing, and working with the revival and performance of early Italian choral music. She wrote at least one book on musical theory.

She studied at the Naples Conservatory. Her first work, a lyrical sketch, *Ave Maria,* appeared in 1908, two years after her graduation. In 1910 *Nada Delvig,* her one-act opera, was performed in Pistoia. She performed widely, both in Italy and abroad. She was responsible for many concerts of early Italian choral music, often conducting them herself. She and her husband, Franco Michele Napolitano, also a composer, founded the Association Alessandro Scarlatti, from which came the first Neapolitan symphony orchestra.

In addition to her opera, she composed many works for the theater, orchestral music, and a Piano Concerto, instrumental works, chamber works, pieces for piano, and vocal works.

Her most notable works include *Cavalcata grottesca, Notturno,* and her Piano concerto (1917).

Operas:

Ave Maria, one-act, Naples, 1906.
Nada Delvig, one-act, Pistoia, 1910.
Fatum, four acts.
Gardenia Rossa, one-act.

Principal source: Norton Grove

Women composers who married composers didn't always fare so well in their careers. **Elsa Olivieri Sangiacomo Respighi** (March 24, 1894, Rome–March 17, 1996) was one of several such women.

She began her studies of piano and solfege when she was very young, then enrolled in the Istituto Nazionale di Musica in Rome in 1905, at age eleven. In 1911 she entered the Liceo di S. Cecilia (forerunner of the Conservatorio di S. Cecilia) where her composition instructor was Ottorino Respighi. Her songs were first published in 1916; additional publications appeared in 1918, 1919 and 1921.

She married Ottorino Respighi in 1919. Ottorino's career took precedence during their marriage, and her own activities were almost entirely subsumed into his career. They performed together in Europe, North America and South America, and collaborated on several compositions, including the ballet version of *Gli uccelli* in 1927 and the transcription of the Bach Passacaglia in 1930–31.

Ottorini Respighi died in 1936, leaving unfinished the score of his opera *Lucrezia.* Elsa Respighi finished that score, which was performed the next year at La Scala. She and Claudio Guastalla, Ottorino's librettist, then prepared a ballet version of the *Antiche arie e danze.* Guastella, who wrote the scenario, gives her the credit for working with the music. She went on to write articles on Ottorino Resphighi's music, then a biography that was published in 1954. (The English translation drastically cut the original.) In 1969 she founded the

Fondo Respighi in Venice, which was dedicated to improving music teaching in Italy. Her most important compositions were done after Ottorino's death.

Her works include *Il pianto della Madonna*, a sacred drama, in 1938; *Tre canti corali* for an a cappella choir in 1944; and a year later, a cantata for soprano and chamber ensemble. (Guastelli was the librettist or supplied the text for many of her compositions.) She also composed an opera, *Samurai*, a fairy opera in three acts, symphonic poem, orchestral suites, and music for viola, flute and harp.

Operas and stage work:

Il pianto della Madonna, a sacred drama, 1938.
Samurai, a fairy opera in three acts.
Fior di neve, a fairy opera in three acts, c. 1920.
Alcesti, one-act, 1941.

Principal source: Norton Grove

Barbara Giuranna (November 18, 1899, Palermo, Italy–July 31, 1998; birth year sometimes listed as 1902) was a prolific composer who received numerous awards and had her music performed in a variety of venues. She studied piano in Palermo, then in 1919 entered the Naples Conservatory where she studied composition. After graduating she continued her study of composition in Milan.

In 1924 she married composer and conductor Mario Giuranna. Shortly after, the two went to the United States, where they stayed for several years. Two of her orchestral works, *Apina rapita dai nani della montagna* (1924) and *Marionette* (1924) had their debut performances in Chicago in 1929 with repeat performances at the Metropolitan. They returned to Italy, and in 1933 she won a competition by the Sindacato Musicisti Italiani. In 1936 she was represented at the Venice Biennale, the first Italian woman composer to be so honored; the piece was Adagio and Allegro for nine instruments.

In addition to her composing she taught at the S. Cecilia Conservatory in Rome from 1937 to 1976. She received honors and prizes throughout her life; in 1990 the International Leonard Bernstein Academy organized a concert in Rome in her honor that included her mass *Sinite parvulos*.

Her music often shows elements of Native American melodies, Corsican folksongs and Indian music. Her works include three operas, all staged, orchestral and vocal works, and solo violin pieces.

Operas and stage work:

Trappolo d'oro, ballet, 1929.
Jamanto, opera, Bergamo, 1941.
Mayerling, opera, Naples, 1961.
Hosanna, opera, Palermo, 1978.

Principal source: Norton Grove

Mexico

Maria Grever (August 16, 1885, Leon, Guanajuato–December 15, 1951, New York) was a child prodigy and reputedly began composing at age four. Her father was a Spaniard, and her mother a Mexican. When she was young she went to Spain with her parents and traveled throughout Europe; she later said she received musical advice from Franz Lehár while on this trip. When she returned to Mexico she studied singing with her aunt, Cuca Torres.

Her husband, whom she married in 1907, was Leo Augusto Grever, an American oil company executive. She became an American citizen in 1916, and by 1917 they were living in New York. She gave four professional recitals in New York over an extended period of years: in 1919, 1927, 1928, and 1939. The 1927 recital included her "song dramas" and the premier of her one-act stage work *The Gypsy*. Her miniature opera *El cantarito* premiered at the recital in 1939. She wrote her own librettos.

Perhaps her best-known compositions are *Munequita Linda* for voice and orchestra and *Júrame* for voice and orchestra.

In addition to her stage works she composed popular songs, several of which became classics: "What a Difference a Day Makes" being one of them. She also composed music for many of the films made by Paramount Pictures.

After her death her bust was placed in the composers' gallery in Chapultepec Park in Mexico City.

Biography:

Maria Grever: poeta y compositora, by Maria Luisa Rodriguez Lee (Washington, D.C: Scripta Humanistica, 1994).

Principal sources: Norton Grove; Esperanza Pulido, "Mexican Women in Music," *Latin American Music Review*, v. 4, no. 1, pp. 120–131.

Emiliana de Zubeldia (December 6, 1888, Salinas del Oro, Navarra, Spain–May 26, 1987, Hermosillo, Sonora) was only eight when she entered the Pamplona Academia Municipal de Música. At fifteen she continued her studies at the Madrid Real Conservatorio, finishing in 1906. Three years later, following the death of her father, she returned to Pamplona to serve as *professor auxiliary de piano* at her former school.

She married Dr. Joaquin Fuentes Pascal in 1919. Three years later she separated from him and moved to Paris, where she studied piano with Blanche Selva and composition with Vincent d'Indy. After her studies she toured extensively, performing in Mexico, Central America and New York,

In 1932 she moved to Mexico. After giving her first recital there in 1933, she embarked on a concert tour in Central America. In 1942 she became a Mexican citizen. She taught in Mexico City for about ten years, until the

University of Hermosillo invited her to come to the university for a year to develop choruses. She stayed there for forty years.

She composed in a variety of genres including orchestral pieces, music for chamber and solo instruments, music for keyboard, choral works and songs. One of her better known works is the *Sinfonía elegíaca*, composed in 1940 in memory of her sister. Some of her compositions were published in Pamplona under the name of Emily Bydwealth.

Principal source: Norton Grove

Netherlands

Although **Anna M. Cramer** (July 15, 1873, Amsterdam–June 9, 1968, Blaricum) was long-lived, all of her published work appears before 1911.

She attended the Amsterdam Conservatory where she studied piano and began composing. She graduated in 1897, and by 1903 she was studying composition in Berlin. Her lieder were soon published, and in 1909 she toured, accompanying her own lieder in many concerts. By 1910 she had published four collections of songs. Her music may have been ahead of its time with its complex harmonies and chromaticism, and some of the critical reviews were negative. Perhaps in reaction to that, she published nothing more after that time.

She moved from Munich to Vienna, then was back in Amsterdam by 1934. Her music was forgotten and she lived as a recluse until she died. Research after her death located more songs, including some with orchestral accompaniment that had been intended for an opera.

Principal source: Norton Grove

Elizabeth Kuyper (September 13, 1877, Amsterdam–February 26, 1953, Viganello, Switzerland) was the first woman to win the Mendelssohn state prize for composition in 1905. She was also the first woman to teach theory and composition at the Berlin Hochschule für Musik.

After earning her piano-teaching certificate in 1895 she left Amsterdam to study at the Berlin Hochschule für Musik. From 1908 until 1920 she taught theory and composition there.

Throughout her life she was a strong proponent of symphonic orchestral work for women, and she founded women's symphony orchestras in Berlin (1910), The Hague (1922), London (1922–23), and New York (1924–25). All were well received. The Hague orchestra was organized to provide music for a conference of the International Women's Council in 1922 and was short lived by intent. The others were eventually discontinued because of financial difficulties.

In 1925 she returned to Europe and settled in Muzanno, Switzerland.

Her compositions include works for orchestra, chamber groups, piano, vocal and orchestral works, and choral works. Among her best-known compositions are *Das Lied von der Seele*, for orchestra with seven solo singers and a dance.

Principal source: Norton Grove

Jeanne Beijerman-Walraven (June 14, 1878, Semarang, Indonesia–September 20, 1969, Arnhem) studied privately at The Hague. She composed for over half a century but because she frequently revised her works, her output was small. Throughout her life she was interested in contemporary music. Many of her compositions derive from her interest in Dutch and French poetry.

She composed orchestral works, including *Concertouverture* in 1910, *Orkestuk* in 1921 and *Feestlied* in 1926; chamber and instrumental works, and works for voice and piano.

Principal source: Norton Grove

Reine Colaco Osorio-Swaab (January 16, 1881, Amsterdam–April 14, 1971, Amsterdam) didn't begin composing until after the death of her husband when she was in her forties. All of her compositions were written between 1930 and 1960.

She first concentrated on composing songs, but as she became drawn to philosophical and religious subjects she began to compose works for narrator and instrumental accompaniment. She wrote a substantial amount of chamber music; larger-scale works, including *Genezing van den Blinde* for orchestra and narrator; and a set of six songs commemorating the death of her son at Dachau.

Principal source: Norton Grove

Dina Appeldoorn (December 24, 1884, Rotterdam–December 4/5, 1938, The Hague) began her music career as a piano teacher and an accompanist for several choirs at The Hague. At that time she was also studying and working at composition, and gradually her emphasis turned to composing.

Her first major work was a symphonic poem that was performed in 1912. Some of her orchestral works, including her symphony *De Nordze* (1925), were premiered by the Utrecht city orchestra. She wrote many choral works, which were frequently performed, two symphonies, a symphonic poem *Pêcheurs d'Islande*, chamber music, *Duinsprookje* (a children's operetta), and songs.

Eventually she became involved with the Esperanto movement and wrote songs in Esperanto.

Stage work:
Duinprookje, children's operetta, 1927.
Principal source: Norton Grove

Bertha Tideman-Wijers (January 8, 1887, Zutphen, Netherlands–date of death not known) first studied with her mother and sister. In 1900 she attended the Stern Conservatory in Berlin, then went on to the Berlin Hochschule für Musik. She lived in the Dutch East Indies for seventeen years, returning to Holland in 1929.

Her compositions include chamber music, piano pieces and songs.
Principal source: Cohen

Rosy M. Wertheim (February 19, 1888–May 27, 1949, Laren) initially considered a career in social work, but she was persuaded by her piano teacher to pursue music instead. After receiving her certificate in piano teaching in 1912 she began her career by teaching piano and solfege while she was taking voice lessons and studying composition. She also conducted a Jewish women's chorus and taught piano to children of poor families.

She was drawn to the music of Debussy, Ravel and Stravinsky, and in 1929 she moved to Paris to study with the composer Louis Aubert. Her home in Paris was a gathering place for other composers. During this time she also worked as a foreign correspondent for Dutch newspapers. She stayed in Paris until 1935, then spent a year in Vienna where she studied with Karl Weigl, husband of composer Vally Weigl (see entry) and continued her work as a foreign correspondent.

She then moved to the United States where she stayed about a year. During that time she took part in a Composers Forum, which was a program of the Federal Music Project under the WPA, where her *String Quartet, Divertimento* for chamber orchestra, and several of her piano pieces were well received. Throughout she continued her work as a foreign correspondent. She returned to Amsterdam in 1937.

The extent of her activities during World War II is not clear. She may have gone into hiding, or she may have had a role in the resistance. She is said to have given clandestine concerts in the basement of her home, often presenting works by Jewish composers.

In addition to her early choral works, she composed works for orchestra, string quartet, and piano. Among her most successful works are her *String Quartet, Divertimento* for chamber orchestra, a trio for flute clarinet and bassoon, and a piano suite.

Principal sources: Norton Grove; Composers Forum Transcripts, Federal Music Project, Record Group #69, National Archives II, College Park, MD.

Hanna Beekhuis (September 24, 1889, Leeuwarden, the Netherlands–February 26, 1980, Bloemendall, the Netherlands) studied in Amsterdam and at the Geneva Conservatory, then spent three years at the Cologne Conservatory. She was a composer and a pianist. She lived in Switzerland during the war; her compositions were performed in Zurich. In 1945 she returned to Amsterdam.

She was a prolific composer. Some of her compositions were influenced by her travels in Corsica, Catalonia, and Morocco. In addition to chamber and orchestral works, she composed many works for voices and instruments.

Principal source: Cohen

Johanna Bordewijk-Roepman (August 4, 1892, Rotterdam–October 8, 1971, The Hague) was primarily self-taught in composing with the exception of lessons in orchestration in 1936–37.

She first studied English but then turned to composing. Her first compositions, which she wrote when she was twenty-five, were songs to accompany pictures in her children's storybooks. In 1940 she had her first major success with a performance of *Les Illuminations* by the Rotterdams Philharmonisch Orkest.

Her husband Frans Bordewijk, who was a well-known writer, wrote the texts for *Rotonde,* her one-act opera, and *Plato's Dood,* an oratorio. She regularly received commissions throughout the 1940s and 1950s, and her work continued to be performed.

In addition to the opera and oratorio her compositions include symphonic pieces, a concerto, works for male voices and other choral works.

Opera and stage work:

Rotonde, one-act opera, 1943.
Plato's Dood, oratorio, 1949.

Principal source: Norton Grove; Cohen

Henriëtte Hilda Bosmans (December 6, 1895, Amsterdam–July 2, 1952, Amsterdam) was the daughter of professional musicians. Her father, who died when she was less than a year old, was principal cellist at the Concertgebouw Orchestra, and her mother, Sarah Benedicts, was a concert pianist and teacher at the Amsterdam Conservatory. Henriëtte studied with her mother at the conservatory, graduating with honors when she was seventeen. She then began teaching as well. Eventually she became a concert pianist and performed with leading orchestras.

She began composing when she was fifteen; her first compositions were for cello, and she continued writing for cello. In the 1920s she studied orchestration and composition. She was considered the most talented Dutch woman composer of her time, and her works were widely performed.

Because of the death of her fiancé in 1935, the impending war, and then the war itself, she did not compose between 1936 and 1945. Performance of her music was banned in 1942. She resumed composing after the war while she continued her performing and accompanying. At that time her compositions were primarily vocal works. Other works include music for orchestra and chamber music.

In 1994 the Society of Dutch Composers began awarding The Henriëtte Bosmans Prize for young Dutch composers.

Principal sources: Norton Grove; Grove's

Norway

Signe Skabo Lund (April 15, 1868, Christiania [Oslo]–April 6, 1950, Oslo) studied in Christiania. Later she studied in Berlin and spent time in Copenhagen and Paris.

From 1902 to 1920 she lived in Chicago, which had a significant Norwegian population at that time, teaching and lecturing on Norwegian topics. She also traveled widely in the United States, giving concerts and lecturing.

In 1914 she composed a Norwegian-American cantata for the centenary of the Norwegian constitution. She was one of the founders of the Norwegian Association of Composers, founded in 1917. Her orchestral works and piano compositions gave her wide recognition as a composer.

Perhaps her best-known works are her piano pieces *Legende* and *Norske smaastubber,* and her orchestral works *Berceuse, Andante,* and *Piano concerto* op. 63.

Primary sources: GDM&M; Norton Grove

Mon Schjelderup (June 16, 1870, Halden, Norway–November 21, 1934, Oslo) was a pupil of Agathe Grøndahl (see entry) in Christiania (now Oslo). She also studied in Berlin, then in Paris with Jules Massenet. She taught at the Christiania Conservatory from 1899 to 1906, when she had to retire because of poor health.

She is particularly known for her songs, but her compositions also include orchestral, piano and chamber works.

Principal source: Norton Grove

Pauline Margrete Hall (August 2, 1890, Hamar, Norway–January 24, 1969, Oslo) studied first in Norway, then from 1912 to 1914 in Paris and Dresden.

From 1926 to 1932 she was theater and music critic for the *Oslo Dagbladet* in Berlin. On her return to Oslo she continued to work as a critic from 1934 to 1942 and from 1945 to 1956. As a critic and as president of Ny Musikk, the Norwegian section of ISCN, from 1938 to 1960, she actively promoted new Norwegian music.

For a time, particularly in the early 1930s, the French voice of her music jarred with the strong national mode of Norwegian musical life and affected the reception of her compositions. This changed after World War II, and she received more positive recognition as a composer. She was considered the most eminent Norwegian composer following Agathe Grøndahl (see entry).

Her compositions include ballet, incidental music to many plays, orchestral works, choral works, chamber music, film and TV scores, and piano pieces.

Principal source: Norton Grove

Poland

Wanda Alexandra Landowska (July 5, 1879, Warsaw–August 16, 1959, Lakeville, Connecticut) played a major role in the revival of the harpsichord in the 20th century. She was also an eminent pianist.

She first studied piano in Warsaw, then in 1896 she went to Berlin to study composition. From the start she composed in a wide range: songs, piano pieces and works for orchestra. *Kolysanka* for piano was performed in Warsaw in 1899; a year later *Paysage triste* for string orchestra also was performed in Warsaw.

That same year, 1900, she married Henry Lew, who was an authority on Hebrew folklore. She credited him for teaching her how to do the methodical research she would later do on the harpsichord and harpsichord music. They moved to Paris where Wanda continued composing and playing; in 1901 she played her *Rhapsodie orientale*. Two or three years later she entered a piano piece and a song in the Musica International Competition, winning first and second prizes.

She began inserting some harpsichord music in her performances; since she also played a considerable amount of Bach and his contemporaries the music fit readily into her concerts. That was also when she gave her first public performance of the harpsichord. In 1909 her book *Music Ancienne* (later reissued as *Landowska on Music*) was published. She was touring widely by this time; she enjoyed relating her visits to the estate of Leo Tolstoy to play for him. Although he and his wife had long been separated, she would come to the estate and enjoy the music as well.

Four years later she began teaching a harpsichord class at the Hochschule für Musik in Berlin. During World War I she and her husband were detained as civil prisoners on parole, which limited her performing and obviously her touring.

After the war she composed fewer pieces and instead focused on writing cadenzas for concertos by Mozart, Haydn, Handel and C.P.E. Bach. She also performed and recorded.

In 1919, before they could return to Paris, her husband was killed in a car accident. Wanda returned alone to Paris via Switzerland where she played and gave some classes.

Six years later she settled in Leu-la-Forêt, north of Paris, where she founded the École de Musique Ancienne.

When the German occupation in 1940 forced her to leave, she had to abandon her instruments, manuscripts of her early compositions, and her library of over 10,000 volumes. She went to the United States and settled in Lakeville, Connecticut. She composed *Liberation Fanfare* in admiration of Charles de Gaulle; the orchestral version (by Richard Franko Goldman) was frequently performed.

Her compositions include piano pieces, songs, and works for orchestra. Landowska was a devotee of Bach from an early age.

Schoenberg gives an intriguing description of one of her performances: "[Landowska] had the stage fixed up as though it were her living room — the harpsichord dominating, a studio lamp to the left of the keyboard, the stage nearly darkened.... Finally the stage door opened and The Presence approached.... Her palms were pressed together in prayer a la Dürer, her eyes were cast to the heavens, and everybody realized she was in communion with J. S. Bach, getting some last-minute coaching and encouragement.... It was one of the great entrances of all time" (Schonberg, *The Great Pianists from Mozart to the Present* [New York: Simon & Schuster, 1963], 397).

Principal sources: Grove's; Howard Schott, "Wanda Landowska: A Centenary Appraisal," *Early Music*, vol. 7, no. 4, pp. 467–472.

Irene Wieniawska Poldowski (Lady Dean Paul) (May 16, 1880, Brussels–January 28, 1932, London) is considered to be a Polish composer although much of her professional life was spent in England. Her father, who died before she was born, was the Polish violinist Henryk Wieniawski, and her mother, who was English, was a niece of the composer George A. Osborne. Because of her father's fame she primarily used the name "Poldowski" throughout her professional life.

When she was about twelve she entered the Brussels Conservatory; several years later she moved to London for further study. She also studied briefly with Vincent d'Indy in Paris. At some point after her marriage to Sir Aubrey

Dean Paul in 1901 she went to Paris for further study. She returned to London for a time, then went back to Paris where she studied with d'Indy.

She is known chiefly for her many songs, particularly for her settings of poetry using texts by Verlaine and William Blake. She also composed orchestral music, an operetta, work for piano and orchestra, a woodwind suite, music for several stage works, and instrumental pieces. From about 1912 to the late 1920s much of her work received regular performances in Europe. *Nocturnes,* her symphonic sketch, premiered at the Queen's Hall Promenade concerts in 1912.

Stage work:

Laughter, operetta.

Principal sources: Grove's; Norton Grove

Anna Maria Klechniowska (April 15, 1888, Borowka, Ukraine–August 28, 1973, Warsaw) took her early studies at the Conservatory of Warsaw and the Conservatory of Lemberg (now L'viv). She then attended the Leipzig Conservatory from 1906 to 1908. Following that she continued her studies in piano at the Kraków Music Institute, and later at the Vienna Music Academy, graduating from there in 1917.

For the next twenty years she developed and taught her own music courses for beginners. Her elementary piano manual stayed in use for decades. She was a pupil of Nadia Boulanger after 1940.

She was best known for her educational music, but she composed in several genres. Among her other compositions are the symphonic poem, *Wawel* (1917), and the ballets *Juria* and *Fantasma.*

Stage works:

Juria, ballet, 1939.
Fantasma, ballet, 1954.

Principal source: Norton Grove

Romania

Mansi Barberis (March 12, 1899, Iasi, Romania–October 10, 1986, Bucharest) attracted the attention of George Enescu at a young age; he suggested she begin to study theory along with her other lessons. Eventually her musical education included study at a variety of places: the Iasi Conservatory from 1918 to 1922, in Berlin from 1922 to 1923 and in Paris as a pupil of Vincent d'Indy in 1926 and 1927. She was a violinist, violist, composer and conductor. She also taught voice.

After Paris she returned to Romania to teach singing and violin. She was well known as choral conductor and founder of the Femina String Quartet.

During the communist rule her activities, particularly her musical activities, were restricted. Eventually she was "rehabilitated" and resumed her teaching and composing.

She utilized folklike melodies, and her operas, some of which are based on Moldavian folklore, have nationalistic themes. She also composed orchestral, choral, and chamber music, incidental music for the theater and many songs.

Operas:

Printesa îndepărtată [The Distant Princess], Iasi, 1946, revised 1976.
Apus de soare [Sunset], Bucharest, 1958.
Kera Duduca, television opera, 1963, revised, 1970.
Caruţa cu paiaţe [The Cart with Clowns], Iasi, 1982.

Principal source: Norton Grove

Berta Bock (March 15, 1857, Sibiu [Hermannstadt]–April 4, 1945, Sibiu) came from a musical family, her grandfather having founded the Hermannstädter Musikverein in Sibiu. As a child she studied piano, theory, and singing.

Her pantomime-ballet *Klein Elschens Traum* was performed in Sibiu in 1907. This was followed by another pantomime-ballet, *Das erste Veilchen*, also performed in Sibiu. Her opera, *Die pfingstkrone*, was based on Saxon folklore in Transylvania in 1927. This was performed throughout Transylvania in 1927, then in Cleveland in 1931. She also composed lieder.

Opera and stage works:

Klein Elschens Traum, pantomime-ballet, Sibiu, 1907.
Das erste Veilchen, pantomime-ballet, Sibiu, 1910.
Die pfingstkrone, opera, based on Saxon folklore, 1927.

Principal source: Norton Grove

Russia

Yuliya Lazarevna Veysberg [Julie Lazarevna Weissberg] (December 25/January 6, 1880, Orenburg, Russia–March 1 [or 4], 1942, Leningrad) was a writer, translator and composer. She studied piano with Rimsky-Korsakov and instrumentation with Alexander Glazunov at the St. Petersburg Conservatory. However, in 1905 she was dismissed from the conservatory for participating in a strike. In 1907 she began studying in Germany with Engelbert Humperdinck and Max Reger and continued until 1912, when she returned to St. Petersburg to take her examinations and receive her degree.

For two years, from 1915 to 1917, she worked at the editorial board of the periodical *Muzïkal'nïy sovremennik*. Four years later she became choral director at the Young Workers' Conservatory, a position she held for two years.

She was married to Rimsky-Korsakov's son.

She wrote primarily in vocal genres: operas, vocal orchestral works and vocal chamber works. Many of her compositions are for children: "opera games," cycles of "song-riddles" and music for children's choirs.

Her translation of the musical writings of Romain Rolland (nine volumes) was published in 1938.

Operas and stage works:

Rusalochka [*The Little Mermaid*], after Hans Christian Anderson, 1923.
Gyul'nara, excerpts published, 1935.
Gusi-lebedi [*Geese-Swans*], children's opera, Moscow, 1937.
Myortvaya tsarevna [*The Dead Princess*], radio opera, 1937, broadcast, 1938.
Zaykin dom [*A Little Rabbit's House*], children's opera, 1937, Moscow, 1938.

Principal source: Norton Grove

Very little is known of the life of **Valentina Ramm** (October 22, 1888, Kharkoff, Russia–date of death not known). She studied in Moscow.

Her compositions include songs, piano pieces, music for voice and orchestra, and incidental music.

Principal source: WON

Spain

The information about **Luisa Casagemas** (December 13, 1863, Barcelona–after 1894) is sketchy, as she somewhat disappears from sight early in her career. The first public performance of her music was in 1893, when *Crepusculo* was performed. That same year her opera *Schiava e regina,* which she composed when she was in her teens, won a prize in connection with the World's Columbian Exposition in Chicago. It was also scheduled for performance in Barcelona in 1893, but that performance had to be cancelled after an anarchist attack on the theater. In 1894 the royal family arranged for a premiere of excerpts from the opera in the royal palace.

Her compositions include music for voice and piano, for various instruments, and the opera *I briganti: Monserrat.*

Operas:

Schiava e regina, c. 1880.
I briganti: Monserrat, four-act opera.

Principal source: Norton Grove

A woman of many dimensions, **Narcisa Freixas y Cruells** (December 13, 1859, Barcelona–December 20, 1926, Barcelona) was a sculptor and painter in addition to a composer and teacher.

She was very active on behalf of children and young men and women. She founded a music school in Barcelona for children and young ladies. The choir of that school performed in asylums, prisons and hospitals. She founded the "Cultura Musical Popular," which promoted cultural music among young people. She established children's theater competitions, founded choirs in Madrid and Barcelona, and helped found a library for young people. In 1917 at the Madrid Atheneum, the Ministry of Public Education put her in charge of a course for teachers on the improvement of singing in schools.

Her compositions, which were mainly for children, often utilized settings of Catalan poets and traditional Catalan music.

Principal source: Cohen; Norton Grove

After finishing her studies at the Conservatorio Real Madrid, **Maria Rodrigo** (1888, Madrid–1967, Puerto Rico) worked in popular musical theater for a while before going to Munich to continue her studies. She returned to Madrid and taught choral and instrumental groups at the Madrid Conservatory from 1933 to 1939. Reputedly, she was also assistant conductor at the Royal Opera House in Madrid.

In 1939 she went to Puerto Rico, in exile. She did not compose during that period.

Her compositions include operas, zarzuelas, a symphony, a symphonic poem, pieces for wind instruments, violin, and chorus and orchestra.

Operas:

Becqueriana, opera, Madrid, 1915.
Diana cazadora, Madrid, 1915.
La romeria del rocio, zarzuela, Barcelona, 1921.
La flor de la vida, zarzuela.
Cancion de Amor, zarzuela, 1925.
El roble de la Jarosa.

Principal source: Norton Grove

Maria Teresa Prieto (1896, Oviedo–January 24, 1982, Mexico) first studied in Oviedo with Saturnino del Fresno, whose strong interest in the traditional Asturian music is reflected in some of Prieto's music. She was also strongly influenced by the music of Bach, and that, too, is reflected in her compositions. She continued her studies at the Conservatorio Real in Madrid.

Because of the Spanish Civil War, in 1936 she went to Mexico to live with her brother. Through him she met Stravinsky, Milhaud, and many Mexican composers as well as other Spanish musicians who were then living in Mexico. From 1937 to 1939 she studied with Manuel Ponce.

She worked with Milhaud at Mills College in California in the late 1940s.

In 1958 she won the Samuel Ros Prize in Madrid. Throughout her career her composing reflected the changes in style taking place in the 20th century.

She composed in many genres: works for piano, piano and orchestra, the *Sinfonia asturiana*, a symphonic poem *Chichen Itza*, many orchestral pieces, music for piano, orchestra and chorus, a ballet suite, fugues, and chamber pieces.

Principal source: Grove's; Cohen

Switzerland

Marguerite Roesgen-Champion (January 25, 1894, Geneva, Switzerland–June 30, 1976) studied at the Geneva Conservatory. She later settled in Paris where she began a concert career as a harpsichordist, appearing with major orchestras in France, Italy, Spain and Holland.

Her compositions include works for chorus and orchestra, symphonic poems, a concerto for harpsichord and orchestra, and a harp concerto.

Principal source: WON

United States

Like so many composers, **Eleanor Everest Freer** (May 14, 1864, Philadelphia, Pennsylvania–December 13, 1942, Chicago) came from a musical family and began playing the piano early. Her father was an organist and her mother a singer, and Eleanor met many musicians during her childhood. She began composing while she was in her teens.

She studied singing and composition in Paris from 1883 to 1886. During that time she had the opportunity to sing for Verdi and for Liszt. When she returned to the United States she taught piano in Philadelphia and singing at the National Conservatory of Music in New York.

In 1891 she married Archibald Freer of Chicago. The next year they went to Leipzig where he studied medicine and she studied music. In 1899 they were back in Chicago. She became very active in music organizations, and she studied with Bernard Ziehn. In 1902 she began composing. She often used English poems for her art songs, feeling strongly that they had been neglected in favor of French, German and Italian texts.

She became active in promoting modern music. In 1921 she established the Opera in Our Language Foundation which combined with the David Bispham Memorial Fund (which was also established by her) to fund productions of English opera in the United States. The two organizations soon merged to become American Opera Society of Chicago. This particular involvement prompted her to begin writing operas.

Her first opera, *The Legend of the Piper* (1922), was performed in 1925. She wrote a total of eleven operas, and all were performed and published. One received a David Bispham Medal. She also wrote songs, including a cycle of forty-four texts of *Sonnets from the Portuguese*, by Elizabeth Barrett Browning.

Operas:

The Legend of the Piper, 1922, South Bend, Indiana, 1925.
Massimilliano, the Court Jester or The Love of a Caliban, Chicago [vocal score], 1925.
The Chilkoot Maiden, her libretto, Skagway, Alaska, [vocal score], 1927.
A Christmas Tale, Milwaukee, [vocal score], 1928.
The Masque of Pandora, her libretto after H. W. Longfellow, Milwaukee, [vocal score], 1929.
Preciosa, or The Spanish Student, her libretto, after H. W. Longfellow, Milwaukee, [vocal score], 1929.
Frithiof, Milwaukee, [vocal score], 1929.
Joan of Arc her libretto, Milwaukee, [vocal score], 1929.
A Legend of Spain, her libretto, Milwaukee, [vocal score], 1931.
Little Women, her libretto, after Louisa May Alcott, Chicago, [vocal score], 1934.
The Brownings Go to Italy, Chicago, [vocal score], 1936.

Memoirs:

Recollections and Reflections of an American Composer, by Eleanor Everett Freer (S I.: s.n., 1929).

Principal sources: New Grove; Cohen

Narcissa, an opera by **Mary Carr Moore** (August 6, 1873, Memphis, Tennessee–January 9, 1957, Inglewood, California), is considered by many to have a claim to being the first major "American" opera.

By the age of ten her family had relocated to Napa. Her early training was in singing, but she soon became interested in composing. She studied composition and singing in San Francisco, and by 1889 she was composing and teaching. In 1894 her career was launched when she sang the lead in her own operetta, *The Oracle*. Within a year she had left her singing career to teach and compose, but there was a hiatus of about fifteen years in her composing, given over to family and children.

The Oracle was followed in 1909 by *Narcissa or The Cost of Empire*, with libretto by her mother. This was a grand opera, based on the 1847 massacre of Narcissa and Marcus Whitman, who were missionaries in the Oregon Territory. No well-known male conductor was willing to take a chance on it, so Mary conducted it herself.

Critics questioned whether it qualified as a "real" opera. The composer's career wasn't on the East Coast. Furthermore, the accepted setting for "American" opera was the East Coast during the colonial time, and the opera was set in the West. There was no love story. With these strikes against it, *Narcissa* didn't draw serious critical attention. It was awarded, belatedly, a David Bispham Medal in 1930.

By then she had moved from Lemoore, California, to Seattle. She lived several places on the West Coast; she left Seattle in 1915 and moved to San Francisco, where she stayed until she moved to Los Angeles in 1926.

Her next opera, *David Rizzio*, finally premiered in 1932. This had a more traditional setting and theme: Mary, Queen of Scots, concentrating on the time of her rule rather than her betrayal and execution, which was usually the focus.

Chapman College, where she was professor of theory and of composition, awarded her the honorary DMus in 1936.

She composed operas and operetta and a vaudeville sketch. Most of her operas were published and performed, though often through her own efforts. She also composed orchestral pieces and chamber works.

Operas and stage works:

The Oracle, operetta, San Francisco, 1894.
Narcissa, or The Cost of Empire, opera, Seattle, 1909.
The Leper, unperformed, 1912.
Memories, vaudeville sketch, Seattle, 1914.
Harmony, operetta, San Francisco, 1917.
The Flaming Arrow, or The shaft of Ku'pish-ta-ya, operetta, San Francisco, 1919.
David Rizzio, opera, Los Angeles, 1927.
Legende provençale, unperformed, 1929.
Los rubios, Los Angeles, 1931.
Flutes of Jade Happiness, Los Angeles, 1932.
Principal source: ANB

Anice Potter Terhune (October 27, 1873, Hampden Massachusetts–date of death not known) often used the pseudonym Morris Stockton to avoid having her work confused that with of her husband, who was the author of the Lassie books.

She wrote many songs as well as music for two operas and numerous piano pieces.

Operas:

The Woodland Princess, 1911.
Nero, opera, 1914.
Principal source: WON

Edith Rowena Noyes (March 26, 1875, Cambridge, Massachusetts–date of death not known) began her studies with Edward MacDowell when she was sixteen. She also studied theory with George Chadwick and counterpoint at the New England Conservatory. She made two tours of Europe, in 1899 and in 1919, in which she played only American music.

Her compositions include a violin sonata, an operetta and two operas.

Operas and stage work:

Last Summer, operetta, 1898.
Waushakum, pageant opera, based on an Indian subject, 1917.
Osseok, 1917.

Principal source: WON

Harriet Ware (August 26, 1877, Waupan, Wisconsin–1962) studied in Berlin. Her compositions were published and performed during her life, and one of her compositions was made the national song of the Federation of Women's Clubs. The New York Symphony Orchestra performed her symphonic poem *The Artisan.*

She also wrote piano works, choral music and operettas.

Operas and stage works:

Priscilla, opera.
Sinner's Secret, opera.
Undine, opera, 1923.
The Love Wagon, operetta.
Waltz for Three, operetta.

Principal source: WON

Mabel Wheeler Daniels (November 27, 1877, Swampscott, Massachusetts–March 10, 1971, Cambridge, Massachusetts) began her piano lessons when she was young and wrote her first piece when she was ten. She also sang well and had a fine voice.

As a student at Radcliffe College she was very active in the choral society and sang lead in several operettas. Composing and conducting were logical next steps for her and she realized that music, and composing music, should be her life's work.

After graduating *magna cum laude* in 1900 she studied orchestration with George Chadwick at the New England Conservatory. Two years later she entered the Munich Conservatory. Among the classes she wanted to take was score-reading, but no woman had ever presumed to ask to be admitted. After long consideration the director finally agreed to her joining.

In 1911 and 1912 she directed the Radcliffe Glee Club and the Bradford Academy, then from 1913 to 1918 she was head of music at Simmons College.

One of her early choral works, *The Desolate City,* attracted the attention of Mrs. Edward MacDowell, who was always interested in promising young composers. She was so impressed by Mabel's music that she invited Mabel to direct a performance at the MacDowell Colony. The following year Mabel was invited to become a resident at MacDowell; she was a fellow there for twenty-four summers. After 1918 she focused entirely on composition, with some financial support from her family.

She worked for women's suffrage and concerned herself with the discrimination against women musicians. She was active in a variety of professional groups that included the American Composers' Alliance, ASCAP, and the College Club of Boston and the Musical Guild.

Tufts College awarded her an honorary M.A. degree in 1933, and in 1939 Boston University awarded her a Doctor of Music Degree. She also received a number of prizes for her compositions.

Many of her compositions were choral works, with orchestra, accompaniment or unaccompanied. She wrote operettas and an opera sketch, ballets, and instrumental pieces. Among her best-known pieces are *Deep Forest*, for chamber orchestra; *Exultate Deo*, for mixed chorus and orchestra; and *The Song of Jael*, scored for orchestra, chorus and soprano solo, based on a poem by Edwin Arlington Robinson.

Opera and stage works:

A Copper Complication operetta, 1900.
The Court of Hearts, operetta, 1900.
Alice in Wonderland Continued, opera sketch, 1902–1904.
The Legend of Marietta, operetta, 1909.

Memoirs:

An American Girl in Munich: Impressions of a Music Student, by Mable Wheeler Daniels (Boston: Little, Brown, 1905).

Principal source; Norton Grove; Cohen

Fannie Charles Dillon (March 16, 1881, Denver, Colorado–February 21, 1947, Altadena, California) earned her degree at Pomona College in Claremont, California, then moved to Berlin, where she studied piano and composition for six years. In 1908 she made her debut as a pianist in Los Angeles. She was a member of the music faculty at Pomona from 1910 to 1913.

In 1918 she was invited by the Beethoven Society of New York to give a concert of her own compositions. That same year she began teaching in Los Angeles public schools, which she continued until her retirement in 1941. She was selected to be California's first representative composer to go to the MacDowell Colony in 1921.

She wrote several orchestra pieces including *Celebration of Victory, The Cloud, A Letter from the Southland, In a Mission Garden, Chinese Symphonic Suite,* music for piano and other solo instruments, and music for plays for the Woodlawn Theater at Big Bear Lake, California, which she founded.

Her papers are at UCLA.

Principal source: Norton Grove

Marion Eugenie Bauer (August 15, 1882, Walla Walla, Washington– August 9, 1955, South Hadley, Massachusetts) had a particularly rich musical education.

By 1899 she had moved to New York, where she lived and studied with her older sister Emilie Frances Bauer who was a successful music critic, teacher, and composer. In 1906 and 1907 Marion was in Paris, where one of her teachers was Nadia Boulanger; Marion may have been her first American pupil. In turn Marion gave Nadia English lessons. She returned to New York in 1907 and continued her studies. There were two additional study trips to Europe: Berlin in 1910–1911 and Paris in 1923–1924.

When Emilie died in 1926, Marion Bauer joined the faculty at New York University where she taught music history and composition until 1951. From 1940 to 1944 she also taught at Juilliard and lectured. In addition, she taught at Mills College, the Carnegie Institute of Technology, and the Cincinnati Conservatory, and during summers she frequently gave public lectures about contemporary music.

She spent many summers at the MacDowell Colony where she met other important women composers including Amy Beach, Mabel Daniels, Mary Howe, Miriam Gideon (1906–1996) and Ruth Crawford (1901–1953).

She wrote orchestral music, chamber music, music for piano, chamber music, and vocal works.

Most of her papers are at New York University.

Principal sources: Grove's; Norton Grove

Although **Mary Howe** (April 4, 1882, Richmond, Virginia–September 14, 1964, Washington, DC) began composing relatively late, she was a prolific composer in several genres.

Her early music education was private, first at home, then in Dresden for a brief time in 1904. After she returned to the United States she studied at the Peabody Conservatory.

She began her composing around 1920. By that time she was living in or near Washington, DC. That same year she and Anne Hull gave their first professional performances as duo-pianists, which they would continue until 1935. She also was active as an accompanist. Then, in 1922 when she was forty years of age, married and the mother of three, she earned the diploma in composition at the Peabody.

In 1933, by which time she had composed a large body of work, she studied briefly with Nadia Boulanger in Paris.

The extent of her participation in music organizations was remarkable. She and her husband helped found the National Symphony Orchestra, and she served as director. With Elizabeth Sprague Coolidge (see entry) and others she was one of the founders of the Chamber Music Society of Washington, which became the Friends of Music in the Library of Congress. She and Amy Beach helped organize the Society of American Women Composers in 1925.

She was a strong supporter of the MacDowell Colony and a participant for many years. From 1935 to 1940, she and her children (known as "The Four Howes") gave programs of madrigals and early music to benefit the MacDowell Colony.

In 1961 she received an honorary doctorate from George Washington University.

Her compositions include over twenty large orchestral works, chamber music, two ballets, piano and vocal music. Among her best-known compositions are *Castellana*, based on four Spanish folk tunes, and *Three Pieces after Emily Dickinson*, a string quartet.

A manuscript catalog of her works was edited by C. Howe in 1992.

Principal source: Norton Grove

Florence Beatrice Price (April 9, 1887, Little Rock, Arkansas–June 3, 1953, Chicago) was the first African American woman to be recognized as a symphonic composer.

She grew up in Little Rock. Her first studies were with her mother, who was a piano teacher. After graduating from high school at age fourteen (class valedictorian), she enrolled in the New England Conservatory of Music in Boston, graduating with honors in 1906. She taught until 1912, when she married Thomas Price, an attorney; she continued teaching and composing even while her children were young. Many of her early compositions and publications were teaching material.

In 1925 she received recognition for "Memories of Dixieland" in a contest sponsored by the magazine *Opportunity*. In 1926 the Price family moved to Chicago, which was booming with black culture, particularly in music and literature.

She won two prestigious Wanamaker Awards in 1932: one for her "Symphony in E Minor" and one for a piano sonata. In 1933 the Chicago Symphony Orchestra performed her "Symphony in E Minor," which made Florence the first African American woman composer in history to have a symphonic work performed by a major American orchestra. Her music was featured in a program at the 1933–34 Chicago World's Fair, the Century of Progress Exposition.

In 1934 her "Concerto in D Minor" was performed at commencement exercises for the Chicago Musical College. Also, her "Concerto in F Minor" was performed by the Chicago Women's Symphony Orchestra. Her music was played on the radio as well, and she was receiving national notice. At her remarkable concert from the steps of the Lincoln Memorial, Marian Anderson closed the program with one of Florence's songs.

In 1940 the Michigan WPA Symphony premiered Florence's Symphony in C Minor No. 3. First Lady Eleanor Roosevelt was present at the rehearsal and wrote glowingly about it in her newspaper column.

During the war there were fewer opportunities for performance, particularly orchestral performances, but after the war her music was performed in Europe and in the United States.

Throughout her life she was active as a composer and teacher. Many of her songs are arrangements of spirituals or original compositions based on spirituals. *Songs to the Dark Virgin*, based on a text by Langston Hughes, is perhaps her best-known art song.

Her orchestral music includes four symphonies, symphonic dance suites, a rhapsody, and concert overtures. She composed choral works in addition to her art songs and her work with spirituals. Her instrumental compositions include music for chamber groups, for piano, and for organ.

A school in Chicago is named after her.

Here papers are at the University of Arkansas, Fayetteville.

Principal sources: Norton Grove; Florence Price papers, University of Arkansas, Fayetteville.

Ruth Lynda Deyo (April 20, 1884, Poughkeepsie, New York–March 4, 1960, Cairo, Egypt) was a student of William Mason, Teresa Carreño and Edward McDowell. When she was nine she made her debut as a pianist at the World's Columbian Exposition. She first performed in Europe at the age of twenty. In 1915–16 she toured America with Pablo Casals.

She settled in Egypt in 1925. Five years later she composed her opera *The Diadem of Stars*. Stokowski and the Philadelphia Orchestra performed the prelude on April 4, 1931.

Her papers are at Wheaton College in Norton, Massachusetts.

Opera:

The Diadem of Stars, 1930.

Principal source: WON

There can be some name confusion about **Zucca Mana** (December 25, 1885, New York–March 8, 1981, Miami), who grew up as Augusta Zuckermann but in her teens changed her name to Zucca Mana. (Adding to the confusion, her birth year is given variously in different accounts.) In her unpublished memoirs she claimed to have performed with major orchestras in New York before the age of ten; this is not verified, however. In 1902 she did perform as part of a concert series for young people at Carnegie Hall.

About five years later she spent time in Europe; during that period she gave concert tours with the Spanish violinist Juan Manon. She also sang professionally; her most significant performance was in London in *Der Graf von Luxemburg* by Franz Lehár. Her articles describing some of the musicians she met were published in American music magazines.

After her return to the United States in 1915, she began publishing her compositions. In 1921 she married Irwin Cassell and located in Miami.

Her catalog of published works lists about 390; however she claimed to have written and published about 2,200 works in total. She was involved in the American Music Optimists, formed to advance the cause of American music and musicians.

Her compositions include *Hypatica,* a Chinese opera, a violin concerto, piano concerto, piano trio and many songs.

Her papers are at Florida International University and University of Miami.
Operas:

Hypatia, c. 1920.
Queue of Ki-Lu, c. 1920.
Principal source: Norton Grove

Elizabeth Gyring (1886, Vienna–New York, 1970) studied at the Vienna Academy of Music and had her earlier compositions performed in concert and on the radio by members of the Vienna and Berlin Philharmonic Orchestras.

In 1939 she came to the United States. Her works were performed in Carnegie Hall and other venues, and on university series throughout the United States. She became a U.S. citizen in 1944.

She wrote several large-scale works: one opera, several cantatas including *The Reign of Violence Is Over* (1943), based on a poem by Henry Wadsworth Longfellow, and *The Secret of Liberty* (1945), about World War II. In addition she wrote chamber pieces primarily for wind instruments, and solo works for piano and organ.

Her papers are at Washington State University.
Opera:

Night at Sea and Day in Court, opera, 1954.
Principal source: Norton Grove

Caro Roma (September 10, 1869, East Oakland, California–September 23, 1937, East Oakland, California) was enterprising from an early age. (Her real name was Carrie Northly; Caro Roma was her stage name.)

As a child she performed in public. When she was a teenager a French Opera company on tour in Canada retained her as its orchestra conductor.

It was evident she had a great talent for music and performing, and her family sent her to the New England Conservatory when she was young. She matured as a performer and developed her compositional skills. She was also a talented writer and wrote many poems.

After graduating in 1890 she pursued a career as an opera singer, singing with the Castle Square Opera Company in Boston and the Tivoli Opera House in San Francisco, and touring widely through the United States, Canada and Europe. In 1906 she sang with the Turner Grand Opera in London. She also sang in vaudeville.

She moved to Miami in 1919 and joined the faculty at the Florida Conservatory of Music and Art. She was a prolific writer of songs, and more than one thousand of them were published.

Her compositions include sea songs, sacred songs and two song cycles, *The Swan* and *The Wandering One*. Her opera *God of the Sea* was unpublished.

Opera:

God of the Sea, unpublished.

Principal sources: Norton Grove; Cohen

Mildred Couper, born Mildred Cooper (December 10, 1887, Buenos Aires–August 9, 1974, Santa Barbara, California) was one of the first musicians to experiment with quarter-tone music. Like many women of that time she studied internationally: in Karlsruhe, Germany, Paris (where she studied with Nadia Boulanger) and Rome. She was married to American expatriate artist Richard Hamilton Couper and spent her early married life in Rome, Italy. At the start of World War I they fled to New York. Her husband died in the flu epidemic of 1918.

She stayed in New York, teaching piano, until about 1927, when she went to California. There she began experimenting with a quarter-tone piano.

Her first composition in quarter-tone was *Xanadu*, a ballet that was written for a 1930 production of Eugene O'Neill's *Marco Millions*. This was followed by *Dirge* and *Rumba*. She also composed instrumental works and works for orchestra. Her piano works that are not quarter-tone include songs and music for children.

Her papers are at the University of California, Special Collections.

Principal sources: Norton Grove: website of Mildred Couper papers at the University of California Special Collections

Mary Edward Blackwell (1887, Milwaukee–January 7, 1987, Sinsinawa, Wisconsin) began her piano lessons when she was six. After graduating from St. John's Academy in Milwaukee she entered the Sinsinawa order of the

Dominicans and made her profession in 1907, taking the name Mary Edward. She was one of the first sisters to teach music at Rosary College in River Forest, Illinois, when it opened in 1922.

She studied at the American Conservatory in Chicago and took degrees in music and music theory, the first woman and first religious sister to do so. Several of her compositions were published.

The head of the American Conservatory sent some of her manuscripts to Ottorino Respighi in Rome. This led to her receiving the American Scholarship, which entitled her to study orchestration and symphonic composition in Rome for three years. She was in Rome from 1933 to 1936. After Respighi died in 1936, Nadia Boulanger invited Sister Mary Edward to join her studio in Paris. Through Boulanger she met Igor Stravinsky; they developed a lifelong friendship.

She returned to the faculty of Rosary College from 1936 to 1941, then taught at Edgewood College in Madison, Wisconsin, from 1943 to 1950. She kept up her friendship with Nadia Boulanger, and from 1941 until 1944, while Nadia taught at Radcliffe, Harvard, Indiana University, or Stanford during the academic year, she came to Sinsinawa Mound (the mother house of the Sinsinawa Order) each summer to teach music to the Sisters. Nadia and Sister Edward kept up their friendship, writing frequently, until Nadia's death in 1979.

In 1950 Sister Edward returned to Sinsinawa Mound, continuing to teach. In her sixties she traveled extensively, lecturing at high schools.

Principal source: personal research of the Dominican University archives; API (Alliance Publications, Inc.) — web

Lily Teresa Strickland (January 28, 1887, Anderson, South Carolina– June 6, 1958, Hendersonville, North Carolina) was always interested in music from a variety of cultures, and much of her music reflects these various influences. Some of her early pieces show the influence of the black music she heard as a child. Later works reflect her interest in Native American music.

She studied at Converse College from 1901 to 1904. The next year she entered the Institute for Musical Art in New York (the forerunner of Juilliard) on a scholarship. Around 1910 she became very interested in Native American music. *Two Shawnee Indian Dances* (1919) and the operetta *Laughing Star of Zuni* (1946) are among her works that utilize Native American melodies.

In 1912 she married J. Courtney Anderson. From 1920 to 1929 their primary residence was in India, where he was the manager of the Calcutta branch of an American company. Lily traveled throughout Africa and Asia, writing travel articles, and composing and painting.

The music of India had a strong impact on her. She studied the music and wrote articles discussing Indian music and European music. *The Cosmic Dance of Siva* and *Oriental and Character Dances,* both written in the 1930s, reflect her study of Indian music.

After their time in India, she and her husband lived in Woodstock and Great Neck, New York, until 1948, when they retired to Hendersonville.

She was a prolific composer. Her works include several operettas, a cantata *St. John the Beloved* (1930), orchestral suites, and many songs and piano pieces.

Her papers are at Converse College.

Stage works:

Jewel of the Desert, 1930.
Laughing Star of Zuni, operetta, 1946.
Joseph.
Woods of Pan.

Principal sources: New Grove; Norton Grove

Lucile Crews (August 23, 1888, Pueblo, Colorado–date of death not known) studied at the New England Conservatory of Music and the American Conservatory in Chicago, then later in Paris with Nadia Boulanger, and in Berlin.

Her one-act opera won a Pulitzer Traveling Scholarship in 1926, and her *Suite for Strings and Woodwinds* won a prize at the Festival of Allied Arts in Los Angeles. Her compositions also include an opera miniature, piano pieces and chamber works.

Operas and stage works:

The Call of Jeanne d'Arc, 1923.
Eight Hundred Rubies, grand opera in one act, 1926.
Ariadne and Dionysius, NBC Music Guild, 1935.
The Concert, 1959.

Principal source: WON

Immediately after she received her diploma in piano in 1908 from the Cincinnati Conservatory, **Ethel Glenn Hier** (June 25, 1889, Cincinnati, Ohio–January 14, 1971, Winter Park, Florida) established a successful piano studio. She returned to the conservatory for further study in 1911. In the summer of 1912 she went to Germany to study composition for several months, perhaps returning to Cincinnati. In 1917 she moved to New York and opened teaching studios in New York and New Jersey, meanwhile continuing to study composition.

Her first publications in 1912 were teaching pieces for piano, but she soon expanded her output. In 1918 she won the first of fourteen fellowships she received to attend the MacDowell Colony. Her works were included in the Festival of American Women Composers in Washington, DC. That same year she, Amy Beach, Mary Howe, Gena Branscome and others founded the Society of Women Composers. Hier frequently lectured on modern music and other topics.

Her work includes orchestral pieces, chamber works, music for piano, vocal and choral works. She also wrote a play, *The Boyhood and Youth of Edward MacDowell* (1926).

Many of her compositions and materials are at the University of Cincinnati Library.

Principal source: Norton Grove

Kathleen Lockhart Manning (October 24, 1890, Hollywood, California–March 20, 1951, Los Angeles) studied composition in Paris in 1908 then toured France and England for the next five years. During that time she was a singer with the Hammerstein Opera Company in London for the 1911–1912 season. She performed only briefly in the United States in 1926.

She wrote primarily vocal compositions, usually with her own texts. She also wrote several operettas, music for piano and four symphonic poems.

Stage works:

Operetta in Mozartian Style, operetta.
Mr. Wu, operetta.
For the Soul of Rafael, operetta.

Principal source: Norton Grove

Helen Eugenia Hagan (January 10, 1893, Portsmouth, New Hampshire–1964) was organist for her church when she was only nine. She attended the Yale University School of Music, and at her commencement she gave a performance of her own Piano Concerto with the New Haven Symphony Orchestra. She was awarded a Yale fellowship, which enabled her to pursue post-graduate studies with Vincent d'Indy and Blanche Selva at the Schola Cantorum in Paris, from which she graduated with honors.

From 1914 to 1918 she toured as a concert pianist. After her return she became head of the music department at the George Peabody College for Teachers. In 1921 she was the first black woman to give a solo concert recital in a New York concert hall.

Her work includes a one-movement concerto, piano pieces, and a violin sonata. Many of her works are lost.

Principal source: Norton Grove

Eva Jessye (January 20, 1895, Coffeyville, Kansas–February 21, 1992, Ann Arbor, Michigan) often lived with relatives during her childhood. She first lived with her grandmothers and aunts. Her parents had separated, and her mother had moved to Seattle. Much of her early appreciation for music came from hearing her great aunt, who had a lovely rich voice, sing spirituals.

She went to Seattle to live with her mother when she was seven. A railroad porter gave her poetry magazines to read on the long trip. This gave her a love for poetry, and she soon was writing her own. At some point she also lived for a while with an aunt in St. Louis.

She was only thirteen when her mother sent her to Western University in Quindaro in Kansas City, Kansas. Because African Americans could not attend public schools in Coffeyville, the university ignored the minimum enrollment age and admitted her a year earlier than normal. She studied music theory and choral music and earned her degree later the same year. She then earned a life certificate in teaching at Langston University.

In 1914, Jessye entered the James A. Handy Literary Society contest. Her poem, "Negroes Are Bound to Rise," won first prize in original poetry.

She taught for several years, then in 1926 she moved to New York to pursue a career in music and theater. Her first break was playing with Major Bowes at the Capitol Theater (later of "Original Amateur Hour" fame).

She began the Original Dixie Jubilee Singers, which later became the Eva Jessye Choir. The choir performed at universities and colleges for more than forty years. She was the choral director for the premier of *Porgy and Bess* and Thomson's *Four Saints in Three Acts*.

In 1963 she directed the official choir for the historic March on Washington. She was an Artist-in-Residence at Pittsburg State University, in Pittsburg, Kansas, in 1979, and remained in Pittsburg until 1981.

In 1987, at age ninety-two, she received an honorary Doctorate of Art from Eastern Michigan University.

Her works include *Paradise Lost and Regained,* a folk oratorio (1934), *The Chronicle of Job* (1936) and folk dramas.

She established the Eva Jessye Collection of Afro-American Music at the University of Michigan in Ann Arbor in 1974. The Eva Jessye Collection, which holds much biographical material, was established at Pittsburg State University in Kansas in 1977. Other materials are at the Atlanta University Center.

She apparently had begun writing her autobiography but had not completed it when she died.

Principal sources: Peter Seidman, "Eva Jessye," *The Black Perspective in Music,* vol. 18, nos. 1–2, pp. 258–263; Norton Grove

Marjorie Eastwood Dudley (November 6, 1891–June 13, 1963) earned advanced degrees and certificates in music and had a rich composing career, in spite of having contracted polio at a young age, which left her handicapped.

She earned the Mus.B. degree in piano from Northwestern University in Evanston, Illinois, two Masters degrees in composing from Chicago Musical College, and a Mus.D. in composition from the University of Toronto. From 1920 to 1956 she was professor of music at the University of South Dakota.

Her compositions include symphonies, string quartets, a piano concerto and many piano pieces.

The Marjorie Eastwood Dudley collection is at the National Music Museum at the University of South Dakota in Vermilion, South Dakota.

Principal source: WON

Frances McCollin (October 24, 1892, Philadelphia–1960), who became blind at an early age, was educated at the Pennsylvania Institute for the Blind at Overbrook and Miss Wright's School, Bryn Mawr. Her compositions were transcribed by Vincent Persichetti and others.

Many of her works were performed with major orchestras, including the Philadelphia Orchestra, the Warsaw Philharmonic, and the Indianapolis Symphony. She won nineteen national awards, including ten awards for her choral works.

Her various compositions include music for orchestra, chamber ensembles, choral pieces, and solo works for organ, piano, and violin.

Biography:

Frances McCollin: Her Life and Music, by Annette Maria DiMedio (Metuchen, N.J.: Scarecrow Press, 1990).

Principal source: WON

Catherine Murphy Urner (March 23, 1891, Mitchell, Indiana–April 30, 1942, San Diego), a student at the University of California, Berkeley, was the first winner of the George Ladd Prix de Paris, which allowed her to go to Paris in 1920 to study composition with Charles Koechlin for a year. He and his music had a substantial impact on her career and her music; likewise, he considered her to be an influence on his music.

She was a talented singer as well as a composer. When she returned to the United States in 1921 she was appointed director of vocal music at Mills College in Oakland, California, a position she held for the next three years. She and Koechlin collaborated on several works, and in 1929 he orchestrated her *Esquisses normands*. She translated Koechlin's treatises and arranged for him to lecture in California.

She was known as a composer and singer in France and Italy as well as in the United States, and many of her works premiered in Paris at the Société Musicale Independante and at the Salle Pleyel. She was particularly interested in Native American melodies and often used them in her compositions.

Her compositions include music for chorus and orchestra, choral works, songs for soprano and piano, and music for chamber and solo instruments.

She was married to the organist Charles Shatto.

Her papers are at the Music Library of the University of California, Berkeley. Charles Shatto's papers, as well as some Koechlin material, are also in the Music Library archives.

Biographical works:

Catherine Urner (1891–1942) and Charles Koechlin (1867–1950): A Musical Affaire, by Barbara Urner Johnson (Burlington, VT: Ashgate, 2003).

Principal sources: Norton Grove; New Grove

Uruguay

Carmen Barradas (March 18, 1888, Montevideo–May 12, 1963, Montevideo) began composing while still very young. Her early education included studies at the Conservatorio Musical la Lira. In 1914 she settled in Spain.

She developed a new system of musical notation that she used in her compositions; Spanish and French musicians and critics didn't approve or utilize her system. Ironically the graphic designs on which her notations are based came into use fifty years later. Using her system she composed *Faricación,* a piano work. That, along with *Asserradero* and *Taller mecánico*, positioned her as a pioneer in modern music.

Following her return to Montevideo about 1928, she taught choral singing at the Normal Institute and continued her composing.

Her later compositions include piano pieces and children's songs.

Principal source: Norton Grove

Opera Timeline

Opera could have begun as it did only in Renaissance Italy. Certainly, as a logical next step from such forms as pageants, masques, and religious dramas, it could have emerged in any number of locations in Europe, but its beginnings would have been of a far different nature.

One of the overriding characteristics of the Renaissance was inquiry — into the glories of the past, the nature of art, aspects of the individual and individual achievement, and science. There was a unique blend of, sometimes tension between, values of the past and the newness of the present. Renaissance Italy had the prosperity and economic resources to support intellectual, artistic, and philosophical pursuits. And one such pursuit was the re-creation of Greek music as an element of ancient Greek drama.

The fact that no one knew what ancient Greek music sounded like was a stumbling block, to be sure, as only the merest fragment survived. But examination of texts and rational consideration could surely determine much about what had been the nature of the combination of drama and music in ancient Greece. And so it did.

Music was changing, with more solo singing and polyphony — where independent lines of music combined to create a harmonic effect — creeping into accompaniment. Some feared that music was in danger of taking over the words. This new music demanded a theory, which in turn demanded examination and attention as well to the application of the theory. "The Camerata," a small group of composers, poets, scholars and amateurs of the arts similar to an academy, undertook the task. Several members, including Vincenzo Galilei, father of the astronomer Galileo, published on the theory of the "new music."

They determined that ancient Greek music had been a perfect union of words and melody. Furthermore, words were dominant and music subordinate. Clearly, what was needed was a solo voice with very simple accompaniment. The words had to be sung naturally, as they would have been spoken, and the melody had to follow the natural speaking. So it was, and in general Italian music ever since has tended to avoid complexity and obscurity, with melody of prime importance.

In the mid–1590s (sources vary on the precise year), *Dafne*, which is widely considered to be the first opera, was performed. The music was by Jacopo Peri and the text was by Ottavio Rinuccini.

And so opera began, and eventually gave rise to what Grout characterizes as its "stepchildren." These offshoots are generally of a humbler nature: less formal and less expensive to produce. Such offshoots include "*opera buffa, opéra comique,* ballad opera, 'intermezzo,' comic opera, vaudeville, operetta, musical comedy and so on." Grout goes on to say, "So far as artistic merit goes they may be equal or even superior to the more pretentious form and must certainly be considered along with it in any historical treatment" (pp. 5–6).

For decades Italy was *the* unparalleled tourist destination in Europe. People from all over Europe made long stays in Italy, as one did in those days, absorbing the art, intellectual discourse and debate, literature, the sunshine and outdoor life, the food and the wine. They also attended the opera and took home stories of the wonderful new entertainment and the life of opera-going.

The intellectual basis of the development of opera might make the performances sound dreary with their restrictions on form, particularly with respect to harmony and choruses. But the development of opera was not static, and the early considerations of what opera ought — and ought not to be — apparently hadn't considered staging.

John Evelyn records his experience at the opera in 1645: "This night ... we went to the Opera, where comedies and other plays are represented in recitative music, by the most excellent musicians, vocal and instrumental, with variety of scenes painted and contrive with no less art of perspective, and machines for flying in the air, and other wonderful notions; taken together it is one of the most magnificent and expensive diversions the wit of man can invent ... the scenes changed thirteen times" (*Diary of John Evelyn*, vol. 1, p. 202).

Moreover, the opera was a place to see and be seen, to socialize, eat and drink, to play cards. Opera became an amusement and a social setting. Several years later, De Brosses would recommend chess for "filling in the monotony of the recitatives" (Grout, p. 198, quoting from Charles de Brosses's *Lettres familieres sur l'Italie* [Paris: Firmin-Didot, 1931]).

Opera follows fashions and can become outdated, perhaps more quickly than most forms of music. In recent years there has been some interest in historic operas, for their music, their historic interest, and their ease of staging. They lend themselves to simple (or minimum) staging. They may be of historic interest. Many contain very good music, although often written in a less complex style than the operas that typically fill the repertoire.

While changes in opera parallel changes in music to some extent, opera has its own rich history. Women composers were part of that history.

The question of "What is an opera?" or more specifically, "Can you talk?" has persisted almost since the genre came into being. Certainly a work that is entirely spoken is not an opera, and a work that is entirely sung is an opera. Between these two bookends there are varying degrees of spoken versus sung text. Classifications are ambiguous and how works are classified tends to be inconsistent.

The time frame is a factor as well. What may have been considered an opera two hundred years ago may not be regarded as an opera today. The questions surrounding the variety of styles, formats and configurations of these works are interesting, but they are not for us to consider here.

In addition to inconsistencies in the sources reflecting the ongoing question "What is an opera?" sources differ on dates of composition and performance dates. Some sources list both if known, or one, or the other, not necessarily distinguishing them. In some cases this probably accounts for a composer's seemingly prodigious output in one year.

It's worth noting that the timeline — being a timeline — includes only operas and stage works that are dated. The preceding text includes many more operas and stage works that do not have dates associated with them, and thus those particular works are not included. Also, obviously, these are only the works that are known. Many, many more probably existed.

One: The Renaissance Transition, 1550–1600

This was a time of much discussion, contemplation, and working out of the "new music" that would become opera. *Dafne*, which is widely considered to be the first opera, was performed in the mid–1590s. The music was by Jacopo Peri and the text was by Ottavio Rinuccini.

Two: The Age of Harmony, 1600–1685

1625   *La liberazione di Ruggiero dall'isola d'Alcina*, musical comedy, Francesca Caccini, Villa Poggio Imperiale, Florence.

Three: The Baroque Era, 1685–1750

1694   *Céphale et Procris*, Elisabeth Claude Jacquet de la Guerre, Paris Opéra.
1707   *Ercole amante*, Antonia Bembo.
1736   *Les Genies, ou Les caractères de l'Amour*, Mlle. Duval, Paris Opéra, Paris.
1740   *Argenore*, Wilhelmina, Princess of Prussia, Margräfin of Bayreuth.

Four: Early Classical, 1750–1800

1753   *Ciro in Armenia*, Maria Teresa d'Agnesi, Regio Ducal Teatro, Milan.
1754   *Frederick II*, Maria Antonia Walpurgis.
         Il trionfo della fedelta, Maria Antonia Walpurgis.
1755   *Daphnis et Amanthée*, Amiens, Helene Guerin.
1756   *Il re pastore*, Maria Teresa d'Agnesi.
1760   *Talestri, regina delle amazoni*, Maria Antonia Walpurgis.
1765   *La sofonisba*, Maria Teresa d'Agnesi, Naples.
1766   *L'insubria consolata*, Maria Teresa d'Agnesi, Regio Ducal Teatro, Milan.
1767   Title unknown, Opéra-comique, Marie-Emmanuelle Bayon-Louis, Salon of Mme. de Genlis.
c. 1771 *Julien et Juliette*, Sophie (de) Charrière.
1771   *Nitocri*, Maria Teresa d'Agnesi, Venice.
1772   *L'Isola Disabitata*, Maria Rosa Coccia.
1776   *Erwin und Elmire*, Anna Amalia, Duchess of Saxe-Weimar, operetta. She may have written the vocal score only.
1780   *The Silver Tankard*, opera, Elizabeth Craven.
1781   *Fleur d'épine*, Marie-Emmanuelle Bayon-Louis, Paris.
         Anacréon, Henriette Adelaide Villard de Beaumesnil.
1784   *Tibulle et Délie, ou Les Saturnales*, Henriette Adelaide Villard de Beaumesnil.
         Le fêtes greques et romaines, Paris Opéra, Henriette Adelaide Villard de Beaumesnil.

1786   *Le Cyclope*, Isabella Charrière, never performed.
        Le mariage d'Antonio, Lucile Grétry.
        L'heureuse erreur, Caroline Wuiet, Paris; her libretto, rehearsed with orchestra at the Comédie-Italienne but not voted for public performance.
        Lucette et Lucas, Florine Dézedé, Paris.
1787   *Toinette et Louis*, two acts, Lucile Grétry.
1788   *Les Phéniciennes*, Isabella Charrière, never performed.
        Title unknown, divertissement, Josephine-Rosalie-Pauline Walckiers, Théâtre de Schaerbeek.
1789   *La folie, ou Quel conte!*, Countess Maria Theresia Ahlefeldt, Anspach.
1790   *Polyphème ou le Cyclope*, Isabella Charrière, never performed.
        Junon, Isabella Charrière, never performed.
        L'Olimpiade, Isabella Charrière, never performed.
        Les Femmes, Isabella Charrière, never performed.
1791   *Ariadne und Bacchus*, opera, Maria Theresa von Paradis, her libretto.
        Zadig, Isabella Charrière, never performed.
1792   *Zwei Landliche Opern*, opera, Maria Theresa von Paradis.
        La repetition villageoise, opera, Josephine-Rosalie-Pauline Walckiers, Théâtre de Schaerbeek.
        Title unknown, Isabella Charrière, never performed.
        Catherine or la belle fermière Emilie (Amélie) Julie Candeille-Simon.
        Les Lêgislatrices, Henriette Adelaide Villard de Beaumesnil.
        Plaire, c'est commander ou le lêgislatrices, Henriette Adelaide Villard de Beaumesnil.
        Telemak på Calypsos Øe or *Telemachus and Calypso*, opera ballet, Countess Maria Theresia Ahlefeldt, Copenhagen Royal Theatre.
        Der Schulkandidat, an operetta or mourning cantata, Maria Theresa von Paradis, Vienna.
1793   *Bathilde, ou Le duc*, Emilie (Amélie) Julie Candeille-Simon.
1794   *Le commissionaire*, comédie, Emilie (Amélie) Julie Candeille-Simon, Paris, Théâtre de la Egalités.
        The Princess of Georgia, opera, Elizabeth Craven, Covent Garden.
        La jeune hôtesse, Emilie (Amélie) Julie Candeille-Simon.
1795   *La bayadère, ou Le Français à surate*, Emilie (Amélie) Julie Candeille-Simon.
c. 1795 *S. Sonnischen*, Countess Maria Theresia Ahlefeldt.
1797   *Rinaldo und Alcina*, opera, Maria Theresa von Paradis, Prague.

Five: The Beethoven Watershed, 1800–1840

1800   *Praxitèle, ou La ceinture*, opera, Jeanne-Hippolyte Devismes, Paris.
1805   *La Méprise volontaire, ou La double leçon*, operetta, Mlle. Le Senechal de Kercado, Opéra-Comique, Paris.
1805?   *Grosse militarische*, opera, Maria Theresa von Paradis.
1807   *Ida, ou L'orphelie de Berlin*, Emilie (Amélie) Julie Candeille-Simon.
1808   *Louise, ou La réconciliation*, Emilie (Amélie) Julie Candeille-Simon.
1811   *Léon, ou Le château de Montaldi*, melodrama, Alexandrine Sophie Bawr, Théâtre de L'Ambigu-Comique, Paris.
1813   *Les deux jaloux*, Sophie Gail.
        Mademoiselle de Launay à la Bastille, Sophie Gail.
1814   *Angéla, ou L'atelier de Jean Cousin*, Sophie Gail.
        La méprise, Sophie Gail.

1816	*Una donna*, Marie Frederike Auguste Amalie, Princess of Saxony.
	Le nozze funeste, Marie Frederike Auguste Amalie, Princess of Saxony.
	Le tre cincture, Marie Frederike Auguste Amalie, Princess of Saxony.
1817	*Il prigioniere*, Marie Frederike Auguste Amalie, Princess of Saxony.
1818	*La sérénade*, Sophie Gail.
1819	*A l'honneur de Nancy*, operetta, Marie Frederike Auguste Amalie, Princess of Saxony.
1820	*L'Americana*, Marie Frederike Auguste Amalie, Princess of Saxony.
1821	*Elvira*, Marie Frederike Auguste Amalie, Princess of Saxony, Dresden.
1822	*Elena e Gerardo*, opera, Marianna Bottini, unperformed.
1823	*Otto der Schutz*, Johanna Mockel Kinkel.
	Elisa ed Ernesto, Marie Frederike Auguste Amalie, Princess of Saxony.
1825	*Guy Mannering*, Louise Angelique Bertin, Bievres.
1826	*La fedelta alla prova*, Marie Frederike Auguste Amalie, Princess of Saxony.
1827	*Le avventure di una giornata*, melodrama, Adelaide Orsola Appignani, Rome, Teatro Valle.
	Le loup-garou, opera, Louise Angelique Bertin, Opéra Comique, Paris.
1828	*Vecchiezza e gioventu*, Marie Frederike Auguste Amalie, Princess of Saxony.
	Der Kanonenschuss, Marie Frederike Auguste Amalie, Princess of Saxony.
1830	*Saul*, Carolina Pazzini Uccelli, Florence.
	Die Räuber und der Sänger, Leopoldine Blahetka.
1831	*Fausto*, Louise Angelique Bertin, Théatre Italien, Paris.
	Il figlio pentito or *Il figlio perduto*, Marie Frederike Auguste Amalie, Princess of Saxony.
1832	*Anna (Emma) di Resburgo*, Carolina Pazzini Uccelli, Naples.
1833	*Il marchesino*, Marie Frederike Auguste Amalie, Princess of Saxony.
	Eufemio da Messina (overture only performed), Carolina Pazzini Uccelli, Milan.
1834	*I riti indiani*, Adelaide Orsola Appignani, not performed.
	Die Siegesfahne, Marie Frederike Auguste Amalie, Princess of Saxony.
1835	*La casa disabitata*, Marie Frederike Auguste Amalie, Princess of Saxony.
	Agnes Sorel, Mary Anne A'Beckett, John Braham's St. James's Theatre, London.
	Francesca da Rimini, Adelaide Orsola Appignani, not performed.
1836	*Le Mauvais oeil*, operetta, Louise Puget, Opéra Comique, Paris.
	La Esmeralda, Louise Angelique Bertin, Paris Opéra, Paris.

Six: Romanticism, 1840–1880

1842	*Little Red Riding Hood*, London, Mary Anne A'Beckett, Surrey Gardens Theatre, London. She declined the invitations to conduct the operas herself.
1843	*I pirati*, Melodrama, Adelaide Orsola Appignani. Rome, Teatro Alibert.
1848	*Die Palastdame*, Caroline Wisender.
1849	*Das Jubelfest* or *Die Drei Gefangenen*, Caroline Wisender.
	Haydée (after Dumas' *Count of Monte Cristo*), Felicita Cassella, Oporto.
c. 1850	*L'elisir d'amore*, Kate Loder.
1857	*La pomme de Turquie*, operetta, Pauline-Marie-Elisa Thys.
	Ugo, Teatro di s Radegonda, Carlotta Ferrari, Milan.
1858	*L'Heriter sans le savior*, operetta, Pauline-Marie-Elisa Thys.
1859	*Le sou de Lise*, operetta, Marie (Felice Clemence) de Reiset Grandval, Paris.
1860	*Dieu le garde*, operetta, Pauline-Marie-Elisa Thys.
1860	*Lost and Found*, operetta, Mary Ann Virginia Gabriel.
1861	*La Perruque du Bailli*, operetta, Pauline-Marie-Elisa Thys.

1862	*Le pays de cocagne*, two acts, operetta, Pauline-Marie-Elisa Thys.
	La Veille, operetta, Charlotte Jacques.
1863	*Les fiancés de Rosa*, opéra comique, Marie (Felice Clemence) de Reiset Grandval, Paris.
	Il Mugnaio di Marlenac, Marie (Felice Clemence) de Reiset Grandval.
1864	*La comtesse Eva*, opéra comique, Marie (Felice Clemence) de Reiset Grandval, Baden-Baden.
	L'Image, Helene Santa Colona-Sourget, Paris.
	The Shepard of Cournouailles, operetta, Mary Ann Virginia Gabriel.
1865	*Manette*, two acts, operetta, Pauline-Marie-Elisa Thys.
	Cristoforo Colombo, Felicita Casella, Nice.
	Widows Bewitched, operetta, Mary Ann Virginia Gabriel.
	Rüdesheim, or Gisela, Alice Mary White Smith.
1866	*Sofia*, lyrical drama, Carlotta Ferrari, Lodi.
	Le sorcier, operetta, Anais, Comtesse de Perriere-Pilt, Paris.
1867	*Trop de femmes*, operetta, Pauline Michelle Ferdinande Viardot-Garcia.
	Die Göttin von Sais, oder Linas und *Liane*, idyllische opera, Ingeborg von Bronsart, Kronprinzliches Palais, Berlin.
	Les vacances de l'Amour, comic opera, privately produced, Anais, Comtesse de Perriere-Pilt, Paris.
1868	*Donna Maria Infanta de Spagna*, Marie (Felice Clemence) de Reiset Grandval.
	La pénitente, opéra comique, Marie (Felice Clemence) de Reiset Grandval, Opéra-Comique, Paris.
	L'ogre, operetta, Pauline Michelle Ferdinande Viardot-Garcia.
1868?	*Cendrillon*, opera, Pauline Michelle Ferdinande Viardot-Garcia.
1869	*La veilleuse, ou Les nuits de milady*, operetta, Louise Puget, Théâtre du Gymnase, Paris.
	Piccolino, Marie (Felice Clemence) de Reiset Grandval, Théâtre Italien, Paris.
	Le dernier sorcier (Der letzte Zauberer), operetta, Pauline Michelle Ferdinande Viardot-Garcia.
1870	*La Dryade*, privately produced, Anais, Comtesse de Perriere-Pilt, Paris.
c. 1870	*Cleopatre*, Mme. la Baronne Maistre.
	Les Roussalkas, opera, Mme. la Baronne Maistre, Brussels.
	Sardanapale, Mme. la Baronne Maistre.
	Who's the Heir? operetta, Mary Ann Virginia Gabriel.
1871	*Eleonora d'Arborea*, lyrical drama, Carlotta Ferrari, Cagliari.
1873	*Jaloux de soi*, operetta, Anais, Comtesse de Perriere-Pilt, Paris.
	Doch' Boyarina ("The Boyar's Daughter"), Ella Georgiyevna Adayevskaya [var. spellings].
	Jery und Bätely operetta, Ingeborg von Bronsart, Weimar.
	Grass Widows, operetta, Mary Ann Virginia Gabriel.
1874	*Sous le masque*, Gabriella Ferrari.
	Flor de los cielos, zarzuela, Soledad Bengoecha de Carmena, Madrid.
	El gran día, zarzuela, Soledad Bengoecha de Carmena, Madrid.
1875	*Héro et Léander*, unperformed, Augusta Holmes.
	Le talon d'Achille, operetta, Anais, Comtesse de Perriere-Pilt.
	Salli Ventadour, Marie (Felice Clemence) de Reiset Grandval.
	La forêt, poème lyrique, Marie (Felice Clemence) de Reiset Grandval, Paris.
	Graziella, operetta, Mary Ann Virginia Gabriel.
1876	*A la fuerza ahorcan*, zarzuela, Soledad Bengoecha de Carmena, Madrid.

Le marriage de Taharin, ou La congiura di Chevreuse, operetta, Pauline-Marie-Elisa Thys, Florence.

Clara di Clevers, melodrama, Adelaide Orsola Appignani, Bologna, Teatro Nationale.

1877   *Fleurette*, two acts, operetta, Emma Roberta Steiner, San Francisco.

Suocera, Florence Marian Skinner.

Zarya Svobodi ("The Dawn of Freedom"), Ella Georgiyevna Adayevskaya [various spellings].

1878   *Le cabaret du pot-casse*, operetta, Pauline-Marie-Elisa Thys.

1879   *Le conte de fêtes*, opéra comique, Pauline Michelle Ferdinande Viardot-Garcia.

The Masked Shepherd, operetta, Florence Ashton Marshall.

Lindoro comic opera, Louise Pauline Viardot Heritte, Weimar.

Seven: Early Impressionism and Romanticism, 1880–1900

1880s   *Marie d'Orval*, Valentina Semenova Bergmann Serova.

c. 1880   *Lancelot du Lac*, Augusta Holmes.

Schiava e regina, Luisa Casagemas.

Nedgeya, operetta, Pauline-Marie-Elisa Thys, Naples.

1881   *L'education d'Achille*, operetta, Pauline-Marie-Elisa Thys.

La congiura di chevreuse, opera, Pauline-Marie-Elisa Thys.

Sais, opera, Marguerite Olagnier.

1882   *Le Prince Noir*, operetta, Eva Dell'Acqua.

La Sevillane, opéra comique, Cécile Louise-Stéphanie Chaminade.

1883   *Maria Regina di Scozia*, Florence Marian Skinner.

1884   *Zuch dziewczyna* (The Brave Girl), operetta, Ludmila Jeske-Choinska-Mikorska, Warsaw.

Le Tresor de l'Emir, operetta, Eva Dell'Acqua.

1885   *Priscilla*, Harriet Ware.

Uriel Acosta 1885, Valentina Semenova Bergmann Serova, Bolshoi, Moscow.

The Uhlans, Christina W. Morison, Dublin.

Don Juan de Marana, Tekla Griebel Wandall.

A cortena roça, Francisca Edwiges Neves Gonzaga.

1887   *Le roi jaune*, operetta, Pauline-Marie-Elisa Thys.

1888   *Le Feude Paille*, operetta, Eva Dell'Acqua.

Les Fiancailles de Pasquin, operetta, Eva Dell'Acqua.

Une Passion, operetta, Eva Dell'Acqua.

Le secret de l'Alcade, operetta, Eva Dell'Acqua.

c. 1888   *Atala*, poème lyrique, Marie (Felice Clemence) de Reiset Grandval.

Hadumoth, Louise Adolfa Le Beau.

Carina, Sophia Julia Woolf, Opéra Comique, London.

1889   *I Firenze*, opéra comique, Helena Munktell, Paris.

L'Oeillet Blanc, operetta, Eva Dell'Acqua.

Le menuet de l'impératrice, comic opera, Hedwige (Gennaro) Chrétien.

Dovetta, Emma Marcy Raymond, New York.

1890   *Prinzessin Lisa's Fee*, children's operetta, Marie Wurm, Lübeck, Stadttheater.

La vision de Jeanne d'Arc, Mlle. Gignoux.

1891   *Hiarne*, Ingeborg von Bronsart, Berlin.

I Quattro Rustici, Adolfa Galloni.

Nephta, Mary Rosselli-Nissim.

Guidetta, three acts, operetta, Pauline-Marie-Elisa Thys.

1892   *Markiz de Créqui* (Marquise de Cresqui), operetta, Ludmila Jeske-Choinska-
        Mikorska, Warsaw.
        Atala, opera, Eugenie-Emelie Juliette Folville, Lille.
1894   *The Oracle*, operetta, Mary Carr Moore, San Francisco.
        Skøn Karen, opera, Tekla Griebel Wandall.
        Khai Dievka (The Brandy Drinker), Valentina Semenova Bergmann Serova,
        Moscow.
        Atala, Gisella Delle Grazie, Turin.
        Day Dreams, Emma Roberta Steiner, operetta.
        Brigands, Emma Roberta Steiner, operetta.
1895   *La Montagne noire*, Augusta Holmes, Paris.
        La trecciaiuola di Firenze, Gisella Delle Grazie, Trieste.
        Le dernier amour, opéra comique, Gabrielle Ferrari.
1896   *La Bachelette*, operetta, Eva Dell'Acqua, Brussels.
        Il Passaporto del Droghiere or *Passaporto*, opera, Gisella Delle Grazie.
        Le tartare, tableau musical, Gabrielle Ferrari.
        L'âme en peine, Gabrielle Ferrari.
1897   *Prince Sprite*, fairy operetta, Florence Ashton Marshall.
1898   *Dal sogno alla vita*, melodrama, Virginia Mariani Campolieti.
        The Snow Queen or The Frozen Heart, operetta, Mary Grant Carmichael.
        Last Summer, operetta, Edith Rowena Noyes.
        The Babes in the Woods, Mary Louise White.
        Max, Mary Rosselli-Nissim.
        Fantasio, opera, Dame Ethel Mary Smyth, Weimar.
1899   *Fritofs saga*, Elfrida Andrée, libretto by Selma Lagerlöf, unperformed.
        Mazeppa, Marie (Felice Clemence) de Reiset Grandval, Bordeaux.
        Il'ya Muromets, Valentina Semenova Bergmann Serova, Moscow.

Eight: Into the Twentieth Century

1900   *Tambour Battant*, operetta, Eva Dell'Acqua, Brussels.
        The Man from Paris, Emma Roberta Steiner, operetta.
        The Court of Hearts, operetta, Mabel Wheeler Daniels.
        A Copper Complication, operetta, Mabel Wheeler Daniels.
1901   *Der verzauberte Kalif*, fantasy opera, Louise Adolfa Le Beau.
        The Legend of Marietta, operetta, Mabel Wheeler Daniels.
1902   *Der Wald*, opera, Dame Ethel Mary Smyth, Berlin.
        Alice in Wonderland Continued, opera sketch, Mabel Wheeler Daniels.
1903   *Une Ruse de Pierette*, operetta, Eva Dell'Acqua.
        La terre bonne, also known as *The Land of the Maple Leaf*, opera, Anne Catherine
        Roberta Geddes-Harvey, Royal Opera House, Guelph.
1904   *Sergeant Brue*, operetta, Liza Elizabeth Nina Mary Frederica Lehmann, London.
        Petit Lunch, operetta, Hedwige (Gennaro) Chrétien, Paris.
1904–05 *Vstrepenulis*, Valentina Semenova Bergmann Serova.
1905   *The House of Shadows*, Louisa Emily Lomax.
1906   *Ave Maria*, Emilia Gubitosi, Naples.
        Ziti, operetta, Eva Dell'Acqua.
        The Wreckers, opera, Dame Ethel Mary Smyth, Leipzig. French, then German.
        Concert version 1908. English translation produced London in 1909.
        The Vicar of Wakefield, romantic light opera, Liza Elizabeth Nina Mary Fred-
        erica Lehmann, Manchester.

	The Wolf, Louisa Emily Lomax.
1907	*The Burra Pundit,* Emma Roberta Steiner, operetta.
	Der Heilige Gral, Mathilde Kralik von Mayerswalden.
	The Brownie and the Piano-tuner, Louisa Emily Lomax.
1909	*Antinoos,* Irma von Halácsy, never performed in a complete form.
	Le Cobzar, lyrical drama, Gabrielle Ferrari, Monte Carlo.
	Narcissa, or The Cost of Empire, opera, Mary Carr Moore, Seattle.
	Die Sühne, Ingeborg von Bronsart, Dessau Hoftheater.
c. 1910	*Ekkehard,* Melbourne, opera, Florence Maud Ewart, Queen's Hall.
1910	*Das Gelöbnis,* music drama, Cornélie van Oosterzee.
	Der Talisman, Adela Maddison.
	Nada Delvig, Emilia Gubitosi.
1911	*La cinquantaine,* comic opera, Hedwige (Gennaro) Chrétien, Paris.
	The Portrait, Dora Estelle Bright.
	For the Queen, musical drama, Mary Frances Allitsen.
	The Woodland Princess, Anice Potter Terhune
1912	*La Princesse Maleine,* Lili Boulanger.
	The Leper, one act, Mary Carr Moore.
	Bindra the Minstrel, romantic opera, Mary Frances Allitsen, published but not performed.
1913	*To apokriatiko oneiro* ("A Dream in Carnival"), Eleni Lambiri.
	Agnete og Havmanden, Hilda Sehested.
	The Boatswain's Mate, comedy, Dame Ethel Mary Smyth, London.
1914	*Nero,* Anice Potter Terhune.
1915	*Diana cazadora,* Maria Rodrigo, Madrid.
	Fiamme, Mary Rosselli-Nissim.
	Becqueriana, opera, Maria Rodrigo, Madrid.
	Everyman, Liza Elizabeth Nina Mary Frederica Lehmann, London.
	Isolma (her libretto), Eleni Lambiri, Milan (said to have been staged).
	Incantesimo, operetta, Vincenza Garelli della Morea, Countess de Cardenas, Teatro Garibaldi, Padua.
1916	*Il viaggio dei Perrichon,* operetta, Teatro Alfieri, Vincenza Garelli della Morea, Countess de Cardenas, Turin.
	Petruccio e il cavalo cappuccino, children's operetta, Elisabetta Oddone Sulli-Rao, Milan.
1917	*Osseok,* Edith Rowena Noyes.
	Waushakum, pageant opera, Edith Rowena Noyes.
	Harmony, operetta, Mary Carr Moore, San Francisco.
	The Snow Queen, Abbie Gerrish-Jones.
1918	*Rose of Destiny,* Celeste de Longpré Heckscher, Philadelphia.
	Pierrot Menteur, operetta, Eva Dell'Acqua.
1919	*The Flaming Arrow, or The shaft of Ku'pish-ta-ya,* operetta, Mary Carr Moore, San Francisco.
1920s	*Ippolita in the Hills,* Adela Maddison.
1920	*A gara colle rondini,* Elisabetta Oddone Sulli-Rao, Milan.
	The Children of Lir, Adela Maddison.
	La capanna ardente, Elisabetta Oddone Sulli-Rao.
c. 1920	*Hypatia,* Zucca Mana [Augusta Zuckerman].
	Queue of Ki-Lu, Zucca Mana [Augusta Zuckerman].
	Fior di neve, fairy opera, Elsa Olivieri Sangiacomo Resphigi.
1921	*Die Mitschuldigen,* opera, Marie Wurm, Leipzig, Stadttheater.

La romeria del rocio, zarzuela, Maria Rodrigo, Barcelona.

Abbé Mouret, Irma von Halácsy, never performed in a complete form.

c. 1922 *Tlass Atka* (Le pays blanc), Marguerite Canal, orchestration unfinished.

1922 *Der Puppenspieler*, Irma von Halácsy, never performed in a complete form.

The Legend of the Piper, Eleanor Everest Freer.

Fête galante, opera, Dame Ethel Mary Smyth, London.

1923 *Undine*, opera, Harriet Ware.

Rusalochka [*The Little Mermaid*], Yuliya Lazarevna Veysberg.

Herz atout, Irma von Halácsy, never performed in a complete form.

The Call of Jeanne d'Arc, Lucile Crews.

1924 *Le nozze di Leporello*, commedia, Vincenza Garelli della Morea, Countess de Cardenas, Teatro Social, Brescia.

1925 *Cancion de Amor*, zarzuela, Maria Rodrigo.

Paraventa e fuoco, children's operetta, Elisabetta Oddone Sulli-Rao.

Massimilliano, the Court Jester, or the Love of a Caliban, Eleanor Everest Freer.

Entente cordiale, comedy, Dame Ethel Mary Smyth, London.

1926 *Eight Hundred Rubies*, opera, Lucile Crews.

The Chilkoot Maiden, Eleanor Everest Freer.

1927 *Duinsprookje*, children's operetta, Dina Appeldoorn.

La commedia di Pinocchio, children's operetta, Elisabetta Oddone Sulli-Rao.

David Rizzio, Mary Carr Moore, Los Angeles.

Die pfingstkrone, Berta Bock, performed in Cleveland in 1931.

1928 *A Christmas Tale*, Eleanor Everest Freer.

The Masque of Pandora, Eleanor Everest Freer.

Preciosa, or The Spanish Student, Eleanor Everest Freer.

1929 *Legende provençale*, Mary Carr Moore.

Frithiof, Eleanor Everest Freer.

Joan of Arc, Eleanor Everest Freer.

1930 *Zoulaina*, opéra comique, Germaine Tailleferre, Opéra Comique, Paris.

The Diadem of Stars, Ruth Lynda Deyo.

The Courtship of Miles Standish, opera, Florence Maud Ewart, concert performance.

1931 *Andrea del Sarto*, Mary Rosselli-Nissim.

Los rubios, Mary Carr Moore, Los Angeles.

A Legend of Spain, Eleanor Everest Freer.

1932 *Cabildo*, Amy Marcy Cheney Beach, chamber opera, unperformed until 1945, Athens, Georgia.

Flutes of Jade Happiness, operetta, Mary Carr Moore, Los Angeles.

The Rose and the Ring, Ethel Leginska ["Ethel Liggins"], Los Angeles.

Their Last War, Clara Anna Korn, Boston.

1933 *Maria*, Francisca Edwiges Neves Chiquinha Gonzaga.

Jewel of the Desert, operetta, Lily Teresa Strickland.

Mateo Falconé, opera, Florence Maud Ewart, unperformed.

Nala's Wooing, opera, Florence Maud Ewart, unperformed.

1934 *Little Women*, Eleanor Everest Freer.

1935 *Gyul'nara*, Yuliya Lazarevna Veysberg.

Old Mr. Sundown, children's operetta, Mirrie (Irma) Hill.

Ariadne and Dionysius, Lucile Crews, NBC Music Guild.

Gale, Ethel Leginska ["Ethel Liggins"], Chicago.

1936 *The Brownings Go to Italy*, Eleanor Everest Freer.

1937 *Le marin du Bolivar*, Germaine Tailleferre, Paris Exhibition, Paris.

Zaykin dom [A Little Rabbit's House], children's opera, Yuliya Lazarevna Veysberg.

Myortvaya tsarevna [The Dead Princess], radio opera, Yuliya Lazarevna Veysberg.

Gusi-lebedi [Geese-Swans], children's opera, Yuliya Lazarevna Veysberg.

Dierdane, Marguerite Beclard d'Harcourt.

c. 1938   *The Bells of Circumstance*, opera, Gina Branscombe.

1939   *El cantarito*, miniature opera, Maria Grever.

1941   *Alcesti*, Elsa Olivieri Sangiacomo Respighi.

Jamanto, Barbara Giuranna, Bergamo.

1943   *Schelmenerbschaft*, Irma von Halácsy, never performed in a complete form.

Rotonde, opera, Johanna Bordewijk-Roepman.

c. 1945   *Pepita's Miracle*, opera, Florence Maud Ewart, unperformed.

1946   *Printesa îndepărtată (The Distant Princess)*, Mansi Barberis, revised 1976, Iasi.

Laughing Star of Zuni, Lily Teresa Strickland, operetta.

1948   *Salambo*, Irma von Halácsy, never performed in a complete form.

1949   *A Game of Chess*, opera, Florence Maud Ewart.

Zlaté ptáče (The Golden Bird), Slava Vorlova.

1950   *Dolores*, operetta, Germaine Tailleferre, Opéra Comique, Paris.

1951   *Il était un petit navire*, satire lyrique, Germaine Tailleferre, Opéra Comique, Paris.

Parfums comedie musicale, Germaine Tailleferre, Monte Carlo Opera, Monte Carlo.

1952   *Rozmarýnka*, Slava Vorlova.

1954   *Night at Sea and Day in Court*, Elizabeth Gyring.

La femme en fleche, chamber opera, Marcelle de Manziarly.

1955   *Náchodská Kasace* (Nachod Cassation), Slava Vorlova.

La fille d'opera, Germaine Tailleferre, Radiodiffusion-Télévision Français.

La bel ambitieux, Germaine Tailleferre, Radiodiffusion-Télévision Français.

Monsieur Petitpos achete un chateau, Germaine Tailleferre, Radiodiffusion-Télévision Français.

La pauvre Eugénie, Germaine Tailleferre, Radiodiffusion-Télévision Français.

1958   *Dva světy*, Slava Vorlova.

Apus de soare (Sunset), Mansi Barberis, Bucharest.

1959   *Memoires d'une bergere*, Germaine Tailleferre, Radiodiffusion-Télévision Français.

The Concert, Lucile Crews.

1960   *Le maître* chamber opera, Germaine Tailleferre, Radiodiffusion-Télévision Français.

La petite sirene, opera, Germaine Tailleferre, Radiodiffusion-Télévision Français.

1961   *Mayerling*, Barbara Giuranna, Naples.

1963   *Kera Duduca*, television opera, Mansi Barberis, revised in 1970.

1964   *Maudlin of Paplewick*, Ina Boyle.

1965   *The Young Kabbarli*, chamber opera, Margaret Sutherland, Hobart.

1978   *Hosanna*, Barbara Giuranna, Palermo.

Bibliography

Ammer, Christine. *Unsung: A History of Women in American Music*. Westport, CT: Greenwood Press, 1980.

Barry, Nicole. *Pauline Viardot*. Paris: Flammarion, 1991.

Bawr, Sophie. *Mes Souvenirs*. Paris: Passard, 1853.

Block, Adrienne F. *Amy Beach, Passionate Victorian: The Life and Work of an American Composer, 1867–1944*. New York: Oxford University Press, 1998.

Bonis, Melanie. *Souvenirs et Réflexions de Mel Bonis, extraits de notes autobiographiques et de pensées de Mel Bonis, recuillis par ses petits enfants*. Editions[cd1] du Nant d'Enfer, 1974.

Bowers, Jane, and Judith Tick, editors. *Women Making Music: The Western Art Tradition, 1150–1950*. Urbana: University of Illinois Press, 1987.

Broadbent, Marguerite, and Terry Broadbent. *Leginska: Forgotten Genius of Music*. Cheshire, England: North West Piano Player Association, 2002.

Brown, Jeanell W. *Amy Beach and Her Chamber Music: Biography, Documents, Style*. Composers of North America Series, No. 16. New York: Scarecrow Press, 1994.

Chissell, Joan. *Clara Schumann: A Dedicated Spirit*. New York: Taplinger, 1983.

Citron, Marcia. *Cecile Chaminade: A Bio-bibliography*. Westport, CT: Greenwood Press, 1988.

_____, compiler, translator, and editor. *The Letters of Fanny Hensel to Felix Mendelssohn*. New York: Pendragon Press, 1987.

Craven, Elizabeth. *Memoirs of the Margravine of Anspach. Written by Herself*. London: H. Colburn, 1826.

Dahm, Cecile. *Agathe Backer Grondahl: Komponisten og pianisten*. Oslo: Solum, 1998.

Daniels, Mabel Wheeler. *An American Girl in Munich; Impressions of a Music Student*. Boston: Little, Brown, 1905.

Dees, Pamela Youngdahl. *A Guide to Piano Music by Women Composers, Vol. I*. Westport, CT: Greenwood Press, 2002.

DiMedio, Annette Maria. *Frances McCollin: Her Life and Music*. Metuchen, NJ: Scarecrow Press, 1990.

Ebel, Otto. *Women Composers: A Biographical Handbook of Woman's Work in Music*. Brooklyn, NY: F.H. Chandler, 1902.

Eckhardt, Ferdinand. *Music from Within: A Biography of the Composer S. C. Eckhardt-Gramatté*. Edited by Berald Bowler. Winnipeg, Manitoba: University of Manitoba Press, 1985.

Elson, Arthur. *Woman's Work in Music; Being an Account of Her Influence on the Art, in Ancient as Well as Modern Times; A Summary of Her Musical Compositions, in the Different Countries of the Civilized World; An Estimate of Their Rank in Comparison with Those of Men*. Boston: L. C. Page, 1903.

FitzLyon, April. *The Price of Genius*. London: Calder, 1964.

Frasier, Jane. *Women Composers: A Discography*. Detroit Studies in Music Bibliography, no. 50. Detroit: Information Coordinators, 1983.

Freer, Eleanor Everest. *Recollections and Reflections of an American Composer*. Chicago: N.p., 1929.

Fuller, Sophie. *Pandora Guide to Women Composers*. London: Pandora, 1995.
_____. "Women Composers during the British Musical Renaissance." Doctoral thesis, University of London, 1998.
Geliot, Christine. *Mel Bonis: Femme et compositeur*. Paris: Harmattan, 2000.
Glickman, Sylvia, and Martha Furman Schleifer, editors. *From Convent to Concert Hall: A Guide to Women Composers*. Westport, CT: Greenwood Press, 2003.
Gray, Dr. Anne K. *The World of Women in Classical Music*. La Jolla, CA: WordWorld, 2007.
Grout, Donald. *A Short History of Opera*. New York: Columbia University Press, 1947.
Guptill, Teresa L. "The Life and Music of Helen Hopekirk." DMA dissertation, University of Washington[cd2].
Hallman, Diana Ruth. "The Pianist Fannie Bloomfield Zeisler in American Music and Society." Master's thesis, University of Maryland, 1983.
Harding, Bertita. *Concerto: The Glowing Story of Clara Schumann*. Revised ed. Ithaca, NY: Cornell University Press, 2001.
Héritte-Viardot, Louise. *Mémoires de Louise Héritte-Viardot: une famille de grands musiciens: notes et souvenirs anecdotiques sur Garcia, Pauline Viardot, La Malibran, Louise Héritte-Viardot et leur entourage*. Paris: Stock, 1923.
Iverson, Jane Leland. "Piano Music of Agathe Backer Grondahl." DMA dissertation, University of Northern Colorado, 1993.
Jackson, Barbara Garvey. *"Say, Can You Deny Me?"* Fayetteville: University of Arkansas Press, 1994.
Jenkins, W. S. *The Remarkable Mrs. Beach, American Composer: A Biographical Account Based on Her Diaries, Letters, Newspaper Clippings, and Personal Reminiscences*. Warren, MI[cd3]: Harmonie Park Press, 1994.
Jezic, Diane Peacock. *Women Composers: The Lost Tradition Found*. New York: Feminist Press at the City University of New York, 1988.
Johnson, Barbara Urner. *Catherine Urner and Charles Koechlin: A Musical Affaire*. Aldershot, England: Ashgate, 2003.
Keegan, Susanne. *The Bride of the Wind: The Life and Times of Alma Mahler-Werfel*. New York: Viking, 1992.
Laurence, Anya. *Women of Notes: 1000 Women Composers Born before 1900*. New York: Richards Rosen Press, 1978.
Lehmann, Liza. *The Life of Liza Lehmann: By Herself*. New York: E. P. Dutton, 1918.
Letzter, Jacqueline, and Robert Adelson. *Women Writing Opera: Creativity and Controversy in the Age of the French Revolution*. Berkeley: University of California Press, 2001.
Litzmann, Berthold. *Clara Schumann: An Artist's Life*. 2 vols. New York: Vienna House, 1972.
_____, editor. *Letters of Clara Schumann and Johannes Brahms, 1853–1896*. New York: Vienna House, 1971.
Mahler, Alma. *The Diaries, 1898–1902*. Selected and translated by Antony Beaumont. London: Faber and Faber, 1998.
_____. *Gustav Mahler: Memories and Letters*. Translated by Basil Creighton. London: Murray, 1968.
Marshall, Kimberly, editor. *Rediscovering the Muses: Women's Musical Traditions*. Boston: Northeastern University Press, 1993.
Merrill, Lindsey. "Mrs. H. H. A. Beach: Her Life and Works." Ph.D. dissertation, University of Rochester, 1963.
Milinowski, M. *Teresa Carreño: By the Grace of God*. New York: Da Capo, 1979.
Muller, Dana G. "The Career and Piano Compositions of Helen Hopekirk." DMA dissertation, University of Hartford[cd4].
Nauhaus, Gerd, editor. *The Marriage Diaries of Robert and Clara Schumann: From Their Wedding Day through the Russia Trip*. Boston: Northeastern University Press, 1993.
Neuls-Bates, Carol, editor. *Women in Music: An Anthology of Source Readings from the Middle Ages to the Present*. Revised ed. Boston: Northeastern University Press, 1996.
Parsons, Charles H. *The Mellen Opera Reference Index*. Lewiston, NY: Edwin Mellen Press, 1986.

Pendle, Karin, editor. *Women and Music: A History.* Bloomington: Indiana University Press, 1991.

Pool, Jeannie G. *Women in Music History: A Research Guide.* New York: Pool, 1977.

Reich, Nancy B. *Clara Schumann: The Artist and the Woman.* Revised ed. Ithaca, NY: Cornell University Press, 2001.

Restout, Denise, editor and translator. *Landowska on Music.* New York: Stein and Day, 1964.

Rogers, Clara Kathleen. *Memories of a Musical Career.* Boston: Little, Brown, 1932.

_____. *The Story of Two Lives; Home, Friends, and Travels, Sequence to "Memories of a Musical Career."* Norwood, MA: Plimpton Press.

Rosenstiel, Leonie. *Nadia Boulanger: A Life in Music.* New York: W. W. Norton, 1982.

Sadie, Julie Anne, and Rhian Samuel. *The Norton/Grove Dictionary of Women Composers.* New York: W. W. Norton, 1994.

St. John, Christopher. *Ethel Smyth, a Biography.* London: Longmans, 1959.

Smyth, Ethyl. *Impressions That Remained.* London: Longmans, Green, 1919.

_____. *Streaks of Life.* London: Longmans, Green, 1921.

_____. *A Three-Legged Tour in Greece.* London: 1927.

_____. *A Final Burning of Boats.* London: Longmans, Green, 1928.

_____. *Female Pipings in Eden.* London: Peter Davies, 1933.

_____. *As Time Went On.* London: Longmans, Green, 1936.

_____. *Beecham and Pharaoh.* London: Chapman and Hall, 1935.

_____. *Inordinate(?) Affection.* London: Cresset, 1936.

_____. *What Happened Next.* London: Longmans, Green, 1940.

Solenière, Eugène. *La Femme Compositeur.* Paris: La Critique, 1895.

Stern, Susan. *Women Composers: A Handbook.* Metuchen, NJ: Scarecrow Press, 1978.

Tchaikovsky, Peter Ilyich. *Autobiographical Account of a Tour Abroad in the Year 1888.* http://www.tchaikovsky-research.net/en/Works/Articles/TH316/index.html

Tillard, Francoise. *Fanny Mendelssohn.* Translated by Camille Naish. Portland, OR: Amadeus Press, 1996.

Weissweiler, Eva, editor. *The Complete Correspondence of Clara and Robert Schumann.* Translated by Hildegard Fritsch and Ronald L. Crawford. 2 vols. New York: Peter Lang, 1994.

Wright, Constance. *Hortense Beauharnais: Daughter to Napoleon.* New York: Holt, Rinehart and Winston, 1961.

Zaimont, Judith Lang, editor in chief. *The Musical Woman; An International Perspective.* Westport, CT: Greenwood Press, 1983.

Discography

CDs

The American Chamber Ensemble. Judith Lang Zaimont, Vally Pick Weigl, Paul Hindemith. LE329.

Baroque for the Mass: Ursuline Composers of the 17th Century. Maria Xaveria Peruchona, Isabella Leonarda. LE346.

A Cello Century of British Women Composers/Wilmers, Marlow. Catherine Wilmers, R. Caroline Bosanquet, Dora Estella Bright, Rebecca Clarke, and Marie Dare. Quicksilva Records CD QS6245

Chamber Works by Women Composers. Fanny Mendelssohn Hensel, Cécile Chaminade, Amy Beach, Clara Schumann, Teresa Carreño, Germaine Tailleferre, Lili Boulanger. Vox Box CDX 5029.

Deferred Voices: Organ Works by Woman Composers. Mendelssohn, Smyth, and Beach. SK 527.

18th Century Women Composers: Music for Solo Harpsichord, Vol. 1. Gasparo 281.

18th Century Solo Harpsichord Music by Women Composers, Vol. 2. Cecilia Maria Barthelemon, Maria Hester Park, et al. Gasparo 282.

In Praise of Woman—150 Years of English Women Composers. Liza Lehmann, Maude Valerie White (composer) and Ethel Smyth, Anthony Rolfe Johnson (tenor), Graham Johnson (piano). H55159 Helios. *Münchner Komponistinnen aus Klassik und Romantik.* Includes music by Danzi, Lang, Menter, and Franziska Lebrun. Musica Bavarica MB 75 121.

Music by Maria Hester Park, Marie Bigot, and Fanny Mendelssohn Hensel. Centaur.

La Musica: 16th & 17th Century Music and a Surprise. Francesca Caccini, Barbara Strozzi, Sigismondo d'India, Alessandro Piccini, Francesca Campana, Settimia Caccini, Fabritio Caroso, Giovanni Kapsperger, Anonymous, Kabat. LE350.

Musica Femina: Celebrates Women Composers. Kristen Aspen, Francesca Caccini, Theresa Clark, Elizabeth-Claude Jacquet de la Guerre. Lilac Records.

Piano Portraits of the Seasons by Women Composers. Ivory Key Music.

Piano Trios; Clara Schumann, Fanny Mendelssohn. Hyperion CDA66331.

Vive la Différence: String Quartets by 5 Women from 3 Continents. Lucie Vellère, Sarah Aderholdt, Ruth Schonthal, Amy Beach, Priaulx Rainier. LE336.

Women at an Exposition: Music Composed by Women and Performed at the 1893 World's Fair in Chicago. Amy Beach, Cécile Chaminade, Kate Vannah, Liza Lehmann, Maude Valerie White, Clara Kathleen Rogers, Mary Knight Wood, Clara Schumann. Koch International Classics.

The Women Composers. Alma Mahler, Fanny Mendelssohn, Clara Wieck Schumann, Jean Micault, and Claudie Verhaeghe. Arcobaleno 9329.

Women Composers. Elfrida Andrée, Laura Valborg Aulin, Agathe Backer-Grondahl, Lili Boulanger, Maria Syzmanowska, and Fanny Mendelssohn. Swedish Society.

Women Composers Across the Centuries. Susan Anthony-Tolbert .Singing Cat and Mule Publishing Company.

Women Composers for Organ—Music Spanning Five Centuries. Violet Archer, Gracia Baptista, Amy Beach, Roberta Bitgood, and Edith Borroff. Gasparo.
Women Composers: Lost Tradition Found. Leonarda LE 353.
Women's Voices: Five Centuries of Song. Anne Boleyn, Caterina Assandra, Francesca Caccini, Barbara Strozzi, Anna Amalia (Duchess of Saxe-Weimar), Josephine Lang, Fanny Mendelssohn Hensel, Clara Wieck Schumann, Maria Theresia von Paradis, Alma Schindler Mahler, Poldowski (Irene Wieniawska Paul), Pauline Viardot-Garcia, Lili Boulanger, Germaine Tailleferre, Cécile Chaminade, Agathe Backer-Grøndahl, Margaret Bonds, Rebecca Clarke, Miriam Gideon, Jean Eichelberger Ivey, Marion Bauer, Judith Lang Zaimont, Ann Silsbee, Libby Larsen, Gwyneth Walker, Elizabeth Vercoe. LE338.

Specific Composers

Several composers whose work is represented on CDs:

Amy Beach
Lili Boulanger
Cécile Chaminade
Chiara Margarita Cozzolani
Agatha Backer Grondahl
Elizabeth Jacquet de la Guerre
Fanny Mendelssohn
Clara Schumann
Germaine Tailleferre

LPs

The work of many women composers is represented on LPs. This selective list includes several composers whose works are not readily available on CD. The following is an excellent source of listings of LPs:

Keyboard Works by Women Composers. Nancy Fierro, piano. Avant Records AV 1012.
Piano Works by Women Composers. Elisabeth Jacquet de la Guerre, Maria Theresa von Paradis, Maria Syzmanowska, Fanny Mendelssohn Hensel, Clara Schumann, Ingeborg von Bronsart, Agathe Backer-Grondahl, Teresa Carreño, Cécile Chaminade, Germaine Tailleferre, Amy Beach, et al. Turnabout TV 34658.
Songs by Lili Boulanger and Alma Mahler. Lili Boulanger, Alma Schindler Mahler. LPI 118.
Women Composers: A Discography. Jane Frasier. Detroit Studies in Music Bibliography, Number Fifty (Detroit: Information Coordinators, 1983).
Woman's Work. Anna Amalia (Duchess of Sax-Weimar), Anna Amalia (Princess of Prussia, Elfrida Andrée, Lili Boulanger, Ingeborg von Bronsart, Francesca Caccini, Cecile Chaminade, Louise Farrenc, Louise Heritte-Viardot, Elisabeth Jacquet de la Guerre, Josephine Lang, Maria Malibran, Fanny Mendelssohn Hensel, Maria Theresa von Paradis, Irene Wieniawska Paul, Clara Schumann, Germaine Tailleferre, and Pauline Viardot. Gemini Hall 1010.
Anna Amalia, the Duchess of Saxe-Weimar: *Erwin und Elmire*; Gemini Hall Records, RAP 1010. *Auf dem Lande und in der Stadt*, also, *Sie Scheinen zu spielen;* Deutsche Gramophone 2533149. Concerto for Twelve Instruments and Cembalo, also, Divertimento for Strings and Piano; Vox Turnabout TV 34754.
Alfrida Andrée: *Quintet in E Minor*, piano and strings. Allegro molta vivache. Gemini Hall 1010.
Josepha Barbara Auernhammer: *Sonata in A major*, piano; EMI 187 28 839/39.
Mansi Barberis: *Cvartettino pentru coarde in stil neoclassic*, strings; Electrecord ST ECE 01545.

Amy Beach: *Cabildo*, chamber opera; Leonarda LPI 119. *Quartet* for Strings, op. 89; Leonarda LPI 111. Sonata in A Minor; New World NW 268.
Settima Caccini: *Gia Sperai, Non Spero Hor'Piu*; Leonarda LPI 123.
Cecile Chaminade: There are many LP recordings of her music.
Isabella Charriere: *Sonata #3 pour Clavecin*, harpsichord; anthology of Swiss Music, CT 64 4.
Rebecca Clarke: *Trio*; Leonarda LPI 103.
Mabel Daniels: *Deep Forest*, orchestra; Composers Recordings 145.
Eva Dell'Acqua: *Villanelle*, voice and orchestra; Court Opera Classics CO 342.
Margarethe Denzi: *Sonata op. 1, no. 1*, violin and piano; Musica.
Sophie Eckhardt-Gramatté: Several recordings of her music are on World Records: WRC 1596, 1597, 1598, 1599.
Rosalind Frances Ellicott: *Second Piano Trio*; Summerhayes Piano Trio. Meridian Records, 2005.
Louise Farrenc: *Nonetto*; Leonarda 110. *Trio in E Minor*; Leonarda LPI 104.
Chiquinha Gonzaga: Several songs are on LPs: Estudio Eldorado ESTEL 13 79 0333
Maria Grever: *Jurame, Magic Is the Moonlight*; Deutsche Gramaphon 2530700.
Agatha Backer Grondahl: *Concert Study in G Minor, Concert Study in Bflat Minor, Serenade op. 15, no. 1*, orchestra; Norwegian Polydor NFK 10008. Also some of her works are on Gramaphon: AL2013; AL2931; AL2980; V181; X2330; X2751; DA1520.
Elizabeth Gyring: *Sonata no. 2*, piano; Composers Recordings 252.
Augusta Holmes: *Petite pieces*, flute and piano; Orion ORS 76257. *Trois anges sont venus ce soir*, choir and orchestra; Phillips 4230215.
Mary Howe: *Castellana for Two Pianos and Orchestra*; Composers Recordings CRI 124. *Allegro inervitable*, string quartet; Victor 11 8126.
Wanda Landowska: She appears on a variety of recordings including *Bourée d'Auvergne*, harpsichord; RCA Victor 630818.
Josephine Lang: Several of her songs are on Leonarda, LPI 107. *Sie liebt mich*; Gemini Hall 1010.
Margaret Ruthven Lang: *Irish Love Song*, arr. voice and orchestr;. Pelican LP 2008.
Ethel Leginska: *Three Victorian Portraits for Piano*; Orion ORS 75188.
Liza Lehmann: *In a Persian Garden; Ah Moon of My Delight*; RCAS Victor CRM 1 2472.
Maria Malibran: *Reveil d'un beau jour*; Gemini Hall 1010.
Mana Zucca: *I Love Life; Rachem*; RCA Victor 1986.
Kathleen Manning: *Shoes*; London OS 1986.
Marianne Martinez: *Sonata in A major*, piano; Pelican LP 2017. *Concierto in A Major*, harpsichord, Sinfonia in C Major; Ethnos 02 A X 1.
Fanny Mendelssohn: *Piano Trio in D minor*; Vox SVBX-5112. *Sechs Lieder*; Leonarda LPI 112.
Mary Carr Moore: *Sixteen Art Songs*; Cambria C1022.
Marguerite Olagnier: *Sais*. Pacific PIZ 1539.
Maria Theresa von Paradis: One of her most popular compositions is "Sicilienne." It has been reworked in several versions and recorded. A selected listing follows. For violin and piano: *Thibaud Violin Recital*; "Sicilienne"; Jacques Thibaud and Tasso Janopoulo; Angel GR-2079. *Encores*, "Sicilienne"; Itzhak Perlman and Samuel Sanders; Angel SZ-37560. 1979. For cello and piano: *A Jacqueline Du Pré Recital*; "Sicilienne"; Jacqueline Du Pre and Gerald Moore; Angel S-37900, 1982. Piano solo: *Frauen als Komponisten*; "Sicilienne," Rosario Marciano; Vox FSM 53036, 1980.
Dora Pejacevic: Numerous pieces are on Juzoton L5Y 66154.
Giula Recli: *Berzerette*; Golden Age, BAR 1002 A.
Louise Reichardt: *Songs* (9); Leonarda LPI 112.
Gilda Ruta: *Addio, Melodia Romantica, Mesta Serenata, Povero Amore*; Edizioni Musicali PAN NRC5016.
Clara Schumann: There is a wide variety of recordings including: Orion ORS 75182. Germany; Bayer-Records; NY, distributed by Qualiton Imports. *Lieder*; Helicon Nine, [1986] .
Ethel Smyth: *Boatswains's Mate*: excerpts; Victor 18155. *Fete Galante*; Victor 18155. *Wreckers*; Gramaphon 3308. *The Wreckers* (complete opera); rare record editions. SRRE 193–4.

Mirrie Solomon: *Avenu Molkeinu*; WRC R 30154.
Barbara Strozzi: *Arie, cantate & lamenti*; Georgsmarienhutte, Germany, CPO. Several of her works are on Harmonia Mundi HARM 1114.
Margaret Sutherland: *Fantasy, Sonata in F Major, Saxophone and Piano*; Columbia DOX 762. *Quartet in G Minor*, clarinet, horn, viola, piano; Columbia DOX 760/61.
Maria Szymanowska: Her music is on several LPs including Musicdixc RC 782. Avant 1012. *Six Chansons Français*; Cambridge 2777.
Germaine Tailleferre: There are numerous LPs with her music.
Lucie Vellere: *String Quartet No. 3;* Leonarda LPI 111. *Quartet for Four Clarinets;* Mixtur MXT DB 276.

Index